Community organisation or Community Based Organisation refers to organising aimed at making desired improvements to a community's social health, well-being, and overall functioning. Community organisation includes community work, community projects, community development, community empowerment, community building, and community mobilisation. It is a commonly used model for organising community within community projects, neighborhoods, organisations, voluntary associations, localities, and social networks, which may operate as ways to mobilise around geography, shared space, shared experience, interest, need, and/or concern.

Community organisation and community development are interrelated, and both have their roots in community social work. According to United Nations, community development deals with total development of a developing country that is economic, physical, and social aspects. Community development seeks to empower individuals and groups of people with the skills they need to effect change within their communities. These skills are often created through the formation of social groups working for a common agenda. Community developers must understand both how to work with individuals and how to affect communities' positions within the context of larger social institutions.

The present GPH book ***'Community Organisation Management for Community Development (MSW-009)'*** deals with various concepts related to community organisation and community development. Further, it elaborates social action for community development and also describes social welfare administration.

The book is written especially in question & answer format to provide students the instant gratification of a correct answer. In this book, we have tried to solve all possible questions from the exams' point of view. Solutions of previous years' question papers have also been included to help students to understand the unique examination structure.

We hope that this book would not be only a favourite study material for the students but also can be a nice resource for teaching. An attempt has been carefully made to present this book more useful and meet the requirements and challenges of the course prescribed by Indian Universities. We wish you a successful and rewarding career ahead. Feedback in this regard is solicited.

**– GPH Panel of Experts**

## Acknowledgements

Our compliments go to the **GullyBaba Publishing House Pvt. Ltd.,** and its meticulous team who have been enthusiastically working towards the perfection of the book.

Their teamwork, initiative and research have been very encouraging. Had it not been for their unflagging support, this work wouldn't have been possible. The creative freedom provided by them along with their aim of presenting the best to the reader has been a major source of inspiration in this work. Hope that this book would be successful.

**– GPH Panel of Experts**


## Publisher's Note

The present book MSW-009 is targeted for examination purpose as well as enrichment. With the advent of technology and the Internet, there has been no dearth of information available to all; however, finding the relevant and qualitative information, which is focussed, is an uphill task.

We at **GullyBaba Publishing House Pvt. Ltd.,** have taken this step to provide quality material which can accentuate in-depth knowledge about the subject. GPH books are a pioneer in the effort of providing unique and quality material to its readers. With our books, you are sure to attain success by making use of this powerful study material. Provided book is just a reference book based on the syllabus of particular University/Board. For a profound information, see the textbooks recommended by the University/Board.

Our site **gullybaba.com** is a vital resource for your examination. The publisher wishes to acknowledge the significant contribution of the Team Members and our experts in bringing out this publication and highly thankful to Almighty God, without His blessings, this endeavor wouldn't have been successful.

**– Publisher**

# Community Organisation Management for Community Development

**MSW-009**

*For*

Master of Social Work (MSW)

***Useful For***

IGNOU, Rai Technology University, KSOU (Karnataka), NIILM University, Bihar University (Muzaffarpur), Nalanda University, Jamia Millia Islamia, Vardhman Mahaveer Open University (Kota), Uttarakhand Open University, Kurukshetra University, Himachal Pradesh University, Seva Sadan's College of Education (Maharashtra), Lalit Narayan Mithila University, Andhra University, Pt. Sunderlal Sharma (Open) University (Bilaspur), Annamalai University, Bangalore University, Bharathiar University, Bharathidasan University, Centre for distance and open learning, Kakatiya University (Andhra Pradesh), KOU (Rajasthan), MPBOU (MP), MDU (Haryana), Punjab University, Tamilnadu Open University, Sri Padmavati Mahila Visvavidyalayam (Andhra Pradesh), Sri Venkateswara University (Andhra Pradesh), UCSDE (Kerala), University of Jammu, YCMOU, Rajasthan University, UPRTOU, Kalyani University, Banaras Hindu University (BHU) and all other Indian Universities.

Closer to Nature

We use Recycled Paper

**GULLYBABA PUBLISHING HOUSE PVT. LTD.**

ISO 9001 & ISO 14001 CERTIFIED CO.

Published by:

**GullyBaba Publishing House Pvt. Ltd.**

**Regd. Office:**
2525/193, 1st Floor, Onkar Nagar-A,
Delhi-110035
(From Kanhaiya Nagar Metro Station Towards Old Bus Stand)
Ph. 011-27387998, 27384836, 27385249
+919350849407

**Branch Office:**
1A/2A, 20, Hari Sadan, Tri Nagar,
Ansari Road, Daryaganj,
New Delhi-110002
Ph. 011-45794768

**New Edition**

**Author:** GullyBaba.Com Panel
**ISBN:** 978-93-90479-66-5

## Topics Covered

# Contents



# Question Papers

# 1 RELATION OF COMMUNITY AND COMMUNITY WORK

## INTRODUCTION

A community is similar to a living creature, comprising different parts that represent specialized functions, activities, or interests, each operating within specific boundaries to meet community needs. A healthy community has well-connected, interdependent sectors that share responsibility for recognizing and resolving problems and enhancing its well-being. Successfully addressing a community's complex problems requires integration, collaboration, and coordination of resources from all parts. From a systems perspective, then, collaboration is a logical approach to health improvement.

Community development is a collaborative, facilitative process undertaken by people (community, institutions, or academic stakeholders) who share a common purpose of building capacity to have a positive impact on quality of life.

**Q1. Explain the concept of community.**

***or***

**What do you mean by community?**

**Ans.** A community is a small or large social unit (a group of living things) that has something in common, such as norms, religion, values, or identity. Communities often share a sense of place that is situated in a given geographical area (e.g. a country, village, town, or neighbourhood) or in virtual space through communication platforms. Durable relations that extend beyond immediate genealogical ties also define a sense of community. People tend to define those social ties as important to their identity, practice, and roles in social institutions (such as family, home, work, government, society, or humanity at-large). Although communities are usually small relative to personal social ties (micro-level), "community" may also refer to large group affiliations (or macro-level), such as national communities, international communities, and virtual communities.

The English-language word "community" derives from the Old French *comunete*, which comes from the Latin *communitas* "community", "public spirit".

Human communities may share intent, belief, resources, preferences, needs, and risks in common, affecting the identity of the participants and their degree of cohesiveness.

In archeological studies of social communities the term "community" is used in two ways, paralleling usage in other areas. The first is an informal definition of community as a place where people used to live. In this sense it is synonymous with the concept of an ancient settlement, whether a hamlet, village, town, or city. The second meaning is similar to the usage of the term in other social sciences: a community is a group of people living near one another who interact socially. Social interaction on a small scale can be difficult to identify with archeological data. Most reconstructions of social communities by archeologists rely on the principle that social interaction is conditioned by physical distance. Therefore, a small village settlement likely constituted a social community, and spatial subdivisions of cities and other large settlements may have formed communities. Archeologists typically use similarities in material culture—from house types to styles of pottery—to reconstruct communities in the past. This is based on the assumption that people or households will share more similarities in the types and styles of their material goods with other members of a social community than they will with outsiders.

The definition of community is linked to its construct. It is useful to look at it from a historical perspective as well as from the geographical and ideological backgrounds in which it evolved.

Robert Bellah defines community as "a group of people who are socially interdependent, who participate together in discussion and decision making, and who share certain practices that both define the community and are nurtured by it".

According to Foundation for Community Encouragement A community is a group of two or more people who have been able to accept and transcend their differences regardless of the diversity of their backgrounds (social, spiritual, educational, ethnic, economic, political, etc.).

This enables them to communicate effectively and openly and to work together towards goals identified as being for their common good."

Bryon Munon (1968) defines "A community is a relatively self-sufficient population, residing in a limited geographic area, bound together by feelings of unity and interdependency."

C. Farrington and E Pine define a community as a "group of people lined by a communications structure supporting discussion and collective action."

Random House Unabridged Dictionary has many meanings on the term community. The meanings that are closest to social worker's profession are as follows.

(1) Social group of any size whose members reside in a specific locality, share government, and often have a common cultural and historical heritage.

(2) A social, religious, occupational, or other group sharing common characteristics or interests and perceived or perceiving itself as distinct in some respect from the larger society within which it exists example the business community; the community of scholars.

(3) Community, hamlet, village, town, city are terms for groups of people living in somewhat close association, and usually under common rules. Community is a general term, and town is often loosely applied. A commonly accepted set of connotations envisages hamlet as a small group, village as a somewhat larger one, town still larger, and city as very large. Size is, however, not the true basis of differentiation, but properly sets off only hamlet. Incorporation, or the absence of it, and the type of government determine the classification of the others.

**Q2. Briefly explain the concept of virtual community.**

**Ans.** A virtual community, e-community or online community is a group of people that primarily interact via communication media such as newsletters, telephone, email or instant messages rather than face to face, for social, professional, educational or other purposes. If the mechanism is a computer network, it is called an online community. Virtual and online communities have also become a supplemental form of communication between people who know each other primarily in real life. Many means are used in social software separately or in combination, including text-based chat rooms and forums that use voice, videotext or avatars. Significant socio-technical change may have resulted from the proliferation of such Internet-based social networks.

It is also possible for virtual networks to be created and used by geographically and interest bound communities for social uplift and collective action. One example is the case of village blogs created by villagers in Goa to tackle the powerful mining lobby.

**Q3. Discuss Community Construct: Sociological Insights.**

**Ans.** In the late 1800s, the Construct of community has been associated with the German sociologist Ferdin and Tonnies. He considered the relationships characterizing communities and accordingly came up with two variants one named as Gemeinschaft and the other Gesselschaft.

The *Gemeinschaft* communities are based on natural personal, informal face to face social relationships, where individuals are accepted for who they are, and not what they have done. People are recognized and accepted for their innate qualities. This sort of human relationship is reflected in families, small groups and traditional communities.

*Gesselschaft* communities are characterized by rational self-interest and are more contrived in nature. They place greater emphasis on specialized segmented social interactions. The interests of the individual supersede the interests of the group. Utilitarian goals as well as contractual agreements dominate interactions between individuals. There is division of labour and social control is more formalized, based on laws and rules with formal sanctions enforced when laws are violated.

This is particularly attributed to the rise of industrial capitalism in Europe and the United States at the end of the 19th century which was bringing about major transformations in the nature of human relationships.

It is however true that both forms of community life form the current reality of Indian Society and one cannot be attributed a higher/superior value than the other. These need to be viewed as different forms of human association that are present in the rural, urban and tribal communities. It is best to view them as ends of a continuum of human interaction wherein communities are grounded in both informal personal relationships and in the formal institutional structures that are part of contemporary life.

**Q4. Explain different aspects to understand communities.**

**Ans.** There are two aspects to understand communities namely, (a) shared physical space or geographic community and (b) community based on shared interest or identity or functional community.

(1) **Community as Bounded by Geographical Space:** According to Brueggemann (2006), community needs to be embodied to have existence, meaning that it requires a physical space that symbolizes the community for its members and for those who are not part of the community. Bounded is referred to as location based community. The boundaries of this community are often established with a recognized authority such as the Panchayat, the Mohalla, the Municipal government, zoning commission etc. Community may also be embodied in a physical structure, such as a panchayat ghar, a chaupal, a temple, a mosque, a church, a satsang, a choir group, or a recreation club etc. these are also known as geographical communities- that is communities are located in a particular space and locality such as communities in Okhla, Harinagar, Ambedkar Nagar etc.

(2) **Communities of Interest:** Communities of Interest refers to Communities where the membership is based not on shared physical space but on shared interests or characteristics that unite members and provide the basis for one's personal identity. Things like race ethnicity, religion culture, social class professional affiliation and sexual orientation often form the basis of communities of interest. Because such communities are based on identity and interest members carry the community with them. For example one can refer to the caste Mahapanchayats that are a way to foster community identity and to protect community interest. Similarly communities can be formed of alumni associations and old boys/girls associations. There could be communities based on professional interests such as that of artists, professional associations such as the Engineers of India, Indian Medical Association, Traders Associations, Industrial associations etc. There can also be linguistic, religious and cultural associations. Say the Karnatic Music group, the West Bengal Mountaineering association etc or even the positive people's network, fish workers forum, the dalit writers association, the schizophrenic association of India, the Association of Professional Social Workers in India etc. Sometimes they are also referred to as functional communities. Thus community workers such as the child labour, the sex

workers and so on sometimes work with functional communities.

Communities of interest sometimes overlap with locality based communities as when a residential area contains a high proportion of people whose personal identity is tied to one or more specific interest groups, such as the slum and shack dwellers associations, Mahila Milan in Mumbai etc. Most people in urban areas belong to more than one community, with varying degrees of identification of interest and engagement. These multiple community affiliations can be thought of as one's personal community network, representing various locality-based and interest based communities that connect the individual to others and to broader society. It is to be understood that the individual is located across various groups, in a range of formal and informal helping/hindering systems in the community. These provide important tools for the location of the individual in a social context for developing more realistic interventions plans that connect the various levels of human interaction, micro to macro.

**Q5. Discuss the sociological understanding of a community. Illustrate with example from your own region.**

**[Dec-2017, Q.No.-1]**

**Ans.** Communities come in an infinite number of shapes, social arrangements, population and compositions. Relationships that form the basis of communal life and the shared perceptions and common interests of its members are the glue that bonds the community into a coherent unit. In understanding communities Social work draws from both sociological and practitioner's insights, shaped by the growth of profession in trying out the community organisation as method of social work practice.

There are three frameworks to be useful to look at a community from a social work practitioner's perspective.

***These are discussed as:***

(1) **Community as a Social System:** General systems theory is used by social workers to understand many of the phenomenon they encounter in social reality. A system is viewed as being composed of multiple interacting components that relate to one another in an orderly, functional manner. Moreover systems are embedded within larger systems, thus providing a framework for understanding the connection between different levels of the systems. For example an individual might be viewed as one element within a family or kinship group, the kinship group exists within a community, the community within a stagnation or society, thus a system perspective provides a useful

framework for understanding the structure of community and the processes that tie the structural elements together.

Social workers need to critically examine how the sub systems meet or fail to meet the needs of their client groups. Tools that could be used here are community assessment, which can identify the community needs as well as community strengths. These also need to be understood with respect to global systems that impact and impinge on these functions. These global effects could be related to the way globalization, privatization and the dismantling of the social safety net impact on the lives and livelihoods of communities.

(2) **Community as an Ecological System:** In this community is seen as having close interrelationship with the environment in a symbiotic manner. There are regular exchange relationships that occur between the various parts of the community where each part gives and receives in symbiotic relationships with others in the system. There is a definite interdependence between various parts so that equilibrium is achieved.

It brings into what is known as geo-cultural perspective where in the spatial features (land use patterns and distribution of services) of a specific location interact with the community - its population characteristics (such as size, density, diversity) and technology (production of goods and services, transportation, communication etc) The physical features play a significant role in community life and determine the patterns of interaction. The location of specific groups vis a vis the location of resources (water, land, road) is determined by the social dynamics of the community. Thus lower caste communities are often located away from important and central places in the village community.

This perspective also enables the social workers to understand the community structures emergence through dynamic processes of (a) competition between various groups for common pool resources and (b) dominance of a particular group or caste in determining service delivery and access to services, (c) centralization (concentration of resources both economic and social in the hands of particular groups – clustering of these in one area- say the Panchayat and Mahila Mandal or temple location as seat of power and important decisions pertaining to the community in of power, (d) concentration location of specific groups – ghettoisation because of affinal and kinship bonds, or regional and linguistic bonds- such as the Bihari colony, Bengali colony or the Madrasi area-location of specific groups in the urban areas, (e) succession the process where in there is population movement as part of a natural process where in the migrants often move to less desirable areas-moving up once situations are favourable or when they could afford better places and (f) segregation where in even when they could move to new areas they cannot because of antipathy by other groups - the sub groups function as isolated communities- say Seelampur Jhuggi clusters in the North east of Delhi.

Such features can be explored over time by using the Geographical Information systems in the spatial distribution, concentration of resources and amenities juxtaposed with the location of communities. These enable us to understand the relationship between the physical and social environment of the community.

Further the social structure of the community as it evolves over time and the correctives needed become immediately visible and also suggest the type of interventions that could be carried out.

(3) **Community as a Seat of Power and Conflict:** The perspective goes beyond the social systems perspective that sees community as constituting of subsystems that have their functional role cut out for them. The conflicts of interests and disagreements as well as domination are not emphasized. In the ecological system even though there is acknowledgment of power processes of domination, concentration and centralization, there is not much thought provided on how to deal with the differences and the inequitable distribution of resources.

The perspective of community as a centre for power and conflict considers power and politics as central to our understanding of community. It assumes that conflict and change are central attributes of most communities. Community Decision-making is not merely seen as rational planning, collaboration and coordination but also as involving confrontation and negotiation.

Communities are seen as arenas where competing groups are constantly engaged in conflict over power and the control of scarce resources. Some groups often based on social class, caste, religious, linguistic and regional affiliations dominate over other groups. There is a constant process of negotiation and confrontation to fulfil the basic needs by those who are involved. Sometimes the conflict is resolved in favour of the marginalized, aided by the institutional presence of law, judiciary and administration and at other times, the institutions take an opposite stand, and conflict is resolved in favour of the powerful. This perspective enables Social workers to understand the community power structures, the way decisions are made to favour or condemn groups, the way conflict positions are taken and perpetuated and the role that change agents should play in strengthening the capacities of those lower in hierarchy to change the situation. Such issues are very well evident in urban, rural and tribal areas where the communities are denied access to resources on their social origins or economic situation or political affiliation. Caste and communal riots are an extreme form of those conflict positions.

**Q6. What are the main characteristics of community?**
**[Dec-2017, Q.No.-4(a)][June-2019, Q.NO.-4(a)]**

**Ans.** Community is a group of individuals having shared space, values and practices. They are seen to be integrated in a network of relationships that foster commonness and spirit of togetherness. Communities are seen to be homogenous entities with a degree of relationship that is seen to be the very essence of community.

***These are some of the dominating characteristics of our community:***

(1) **Human Scale:** Communities have individuals engaging in face-to-face interactions. They are in that sense primary groups who are in direct contact with one another. People know each other and in this sense are in control of the range of interactions they are engaged in. Social structures are sufficiently small and people are able to own and control them.

(2) **Identity and Belonging:** There is feeling of belonging and acceptance of each other as well as security. Thus one feels a part of the community or a member of a community. Membership involves acceptance by others, allegiance or loyalty to the aims of the group concerned. This sense of belonging is significant and positively regarded. Community can become the person's self concept. Identity also plays a role in the person not only feeling a sense of belongingness to one community but a sense of difference from the other groups. Institutions within community and shared practices also play a role in identity formation and foster a sense of belonging. It also means that people can face a change in the sense of belonging to changing

institutions. These can be seen to erode the togetherness within a community.

(3) **Obligations:** The belongingness carries with it certain sense of rights and responsibilities. There is a mutuality of trust and reciprocity involved firstly in maintaining community life in terms of participating in the collective activities of community, sharing and interacting with others. Participating in community events with adherence to customs and traditions are ordained by collective will of the members.

(4) **Gemenischaft:** This implies that the people have a wide variety of roles in which they interact with each other. These interactions are not contractual but are obligatory. These are important for self-enhancement of individuals as well as for fostering the use of a range of talents and abilities for the benefit of others and the community as a whole.

(5) **Culture:** A community has a specific culture that is reproduced and continuously being shaped by the members of the community, through its social structures, economic systems and power relations. A culture in that sense is all encompassing and all embracing the way of life of a group of people.

**Q7. What is the historical perspective of community work within social work practice?**

**Ans.** Social work in the 19th century was often conceived in terms of a much broader setting than casework. The settlement movement and charity organisation society movements formed the context for the development of social work as a profession and from its genesis community practice has been an essential constituent.

Reform movements to change the situation of the distressed were at the heart of community development and organizing efforts. In the settlement houses in America and in the charity organisation societies with which the social work profession began had the reform element as core. Community organisation emerged in two traditions in England- one with the community worker taking the place of the churches in their role of moral alleviation. Community work is seen to be an attempt to respond to moral confusion because of the erosion of religious faith in the middle of last century; second with the view that the degradation of the poor is a consequence rather than the cause of their poverty.

Community organisation as a method of social work emerged in Great Britain with a growing dissatisfaction of Casework as a method of social work practice.

***The reasons can be seen as follows:***

(1) The influence of the pioneers in community based teams and the evidence that their work offers alternative methods;

(2) The deficiencies of case work, as a method of social work seems to be one major force in the development of community organisation;

(3) Increasing knowledge and understanding of the nature of informal caring systems and other forms of voluntary action in their society and the potential for interweaving statutory services with such systems;

(4) The impact of cut-backs in local government spending which have compelled the serious consideration of alternative;

(5) Political changes on both right and left which for different reasons have favoured the introduction of policies of decentralization. On the right these tend to be founded on policies of self-help and local responsibility. On the left they are likely to derive from local socialism that seeks to revitalize relations between representatives and electorate founded on the local delivery and control of services.

**Q8. What are the purposes of intervention?**

**Ans.** The purposes of Community work vary with the issues of each community that are the focus. Developed industrial countries have seen the post world war II period. The diversity of purpose of community organisation has reflected the complex character of societies with their many groupings and the basic differences among them in their conditions, status, needs and orientation towards maintenance or change of existing institutions. The purposes of community organisation are therefore said to be not uniform but as the reflection of diverse purposes of groups, organisations and movements.

Indian society is multi cultural and represents a diverse reality that had seen practice of community interventions stemming from various social, religious and political movements. These did consider a change in the social reality and a better life for the marginalized howsoever paternalistic they may have been. The diversity of groups, populations with diverse geo-cultural positions and livelihoods brings with it diverse needs that are more commonly concentrated towards economic improvement. Community efforts in India have been fostering these efforts to improve the lot of the down trodden, the powerless in rural, urban and tribal locations.

These efforts have been at the beginning of the century holistic and encompassing all round improvement in the life and living of people in health, education, livelihoods and political empowerment.

A major purpose of community work practice is concerned with improving the way in which social welfare services are organized and delivered with the targeted population being involved in the solutions to their problems hence their participation is a key. Participation and self-help are key concepts in community work.

**Q9. Discuss social action as a part of community work.**

**Ans.** Direct problem solving but the organisation of a population to obtain resources and power that it did not have before. This may take form of bringing pressure upon existing social institutions, the development of new channels of representation whereby the voice of the groups previously excluded may be heard in the decision making process or the creation of new political and economic arrangements that will actually transfer resources to them.

It was the emphasis of enabler role for a community work practitioner that made it possible for it to find a place for community work within the general framework of professional social work. It also provided a formulation that was broad enough to unite community workers operating in many different settings and fields.

As an enabler, the community worker would help people to clarify their problems, identify their needs, and develop the capacity to deal with their own problems more effectively. The emphasis is clearly on skill in developing relationships.

**Q10. Define community development approaches.**

**Ans.** Community development is a continuous process of interaction, consciousness raising, education and action aimed at helping the people concerned to determine and develop their own version of community. No single right formula for what constitutes community and no single right way to develop it. Community Development is a much more complex process full of dilemmas and problems which require unique and creative solutions. Models of community work are thus valuable if they provide frameworks within which these problems and dilemmas can be understood and creative solutions derived.

In the real life experiences, sufferings and aspirations of the people Community programmes must be grounded as articulated by the people themselves, while at the same time these subjective experiences must be linked to an analysis of broader social economic and political structures which are the cause of people's oppression and disadvantage.

Implications for social worker and client groups relationship consciousness raising has important. In this the social worker is not in an expert of the situation but in a role of service as a resource and is answerable to them. This change in relationship between the professionals and the consumers of human services facilitates their empowerment rather than disempowerment.

Structures of domination and oppression have resulted in the legitimation of the wisdom of the dominant groups, while alternative wisdoms of the oppressed groups are unrecognized. An essential component of community development is not only to acknowledge the wisdom of the oppressed, and their right to define their own needs and aspirations in their own way, but to facilitate the expression of that wisdom within the wider society as an essential contribution to the welfare of the human race, Thus community development must incorporate strategies of consciousness raising and of ensuring that the voices of the oppressed are heard, acknowledged and valued. Social justice perspective also means that some who are disadvantaged will continue to be disadvantaged if seen in functional terms. Functional communities can be there at the expense of local communities, then it is to be discouraged and geographical communities be supported instead.

For this geographical communities represent preferred option for community development and community based services. Functional communities both of the elite and the powerless have to be recognized to exist and the latter encouraged and former discouraged.

At grass-roots level, Community based strategy involves giving central place to the initiative of ordinary, people recognizing their voice and efforts in changing their social situation.

**Q11. Explain the meaning of urban community.**

***or***

**What are the census definition of urban community?**

**Ans.** 'Urban' means relating to or located in a city. It represents the characteristics of the city or city life. It has its roof in the Latin word Urbnus - the root urb means city. An urban area is a human settlement with high population density and infrastructure of built environment. Urban areas are created through urbanization and are categorized by urban morphology as cities, towns, conurbations or suburbs. In urbanism, the term contrasts to rural areas such as villages and hamlets and in urban sociology or urban anthropology it contrasts with natural environment. The creation of early predecessors of urban areas during the urban revolution led to the creation of human civilization with modern urban planning, which along with other human activities such as exploitation of natural resources leads to human impact on the environment.

The world's urban population in 1950 of just 746 million has increased to 3.9 billion in the decades since. In 2009, the number of people living in urban areas (3.42 billion) surpassed the number living in rural areas (3.41 billion) and since then the world has become more urban than rural. This was the first time that the majority of the world's population lived in a city. In 2014 there were 7.2 billion people living on the planet, of which the global urban population comprised 3.9 billion. The Population Division of the United Nations Department of Economic and Social Affairs at that time predicted the urban population would grow to 6.4 billion by 2050, with 37% of that growth to come from three countries: China, India and Nigeria.

Max Weber considers urban areas to be more evolved organisationally based on the principles of rationality with the presence of a market and a specialized class of traders. Other religious, political, economic technological and complex administrative structures found in a city complement the trade and commerce network. There is a predominance of industrial and service sectors. City is also characterized by heterogeneity, impersonality, anonymity etc.

Louis Wirth (1938) considers urban areas as relatively large, dense, permanent settlement of socially heterogeneous individuals. Here secondary groups such as the corporation, voluntary associations, representative forms of government and mass media replace the primary group associations that are found in a village. Such relationships are also considered impersonal, segmental, superficial, transitory and often predatory in nature.

Robert Redfield in the 1940s proposed a folk –urban model in which he contrasted the image of city life with an image of the folk community (invariably rural). The latter is considered as small, sacred, highly personalistic, and homogeneous in contrast to the urban as invariably impersonal, heterogeneous, secular, and disorganizing.

**Census Definitions:** As per the 1961 census, an area is considered urban if it meets the following criteria : (1) all places having a municipal corporation, municipality, notified area committee and cantonment board, (2) the places which satisfy the following criteria, (3) population not less than 5,000, (4) Density of Population 1,000 persons per sq mile 9400per sq km, (5) seventy five percent of workers engaged in non-agricultural sector. Census 2001 distinguishes between statutory towns and census towns:

Statutory towns are all places with a municipality, corporation, cantonment board or notified town areas committee etc so declared by a state law. Whereas census towns are places which satisfy the following criteria of: (a) a minimum population of 5,000, (b) at least 75% of male working population engaged in non-agricultural pursuits and (c) density of population being at least 400 persons per sq.km.

Another term urban agglomeration is used to understand the urban spread and growth. It refers to a continuous urban spread constituting a town and its adjoining urban outgrowths, or two or more physical contiguous towns together and any adjoining urban outgrowths of such towns. Examples of outgrowth are railway colonies, university campuses, port areas, military camps etc that may have come near a statutory town or city but within the revenue limits of a village or villages contiguous to the town or city. As per census 2001, it was decided that the core town or at least one of the constituent towns of an urban agglomeration should necessarily be a statutory town and the total population of all the constituents should not be less than 20,000. With such basic criteria the urban agglomerations could be constituted in the following way:

(1) A city or town with one or more contiguous outgrowths,
(2) Two or more adjoining towns with or without their outgrowths, and
(3) A city and one or more adjoining towns with their outgrowths all of which form a continuous spread.

Urban communities live in urban areas. There is tremendous diversity and complexity that characterizes these communities. Urban community is a complex multi-group society.

**Q12. Write the historical development of urban areas.**

**Ans. Colonial Influences:** While earlier cities developed because of their importance as trading centres, port towns, as pilgrimage places, the colonial history has changed all these and made their importance hinge on their ability to serve the colonial rulers for processing and marketing of raw material from hinterland and finished goods from the empires. The processing also meant establishment of factories notably the cotton mills for processing raw cotton aided by the development of railways with each of the trading centres. Industrialization has led to the rapid rise in urban populations, urban centres, and development of urban culture that was starkly different from the pre-colonial city development.

The cities were seen as commercial and trading zones for primary exports and manufactured imports. This continued even after the colonized countries became independent.

**Postcolonial Influences:** The neocolonial city represents city development that has taken place in third world countries with the capital from advanced industrial nations, creating enclaves of industrial production. The commodities produced in neocolonial cities generally are destined for export rather than for home consumption, except perhaps by a small home elite. There are urban factories and urban-resident wage labourers. There is a developing infrastructure of urban transport and communication by which these commodities and labourers are allocated. There is massive urban-ward migration from neighbouring rural areas. The neocolonial city has given rise to informal economy consists of urban services and products provided by the neocolonial city's poorest denizens, the petty hawkers, the shoeshine boys, the household help, the rag pickers, and others who form a class of petty commodity producers and sellers.

**Q13. Discuss urbanization and spread of urban communities.**

**Ans.** Urbanization refers to the population shift from rural to urban residency, the gradual increase in the proportion of people living in urban areas, and the ways in which each society adapts to this change. It is predominantly the process by which towns and cities are formed and become larger as more people begin living and working in central areas. Although the two concepts are sometimes used interchangeably, urbanization should be distinguished from urban growth: urbanization is "the proportion of the total national population living in areas classed as urban," while urban growth refers to "the absolute number of people living in areas classed as urban". The United Nations projected that half of the world's population would live in urban areas at the end of 2008. It is predicted that by 2050 about 64% of the developing world and 86% of the developed world will be urbanized. That is equivalent to approximately 3 billion urbanites by 2050, much of which will occur in Africa and Asia. Notably, the United Nations has also recently projected that nearly all global population growth from 2017 to 2030 will be absorbed by cities, about 1.1 billion new urbanites over the next 13 years.

Urbanization is relevant to a range of disciplines, including urban planning, geography, sociology, economics, and public health. The phenomenon has been closely linked to modernization, industrialization, and the sociological process of rationalization. Urbanization can be seen as a specific condition at a set time (e.g. the proportion of total population or area in cities or towns) or as an increase in that condition over time. So urbanization can be quantified either in terms of, say, the level of urban development relative to the overall population, or as the rate at which the urban proportion of the population is increasing. Urbanization creates enormous social, economic and environmental changes, which provide an opportunity for sustainability with the "potential to use resources more efficiently, to create more sustainable land use and to protect the biodiversity of natural ecosystems."

**Spread of urban communities:** As per census 2001, 742 million live in rural areas and 285 millions in urban areas comprising of 72-2% and 27.8% of the population respectively. Delhi has the highest percentage of urban population (93%) and Himachal Pradesh has lowest (9.8%). In 2001, India has 35 cities/urban areas with a population of more than one million people. In total, some 108 million Indians, or 10.5 percent of the national population, live in the country's 35 largest cities. Mumbai with a population of more than 16 million is now the world's fourth largest urban area followed by Kolkata in fifth place.

Maharashtra has the largest share of urban population of the country (12.1%) and Tamil Nadu (9.5%). About half the urban population of the country lives in the five states namely Maharashtra, Uttar Pradesh, Tamil Nadu, West Bengal, Andhra Pradesh. In the 2001 census nine districts were considered as fully urbanised- these were New Delhi, Kolkata Mumbai, Mumbai, Hyderabad, Chennai, Yanam and Mahe. While in 1991 census there were 129 district that had 30% of its population living in rural areas, in 2001 it increased to 148. Urban slum areas are home to more than 40 million Indians or 22.6 percent of India's urban population. More than 600 Indian towns and cities incorporate slum areas. The largest slum population in cities with population more than one million is found in Mumbai (48.9%) and the lowest in Patna (0.25%).

**Q14. What are the characteristics of urban communities?**

***Or***

**Discuss briefly the social and economic aspects of urban communities. [June-2018, Q.No.-4(b)]**

**Ans.** The characteristic features of urban communities relate to the economy, social structure, the political system, the cultural life and the spatial organisation and their linkage and importance in contributing to the institutional and economic growth of the region and state in particular and the nation at large.

**Social Aspects:** Secondary relations dominate such heterogeneous communities. The formal means of social control such as law, legislation, police, and court are needed in addition to the informal means for regulating the behaviour of the people. There is mobility and openness. The social status is achieved than ascribed. Occupations are more specialized. There is widespread division of labour and specialisation with plenty of opportunities for pursuing various occupations. Family is said to be unstable. More than the family individual is given importance. Joint families are comparatively less in number. People are more class - conscious and progressive and supposed to accept changes.

**Caste and Class in Urban India:** Caste affiliation, kinship ties continue in urban areas despite the modernizing and secularizing effects of urban living. In terms of the urban social structure it is seen that there is persistence of social relationships resembling those of rural areas. The so-called secular, formal and rational behaviour that is portrayed by the traditional understanding of urban areas does not entirely apply to the Indian situation. There is evidence of inter-caste/religious/ethnic competition which may turn into conflict situations too. The power structure thus is not only constituted by the hostilities and opposition that are derived from ones' affiliations, but also those derived on account of one's class. The pattern of conflict and cooperation thus cut across caste, religion and class lines.

**Families in Urban Areas:** The three major family types of nuclear, joint and extended families are found in urban areas.

Since the majority of urban families have to live in areas that have cheaper accommodation, often their place of work is located at a considerable distance.. This creates pressures on the time available for house care, childcare and maintenance of family bonds. Consequently families suffer a lot of strain. The frustrations experienced at the work place and the degradation of environment contributed by both indoor and outdoor air pollution, takes a heavy toll on the health and mental health aspects of urban families. This is compounded by the rising costs of urban living and privatisation of healthcare.

**Economic Aspects:** The urban economy is predominated by industrial and service sectors. The secondary and tertiary sectors predominate. The mode of organisation of the economy is to achieve the above results in various groups and classes, with an uneven distribution of social and economic resources. There is great diversity of the labour force with a few in the organized sector, receiving a high salary packages and a larger number in the informal economy receiving marginal and sustenance incomes with lack of social security benefits.

There are two types of sectors – the organized or the formal sector and the unorganized or the informal sector. Organized sector consists of large-scale operations in terms of capital labour wage labour with the use of advanced and modern technology- with institutional arrangements known as public and private sector partnerships. This sector is also closely linked with the global financial and economic systems. With the result any changes in the global economy affect it directly.

The unorganized sector on the other hand consists of smaller scale of operation in terms of capital and labour, private or family ownership, labour intensive, less advanced technology, unregulated markets and unprotected labour (almost no social security benefits) this is being modified with the social security bill for the protection of unorganized (recently ratified by the Rajya Sabha). This also is affected by government policy regulation as in the case of protection of industry for capital or for labour. The small-scale industrial policy, the programmes of National Institute for micro, small and medium industries institute are some such examples. 93% of the labour force is employed in unorganized sector.

**Inter Relations between the Social and Economic Characteristics:** It is necessary to view the social and economic characteristics of urban communities as interrelated aspects. The economic structure is closely linked to the social settlements. Social and economic features of the city thus get enmeshed in a complex web of local economic relations and global economic transactions.

The economic structure is closely linked to the social settlements. Social and economic features of the city thus get enmeshed in a complex web of local economic relations and global economic transactions. The settings for the local economy are influenced by the local governance systems.

**Urban Poverty:** It is important to understand urban poverty for social workers to design appropriate interventions. Workers engaged in the urban informal economy constitute the bulk of the urban poor. A large section of this population consists of low skilled rural migrants or migrants from smaller towns.

23.62 percent of India's urban population is living below the poverty line. The urban poor population is 3.41 percent less than the rural poor.

The tenth five year plan notes that urban poor can be defined in a declining scale such as core poor, intermediate poor, and transitional poor. Or they can also be classified in terms of declining poor, coping poor, and improving poor, with different degrees of priority for the three basic needs of survival, security, and quality of life.

**Urban-rural Linkages:** It is to be recognized that many poor households have livelihoods that draw on rural and urban resources or opportunities. Urban and rural areas are closely linked, each contributing to the other. These linkages need to be taken into account while planning for community development programmes.

**Q15. Discuss Spatial Segregation of urban communities.**

**Ans.** All urban communities are spatially segregated. That is, communities can have particular location because of their occupations, linguistic, regional, class and caste affiliation. Further the migrants to a city can settle down owing to group affiliations and informal ties. For example in the case of Delhi, the colonial administration ensured that the city development was to benefit the rulers, after annexation of Bahadur Shah Jaffer, the earlier walled city was neglected as the colonial rulers developed the vast New Delhi area, with wide roads, gardens and parks. There was more spatial segregation after partition, when refugees settled in new areas followed by continued influx of surrounding urban populations. Spatial segregation of city thus was not a one time phenomenon, but took place because of the waves of migrations and political upheavals in the subcontinent.

Segregation of the city also took place as the migrants cluster to one particular area because of the informal connections and networks that had with city dwellers. As the refugees because of partition or other political conditions came into the city, the city got its ethnically based groups like the Tibetan community, the Nirankari Colony, the Nizamuddin Basti etc.

*This Can be discussed as:*

(1) **Refugee and Displaced Communities:** The partition of Indian sub-continent into India and Pakistan had deleterious effects on millions of people. There was not only the trauma of leaving one's place of residence, occupation and property but also the apprehension of reaching a safe place. Refugee communities have placed a tremendous strain on the resources of the state/area to which they move. Besides these there is also the trauma experienced when leaving loved ones behind or on the way to a safe destination, they are subjected to violence and loss of dignity. These problems were compounded by the settlements that were established for refugee populations that had the bare minimal facilities. Communities had to establish their lives all over again.

The problem of urban resettlement of the refugees and displaced (2-5 million displaced persons from West Pakistan) was accentuated with the differences in the economic situations of the incoming and outgoing population. This difference has been the more marked in the case of displaced persons from West Pakistan. There was also a difference between refugees related to their origin.

Also there is displacement as a result of ethnic or caste violence that makes communities to move to newer areas within a city or elsewhere- through either a government rehabilitation scheme or on their own. Urban areas are made of many such people and major metropolitan areas are seen strewed with such communities.

**(2) Slums:** Areas that are overcrowded with dilapidated structures, faultily laid out and lacking in essential services are generally termed as slums.

Slums are considered as the physical and social expression of inequalities in the distribution of the benefit of economic growth. Slums are neglected parts of cities where housing and living conditions are appallingly lacking. Slums range from high density, squalid central city tenements to spontaneous squatter settlements without legal recognition or rights, sprawling at the edge of cities. Some are more than fifty years old, (infact in Kolkata some of the slums are 150 years old).

Slums have come to form an integral part of the phenomena of urbanisation in India. It is for this reason that first time in the history of census in this country, the census 2001 has compiled slum demography.

As per the Census of India, 2001, the slum areas broadly constitute of:

(a) All specified areas in a town or city notified as 'Slum' by State/Local Government and UT Administration under any Act including a 'Slum Act'.

(b) All areas recognized as 'Slum' by State/Local Government and UT Administration, Housing and Slum Boards, which may have not been formally notified as slum under any act;

(c) A compact area of at least 300 population or about 60-70 households of poorly built congested tenements, in unhygienic environment usually with inadequate infrastructure and lacking in proper sanitary and drinking water facilities.

**Q16. Discuss the Characteristic Features of the Slums.**

**Ans.** Physically, slums consist of clusters of huts comprising several rooms constructed with temporary building materials, where each room is inhabited by a family sharing a common latrine, without arrangements for water supply, drains, disposal of solid waste and garbage within the slum boundaries.

Slums are characterized by (1) Lack of basic services, (2) Overcrowding, (3) high density doubtful and insecure tenure, (4) Inadequate housing, (5) Hazardous or precarious environments, (6) Lack of access to basic facilities, (7) Poverty or social exclusion.

It is to be understood that each locality, each metropolitan area has different slum types and none of them could be subsumed in one broad category. They are locally known with different names and different features with differing histories, different physical layout, pattern of ownership, political patronage and social make-up.

In case of Kolkata, these slum types could be categorized as the unauthorized bustees located on the sides of canals, large drains, garbage dumps, railway tracks and roads.

Among the **unauthorised slums** types are those, which are simply encroachments by the poor people either displaced from the city itself or retrenched from their work place, on the roadside (locally called jhupri), canals (called khaldhar), or any vacant place (called udbastu) another type of displacement is reported as displacement due to an excessive increase in family size. It has been found that the predominant structure types in the slum areas are pukka, semi-pukka and kutcha (crude or imperfect).

The **authorized slums** are the hut type settlements on leased land from landowners, which is let out to migrants; The second type of slum called "thika tenant slums" where the slum dwellers have taken possession at a fixed rent and have constructed their houses; Third types of slums are those constructed by zaminders (landowners) themselves and let out to the slum dwellers. These types of slums are locally called bustees; The fourth type of slums is Refugee Resettlement Colonies (locally called udbastu colonies) where land has been leased out for 99 years to the refugees from present-day Bangladesh by the government at nominal rents. (These types of houses are called Berar Ghar).

**Q17. What is the meaning of rural community and rural urban continuum?**

***Or***

**Write the short note on meaning of rural community.**

**[Dec-2018, Q.No.-5(e)]**

**Ans.** Rural communities reside in rural areas. Rural area is a geographic area that is located outside towns and cities. The Health Resources and Services Administration of the U. S. Department of Health and Human Services defines the word *rural* as encompassing "all population, housing, and territory not included within an urban area. Whatever is not urban is considered rural."

Typical rural areas have a low population density and small settlements. Agricultural areas are commonly rural, as are other types of areas such as forest. Different countries have varying definitions of *rural* for statistical and administrative purposes.

Conventionally, rural-urban continuum proposes a linear depiction of the contrasting natures of social relationships characteristic of rural and urban settlements. This was a popular conceptual tool to classify different types of community and the transition between them. It arose from early 20th century sociology attempting to understand the social changes consequent upon rapid urbanisation. Life in the countryside occurred in small, geographically isolated settlements which were socially homogeneous, with high levels of mutual communication and social solidarity, and which changed very slowly. Urban communities were attributed the opposite characteristics: **L. Louis Wirth** of the Chicago School, in his highly influential essay 'Urbanism as a Way of Life', thought cities distinctive because they were large, dense and heterogeneous and that this produced the transient, disorderly, anonymous and formal associational relationships of urban living.

Such understandings had affinities with **Ferdinand Tonnies** a-spatial distinction between gemeinschaft (community) and gesellschaft (association). In principle, if all settlements could be placed on such a continuum we would have a strong account of spatial arrangement influenced social life.

The **rural urban continuum** is experienced in some states but not in others. For example in some states like Kerala the distinction of a village and town is impossible to discern. Instead there is a continuum. The left end of the continuum consists of the rural whilst the right of the urban having a mix of characteristics. Those which are having mixed features are placed in the middle. Changes from rural to urban are called urbanisation. There is nothing like the ideal model of rural or urban but an increasingly urban flavour to rural locales. The rapid process of urbanisation through the establishment of industries, urban traits and facilities has decreased the differences between villages and cities.

Some sociologists have used the concept of rural-urban continuum to stress the idea that there are no sharp breaking points to be found in the degree or quantity of rural-urban differences. **Robert Redfield** has given the concept of rural-urban continuum on the basis of his study of Mexican peasants of Tepoztlain. The rapid process of urbanisation through the establishment of industries, urban traits and facilities has decreased the differences between villages and cities.

There are some sociologists who treat rural-urban as dichotomous categories have differentiated the two at various levels including occupational differences, environmental differences, differences in the sizes of communities, differences in the density of population, differences in social mobility and direction of migration, differences in social stratification and in the systems of social interaction.

Another view regarding rural and urban communities has been given by Pocock who believe that both village and city are elements of the same civilisation and hence neither rural-urban dichotomy, nor continuum is meaningful.

**Q18. Explain diversity of rural communities.**

**Ans.** Rural society includes a number of communities that live in what are known as villages. Villages in India vary with respect to their natural resource base, population density, demographic features, amenities, connectivity, historicity, and diversity of lifestyles, languages, cultural features and their proximity to city centres. Some villages have very old population as the majority of younger generation migrates in search of jobs. Such villages are known as Gray villages. Some of the villages are also uninhabited. There are other villages which are known as fringe villages which are located in the outskirts of the towns that eventually become parts of the urban whole.

One major understanding was that communities, which are non-tribal as well as tribal, tend to live in rural areas. Persons belonging to the former are often known as peasant societies or communities in which there is a definite bonding with the nearby market towns. These communities are not isolated like the tribal communities. Their linkage with the nearby towns is also through some forms of shared governance that bind them within the region to other constituents.

Villages are primarily food producing units and they are agriculture based. They produce not only for their own subsistence but also for the urban societies, which are non-producing. Land and the natural resources are the primary means/unit of production in rural societies. Ecological conditions influence the pattern of their stay, with hamlets that are stringed together or individual houses surrounded by their fields.

***Housing Patterns and Settlements in Rural Areas:***

(1) Different kinds of villages are found all over the country. In some, the fields of the village surround a tight cluster of houses. An outlying hamlet or several satellite hamlets are also found attached to some villages in this case.

(2) Linear settlements – e.g. in Kerala and Konkan and in the delta lands of Bengal. In such settlements houses are strung out each surrounded by its own compound. However there is little to physically demarcate where one village ends and another begins.

(3) Here there is scattering of homesteads or clusters of two or three houses. In this case also physical demarcation of villages is not clear. Such settlements are found in hill areas, in the Himalayan foothills, in the high lands of Gujarat and in the Satpura range of Maharashtra.

Usually a village is conceived as a physical entity having an aggregation of houses of mixed architecture (some of mud and thatch and some of cement) in the midst of surrounding agricultural fields. Of course there may be some exceptions to the general image of a village. Village can have more than ten thousand population as in the case of Kerala.

**Size of the Villages:** In 1981 census there were 5, 57, 137 inhabited villages in the country. By the year 1991 this number increased to 4689 towns and 5, 80,781 villages. According to 2001 census there are 5161 towns and 6,38,365 villages including uninhabited villages with 72% of the total population living in villages. Further rural life is characterized by direct relationship of people to nature i.e, land, animal and plant life.

Agriculture is their main occupation. Agriculture provides livelihood to about 58% of the labour force.

**Q19. Discuss rural social structure.**

***Or***

**Write the short note on Jajmani System.**

**[Dec-2017, Q.No.-5(e)]**

***Or***

**Explain the main features of rural social structure in India and discuss the linkages between caste and class in rural society. [June-2018, Q.No.-1]**

***Or***

**What are the basic features of power relation in rural area.**

**[June-2018, Q.No.-4(a)]**

**Ans.** Rural social structure would refer to the inter-relationship, inter-connectedness and inter-dependence of the different parts of the rural society. Caste system is one unique social structure and the inter relationship of the different units (castes) constitutes the structure of the rural society. Society, caste and Panchayat have control over the individual.

**Caste System:** Caste is the fundamental principle of social organisations in the Indian village. The structural basis of Hinduism is the caste system.

Caste is also seen as a 'monopolistic guild'. The occupation on which a caste has monopoly may be very simple. Village is conceptualized as an aggregate of castes, each traditionally associated with an occupation. The members of the caste are spread over a region in more than on village. The members of a caste have matrimonial relations with the neighbouring villages.

**Inter-caste Relations:** Inter-caste relations at the village level constitute vertical ties. The castes living in a village are bound together by economic ties. Generally peasant castes are numerically preponderant in villages and to perform agricultural work, they need the services of carpenter, blacksmith and leather worker castes. It is unlikely that all castes are located within a village, consequently they depend on neighbouring villages for certain services, skills and goods.

Inter-caste relations are mediated by a system known as Jajmani System. Jajmani is sort of mutual give and take form of relationship in which one family is hereditarily entitled to supply goods and render services to the other in exchange of the same. The person rendering the services or supplying the goods is known as kameen or prajan and the person to whom the services are rendered is called a jajman. Thus under jajmani system a permanent informal bond is made between jajman and kameen to meet each other's need for goods and services.

**Family and Kinship Relations:** Rural family functions as the unit of economic, cultural, religious and political activity. In agricultural societies the family becomes the unit of production, distribution and consumption. Marriage is a decision of the family governed by rules of kinship. Family has a strict control and administrative powers over the individual.

Both nuclear and joint family with their modifications are found in rural India.

There are Inter regional variations and in the distribution of family types.

Currently the family is changing in rural India with changes in the social and economic situation. The family as a unit of production has changed more into a unit of consumption. Rules of marriage vary between South and North India.

**Political and Economic Connections:** Political power centered in cities controls villages. The conflicts between different people pertain mainly to the matters of land disputes, traditional power arrangements, sharing of common resources such as the community pastures, water and forest resources and transgressing caste boundaries. Panchayats are usually the forums for dispute resolution. There are two types, one the Village Panchayat and the other Jati Panchayat. The former deals with the welfare of the families living in that village undertaking collective tasks of the village such as performing rituals for the welfare of the entire village or organizing programs for the collective welfare such as building tanks, roads, granary. A traditional caste council called Panch or five, comprises of a small but always an odd number, deals with issues related to caste matters and inter-caste relations. A particular caste is dominant implying either a numerical predominance, or control over economic resources, political power or having a high ritual status, or first ones to take advantage of the Western Education system.

Lower castes are often reduced to a marginal status. The dominant castes have often resorted to violence to keep other castes submissive. The power of the Panchayat is being reduced by the presence of the secular formal institutions, of the dominant castes. There is also conflict between the traditional caste Panchayats and the secular institutions such as the Gram Panchayat. Class has an economic dimension. Upper castes are the landed, and lower castes are the landless, generally.

The power relations are also closely related to the gendered location one has. Thus in rural society women have less power in decision-making and their needs and concern do not seem to be well articulated at the household level and in the larger community. Their institutional presence is also considerably less as compared to men. These are compounded when class and caste are joined together.

**Q20. Discuss rural economic structure.**

**Ans.** The salient features of a rural economy are related to the conditions of agriculture that is the predominant economic activity. The rural sector consists of agriculture and non-agriculture related activities, which are known as farm and non-farm economy.

**Agricultural Sector:** The agricultural sub sector consists of agriculture and allied economic activities such as crop husbandry, animal husbandry, and dairying, fisheries, poultry, and forestry. The non-agricultural sector consists of economic activities related to industry, business or services. This refers to the cottage and village industries, khadi, handloom, handicrafts etc. Business refers to micro enterprises, trading of general goods, small shops petty traders etc, whereas services refer to transport, communication banking and input supply, marketing of farm and non-farm produce etc. The main stakeholders of rural sector include farmers-agricultural and non-agricultural laborers, artisans, traders, money lenders and those engaged in providing such services as transport, communication, processing, banking and education and extension.

**Dry Land Agriculture:** Dry land agriculture is usually unaccounted for in mainstream agriculture. In India, it is estimated that 410 million people depend on the dry lands for a living. Dry land agriculture is another economy in rural areas that closely enmeshes with the 'poverty geography' of the country. Other than the arid zones where even rainfed farming is quite difficult, the heart of the dry lands is in the semi-arid zones. Dry lands in this country constitute more than 70% of the cultivable lands and despite several odds stacked against them, produce about 42% of the country's food. It is reported that nearly 83% of sorghum, 81% of pulses and 90% of oilseeds grown in the country come from these areas.

**Allied Agricultural Activities:** Animal husbandry and horticulture, pisciculture, apiculture and sericulture are examples of allied activities which are closely related to agriculture and provide marginal or substantial source of income for rural communities.

**Non-agricultural Activities:** This sector in rural areas constitutes an important component of the rural workforce constituting 20 to 25% of the rural workforce. This includes manufacturing of implements and work of artisans and crafts persons that support the agricultural work.

Rural industries that fall into the Khadi and village industries serve as an important support for employment. Also some of the people are employed in rural services such as health, education and the markets. In 2001 the workers in rural industries accounted for 3.8% of the rural workforce and above 3% for the total workforce of the country.

The picture of assets in rural areas is skewed. Over 78% of the cultivators belonging to the category of marginal and small operators cultivate less than one third of the land. In contrast less than two percent of the cultivators having holdings of more than 10 hectares each cultivate about 29% of the land.

The average size of holding is bigger in states such as Punjab, Haryana and Gujarat. On the other hand in eastern states like Bihar and West Bengal the operational size of these holdings is relatively small. It may be remembered that the regional differences in the structure of holdings are related to the pressure of population on the land, soil, agro climatic conditions and the extent of irrigation. It is also true that the economic value and productive potential of small holdings in irrigated areas might be higher than relatively large landholding in areas where agricultures is largely dependent on rains.

***Basic features of rural economy are:***

(1) **Excessive dependence on Nature:** With 64% of the net sown area in 1993-94 was rainfed that is crop production depended on the quantum and distribution of rainfall over the growing season. Indian agriculture is vulnerable to natural calamities, such as droughts, floods, hailstorms, and cyclones. This means that the degree of nature induced risk and uncertainty in agriculture is higher than in the non-agricultural sector, with the burden of risk falling on the farmer.

(2) **Low capital labour ratio:** This refers to the amount of capital available per worker. As there is a large workforce depending on agriculture this makes the capital available per capita low.

(3) **Small economic holdings and livestock holdings:** The existing land inheritance law means that the process of subdivision and fragmentation of landholdings continues unabated affecting generation after generation. Almost all the marginal and small farmers are poor, producing very little marketable surplus. It is estimated that the farmers having less than four hectare of land are not financially viable. Thus over 90% of farms in India are not financially viable. Compounded with this is the factor of continued low returns which is making the cultivators to join the ranks of agricultural labour.

(4) **Low factor productivity:** There is low average crop yields per hectare compared to other nations. The inadequate capital in the form of production of inputs, raw material and improved machinery and equipment available per worker/unit of enterprise

(5) **Long gestation and low rate of turnover:** The gestation period for investments in agriculture is long compared to non-agricultural enterprises. Three to four month period for crops to mature, six years for a calf to the stage where milk production is possible, and in horticulture the fruit tree takes about 5-10 years

for bearing fruit. Longer time is taken for a return on investment.

(6) **High incidence of poverty and unemployment:** The poverty in terms of absolute numbers as per official figures is 22%. But the incidence of poverty and the conditions for the above poverty line to turn into poverty situations are plenty. There is increasing rural debt experienced even by the rich farmers specially those in the cotton belt. The uncertainties unleashed by the economic reforms make the poor suffer more. Low skills are compounded by low work availability. Similarly unemployment conditions are increasing.

(7) **Preponderance of illiterate and unskilled workforce:** The labour force in rural areas is less skilled because of the disadvantaged class and caste status. They are unable to complete basic schooling. Both individual and collective structural factors make it difficult for the labour force to acquire skills required to move them from primary sector to the secondary and tertiary structures.

(8) **Lack of basic infrastructure:** Basic infrastructure in terms of connectivity and health and education facilities as also market facilities related to cold storage, etc are still to be achieved in adequate numbers and quality.

**Rural Assets and Poverty:** The picture of assets in rural areas is skewed. Over 78% of the cultivators belonging to the category of marginal and small operators cultivate less than one third of the land. In contrast less than two percent of the cultivators having holdings of more than 10 hectares each cultivate about 29% of the land.

The average size of holding is bigger in states such as Punjab, Haryana and Gujarat. On the other hand in eastern states like Bihar and West Bengal the operational size of these holdings is relatively small. It may be remembered that the regional differences in the structure of holdings are related to the pressure of population on the land, soil, agro climatic conditions and the extent of irrigation. It is also true that the economic value and productive potential of small holdings in irrigated areas might be higher than relatively large landholding in areas where agricultures is largely dependent on rains.

**Rural Credit Markets:** Credit is required in rural areas for consumption and production purposes. Consumption needs require small amounts of credit that meet needs such as food, clothing, shelter, education and health. Credit requirements are usually met from the shaukar/money lender informal institutions. However there is increasing evidence that the growing SHG movement in several parts of the country especially south is able to make inroads into traditional money lending institutions. Their share is less but growing. The traditional institutions survive because of their timely, ready availability of credit and their informal linkages that could be caste or kinship or village based with the client groups. There has been an effort to meet credit needs from the formal institutions but there has been a low presence of these with addition to bureaucratic hurdles in the way.

**Q21. What are the policies and practices of rural communities?**

**Ans.** Policies and prescriptions related to institutional presence, and procedures which govern access or that control and constrain legitimacy related to citizen participation etc strongly influence rural communities.

Reform measures such as reduction in fiscal deficit, reduction of subsidies, devaluation of rupee, export orientation and reduction of agricultural credit adversely affect the rural poor especially in terms of food security, which relates to production, distribution and pricing of the food grains. The agricultural sector is worst affected by the fiscal contraction which invariably result in a disproportionate cut in capital expenditure. Agricultural sector is the mainstay of the rural Indian Economy which is closely related to the existing pattern of the social equity. The shrinkage of the flow of resources to the rural sector, a misconceived interest rate policy which discriminate against agriculture, a sickening rural delivery credit system, the emergence of a new banking culture nurtured by reforms which is far from friendly to agriculture and rural development all go against the interests of rural economy.

Reform and post reform period impact on agriculture are found to be deleterious to the rural poor and the rural landless. Reforms have increased the vulnerability of these masses and this forms one of the critical issues for rural community development.

There are many policies that the government makes with regard to the rural sector directly-such as policies related to agriculture, rural credit policy, policy on investments to be made in social sectors-policies related to the provision of infrastructure in rural areas such as in health, education, employment (NREGA) road connectivity, housing and sanitation, drinking water supply etc. At the same time policies related to industry such as mining, availability of land for real estate for urban areas affects villages located in urban fringes.

Similarly the fiscal policy, which promotes export promotion, favouring areas for tourism development such as in the coastal areas affects the rural people who arc living in thcsc areas. These play a role in affecting the livelihoods of these communities and make them vulnerable to the point of crisis in survival. Thus these become critical for social workers to working with rural communities. Thus any thing that affects the rural populace be it with governance issues such as service delivery or with lack of institutional presence, is of great concern for rural community work.

**Q22. Explain the meaning of tribe.**

**Ans.** A tribe is a human social group. Exact definitions of what constitutes a tribe vary among anthropologists, and the term is itself considered controversial in academic circles in part due to its association with colonialism. In general use, the term may refer to people perceived by a population to be primitive and may have negative connotations. The concept is often contrasted with other social groups concepts, such as nations, states, and forms of kinship. The word tribe first occurs in English in 12th-century Middle English-literature, in reference to the twelve tribes of Israel. The Middle English word is derived from Old French tribu and, in turn, from Latin tribus (plural tribus), in reference to a supposed tripartite division of the original Roman state along ethnic lines, into tribus known as the Ramnes (or Ramnenses), Tities (or Titienses), and Luceres, corresponding, according to Marcus Terentius Varro, to the Latins, Sabines and Etruscans respectively. The Ramnes were named after Romulus, leader of the Latins, Tities after Titus Tatius, leader of the Sabines, and Luceres after Lucumo, leader of an Etruscan army that had assisted the Latins. In 242–240 BC, the Tribal Assembly(comitia tributa) in the Roman Republic included 35 tribes (four "urban tribes" and 31 "rural tribes"). According to Livy, the three "tribes" were squadrons of cavalry, rather than ethnic divisions.

The term's ultimate etymology is uncertain, perhaps from the Proto-Indo-European roots tri- ("three") and bhew ("to be"). The classicist Gregory Nagy says, citing the linguist Émile Benveniste, that the Umbrian trifu (equivalent of the Latin tribus) is apparently derived from a combination of *tri- and *bhu-, where the second element is cognate with the Greek root "to bring forth" and the Greek "clan, race, people" (plural phylai ). The Greek polis ("state" or "city") was, like the Roman state, divided into three phylai.

In Europe during the late medieval era, the Bible was written mostly in New Latin and instead of tribus the word phyle was used, derived from the Greek phule. In the historical sense, "tribe", "race" and "clan" have often been used interchangeably.

In his 1975 study, The Notion of the Tribe, anthropologist Morton H. Fried provided numerous examples of tribes that encompassed members who spoke different languages and practiced different rituals, or who shared languages and rituals with members of other tribes. Similarly, he provided examples of tribes in which people followed different political leaders, or followed the same leaders as members of other tribes. He concluded that tribes in general are characterized by fluid boundaries and heterogeneity, are not parochial, and are dynamic.

Fried proposed that most contemporary tribes do not have their origin in pre-state tribes, but rather in pre-state bands. Such "secondary" tribes, he suggested, developed as modern products of state expansion. Bands comprise small, mobile, and fluid social formations with weak leadership. They do not generate surpluses, pay no taxes, and support no standing army. Fried argued that secondary tribes develop in one of two ways. First, states could set them up as means to extend administrative and economic influence in their hinterland, where direct political control costs too much. States would encourage (or require) people on their frontiers to form more clearly bounded and centralized polities, because such polities could begin producing surpluses and taxes, and would have a leadership responsive to the needs of neighbouring states (the so-called "scheduled" tribes of the United States or of British India provide good examples of this). Second, bands could form "secondary" tribes as a means to defend against state expansion. Members of bands would form more clearly bounded and centralized polities, because such polities could begin producing surpluses that could support a standing army that could fight against states, and they would have a leadership that could co-ordinate economic production and military activities.

**Q23. Describe the common features between a tribe and a caste.**

**Ans.** However such features are not just the characteristic of tribes but also of castes. Further there is also tremendous variability among tribes. Hence other attempts to define tribes consider them as a stage in the social and cultural evolution. Also with respect to their economic life, the production and consumption among the tribes is household based and unlike peasants they are not part of a wider economic, political, and social network. This could be resolved by considering the tribes and castes as belonging to one continuum. The tribes have a segmentary, egalitarian system and are not mutually inter-dependent, while castes are in a system or organic solidarity. They have direct access to land and no intermediary is involved between them and land.

In comparison, tribes are always understood to mainstream civilisations –that it may fight, serve, mimic, or adopt but cannot ignore. In India it has been found that tribes have been transforming themselves into larger entity of the caste system; others have become Christians or Muslims. There is further a change in their economic life – that is a change in the livelihoods from hunting and gathering to peasantry, and in modern times become wage labourers in plantations, mining, and other industries. There is a changing notion of tribe- which has to be the frame work for understanding tribes.

**Q24. Discuss the tribal communities spread across regions and democratic.**

**Ans.** The tribal communities are spread in all regions of the East, West, North and South of India with varying altitudes, terrain and resources. This means that each tribe has a different history, ecology and political economy and socio-cultural complexities. Further there is contiguity of the spread both within India and the neighbouring countries. Some of the Scheduled Tribes within the borders of Arunachal Pradesh,

Nagaland, Manipur and Mizoram have their counterparts across the borders of China, Thailand, Laos, Cambodia.

Tribals constitute only 8% of the population but occupy nearly 20% of the geographical area, which contains over 70% of the minerals and the bulk of forests and water resources.

**Demographic Distribution:** The population of Scheduled Tribes number only 19 million people distributed among 212 communities in the 1951 census. Their strength has increased to 38 and 52 million in 1971 and 1981 census. As per 2001 census, the Scheduled Tribes population is 84.32 million, constituting over 8.2 percent of the country's population. Some tribes were temporarily accommodated in the other backward classes' category. In 1950 there were 212 and in the year 2003, there are 533 tribes as per notified schedule under Article 342 with largest of them being in Orissa (62). Of the 698 scheduled tribes, seventy five are considered as primitive tribes. They are considered more backward than scheduled tribes and continue to live in pre-agricultural stage having very low literacy rates. The listing of tribes in the schedule depends on whether synonyms and sub-tribes are treated separately or not. There are also variations in the size of the communities, from 31 people of Jarwa to over 7 million Gonds. The numerically small tribal communities comprising of less than 1000 people are Andamanese, Onges and Toda etc. On the other hand, tribes like the Bhil, Santhals, Oraon, Munda, Mina, Khond and Saora and the like had more than 1 million population each.

The demographic and geographic spread has implications for the policies and programmes they are subject to as well as their social and economic life. For example large population of a tribe means that it is spread over a number of states and therefore the same group is treated differently by different state policies and development programmes which influences its social and economic structure. Also they may be educated in the language of the state in which they reside – these have far reaching implications for questions of identity and entity of the tribal communities.

**Q25. Describe the social and economic structure of tribal communities.**

**Ans.** The social and economic structure of tribal communities can be discussed as:

**(1) Social Structure:** The social structure is unique for each tribe. This comes with the way the family is organized, the customs and beliefs and the place of habitation, racial and linguistic features.

There is a wide variation across the communities with respect to the above. There arc also widc variations with regard to the particular social institutions that characterize all communities such as their family, marriage and kinship relations as also their particular modes of economy, that are much dependent on the ecological conditions of living. Further the relationship of the community with the nature and the kind of rituals associated with it is another facet that distinguishes them from other communities.

The social life of Indian tribes can be said to have a design with the individual forming families, families forming lineages, lineages in sub-clans or sub-local groups and sub-clans in clans or local group and clans in phratries or territorial groups phratries in moieties; moieties in sub tribes and finally sub-tribes making up the tribe. In this social design the smallest unit is the individual who forms the minimum or the smallest group like family or household. The smaller groups are combined into a larger one through several levels of incorporation.

The Family is the basic social and economic unit. There are well established roles for the various members of the family that are closely related to their authority and power within their social group. The economic, political, ritual rights are also associated with the development of the family.

(2) **Economic Structure:** In India tribals belong to different economic stages, from food-gathering to industrial labour which presents their overlapping economic stage in the broader framework of the stages of economy. A tribe is usually considered as an economically independent group of people, having their own specific economy and thus having a living, pattern of labour, division of labour and specialisation, gift and ceremonial exchange, trade and barter, credit and value, wealth, consumption norms, capital formation, land tenure and good-tangible and intangible–economic status. All these are significant markers for a special tribal economy in the broader set-up of Indian economy. The interdependence between the cultural, social life and the natural surroundings is of great significance in understanding tribal economy.

The mode of production in tribal economy is traditional, indigenous and culturally predominant. This needs to be understood in its structural arrangements and enforced rules for the acquisition and production of material items and services in the context of their cultural, social and natural living conditions. Further there are no class divisions within the tribes as the production relations are governed by the social arrangements. They are culturally a social unit, with being an enterpriser and worker as well as producer and consumer, all at the same time. The system of distribution is linked to the barter system or mutual exchange.

Some of the elements of this economic system are seen to be:

(a) Small economy-smallness of scale which is the fundamental characteristic of tribal communities-the resources, goods and service transactions take place within a small geographical area and within a community of persons numbered in hundreds or thousands. Further one or two good crops are considered staple and produced in bulk. Within the small framework of the tribe and a relatively small number of goods and services are produced and acquired.

(b) Use of simple technology compared to the industrialized economies – may be made by the producer himself or herself or acquired from others for a small sum. This also means that large-scale production processes are ruled out.

(c) Geographical and cultural isolation-in that they are self-contained and have very little transaction with outside communities in a majority of tribal communities.

(d) The profit motive is usually absent, and the role of an incentive is fulfilled by a sense of mutual obligation, sharing and solidarity.

(e) Cooperative and collective endeavors are emphasized.

**Q26. Describe the interdependence of tribes and non-tribal communities.**

**Ans.** Interdependence quite similar to the Jajmani system characterized the functional relationship between tribes or within tribes or tribal people and non-tribal of the tribal villages or the region. Under the system each caste group, within a village is expected to provide certain standardized service to the people of other castes. The head of the family who is served by an individual is known as his Jajman while the man who performs the service is known as the Kamin of Jajman. The Jajman pays his Kamin in cash or kind on a daily monthly or yearly basis.

For example, in the Jaunsar Bawar there is a typical interdependence seen in the agriculturalist, the artisan and the community servant and the free professional of the area. They help each other out. The Koltas till the lands of the Brahmans and Rajputs (khasas) for years together on some annual or periodical agreements and on payment. The Bohars make iron implements for agriculturists. The drummer Bajgis or Dhakis are an indispensable artisan community in Jaunser - Bawar. Their services are required in the temple on communal and ceremonial occasions.

**The Economic Institution of Dhangar:** This institution facilitates the agriculturalist activity. One gets the agricultural labour ryotwaris for cultivating one's own vast land. The person who is employed by a big landowner is commonly known as Dhangar in tribal Bihar. Dhangar is a most familiar word for the tribes like the Oraon, Minda and HO.

In tribal Bihar the big landowners keep agricultural labour land the year round. A labourer is engaged the month of magh on annual basis. Apart from annual payment in cash or in kind he is provided with food and a roof. From the day he is engaged he becomes a family member of the employer and gets the same social privileges. There is no difference in status between the employer and his Dhangar or agricultural labourer. He can even marry the land owner's daughter or sister if he belongs to a different clan. Generally the Dhangars are drawn from the same village.

Thus Tribals practice a mixed economy. The economic system of any Indian tribe cannot be exclusively placed in a particular typology in its strict sense. The fact that a tribe uses all available means to eke out its subsistence and combines minor forest produce collection with cultivation or shifting cultivation, simple cultivation with food collection indicates the complex economy of these people.

**Q27. Explain denotified and nomadic tribes.**

***or***

**Write the short note on Nomadic tribes.**

**[Dec-2017, Q.No.-5(a)] [June-2019, Q.No.-5(a)]**

**Ans.** The **Nomadic Tribes** and Denotified Tribes consist of about 60 million people in India, out of which about five million live in the state of Maharashtra. There are 315 Nomadic Tribes and 198 Denotified Tribes.

A large section of these tribes are known as 'free/liberated jatis' because they were classed as such under the Criminal Tribes Act 1871, enacted under British rule in India.

After Indian Independence, this act was repealed by the Government of India in 1952. In Maharashtra, these people are not been included in the list of Scheduled Tribes due to historical circumstances, but are listed as Scheduled Castes or "Nomadic Tribes. The tribes designated as "Denotified", "Nomadic" or "Semi-Nomadic" are eligible for reservation in India.

The Government of India established the National Commission for De-notified, Nomadic and Semi Nomadic tribes in 2005 to study the developmental aspects of such tribes.

In order to acquire a comprehensive picture of the situation of these communities and to suggest action for their socio-economic development, a National Commission for De-notified tribes, nomadic tribes were set up in 2005 whose report was submitted recently to the Prime Minister. In the Eleventh plan, special attention is to be accorded to the well-being of these groups as per the recommendations of the commission.

Despite these there are still some old issues plaguing these communities. Some of these are:

- Classification and enumeration of denotified and nomadic tribes, thereby providing constitutional safeguards and covering them under the prevention of Atrocities Act (1989).

- Strict scrutiny of these certificates of DNTs and penalisation of bogus DNTs.
- Sensitisation of the police force by information dissemination and in-service training, and setting up of social cells for legal aid and counseling, especially for women.
- Free and compulsory education to genuine DNT children till at least they are up to higher secondary level.

**Q28. Write the current issues faced by the tribal communities.**

*or*

**What are the major issues faced by tribal communities?**

**[Dec-2019, Q.No.-3(a)]**

**Ans.** These are the some of the major issues faced by the tribal communities:

(1) They possess small and uneconomical landholdings because of which their crop yield is less and hence they remain chronically indebted.

(2) Only a small percentage of the population participates in occupa-tional activities in the secondary and tertiary sectors.

(3) Literacy rate among tribals is very low. While in 1961, it was 18.53 per cent, in 1991 it increased to 29.60 per cent which compared to general literacy rate of 52.21 per cent in the country is very low, because while the growth of literacy rate in the past three decades in the country was 28.21 per cent, among the STs it was only 11.7 per cent. Though tribal literacy rate in Mizoram is 82.71 per cent and in Nagaland, Sikkim and Kerala it is between 57 per cent and 61 per cent, lack of literacy among tribal people has been identified as a major development problem.

(4) A good portion of the land in tribal areas has been legally transferred to non-tribals. Tribals demand that this land should be returned to them. In fact, tribals had earlier enjoyed considerable freedom to use forests and hunt animals. Forests not only provide them materials to build their homes but also give them fuel, herbal medicines for curing diseases, fruits, wild game, etc. Their religion makes them believe that many of their spirits live in trees and forests. Their folk-tales often speak of the relations of human beings and the spirits. Because of such physical and emotional attachment to forests, tribals have reacted sharply to restrictions imposed by the government on their traditional rights.

(5) Tribal government programmes have not significantly helped the tribals in raising their economic status. The British policy had led to ruthless exploitation of the tribals in various ways as it favoured the zamindars, landlords, moneylenders, forest contractors, and excise, revenue and police officials.

(6) Banking facilities in the tribal areas are so inadequate that the tribals have to depend mainly on moneylenders. Being miserably bogged down in indebtedness, tribals demand that Agricultural Indebtedness Relief Acts should be enacted so that they may get back their mort-gaged

land. vii. About 90 per cent of the tribals are engaged in cultivation and most of them are landless and practise shifting cultivation. They need to be helped in adopting new methods of cultivation.

(7) The unemployed and the underemployed want help in finding secon-dary sources of earning by developing animal husbandry, poultry farming, handloom weaving, and the handicrafts sector. Most of the tribals live in sparsely populated hills and communications in the tribal areas remain tough. The tribals, therefore, need to be protected against leading isolated life, away from towns and cities, through a network of new roads.

(8) The tribals are exploited by Christian missionaries. In several tribal areas, mass conversion to Christianity had taken place during the British period. While the missionaries have been pioneers in educa-tion and opened hospitals in tribal areas, they have also been responsible for alienating the tribals from their culture. Christian missionaries are said to have many a time instigated the tribals to revolt against the Indian government.

**Q29. What is the concept of community development?**

**Ans.** The concept of community development programmes focuses on the interventions for community development to be people centered and people led, that seek to change for better, the conditions of living of these communities.

Questions such as what is better for the community, who decides on these, who implements the programmes what are the ways in which the programmes are monitored or implemented, who takes decisions regarding funding and allocations, who is accountable to whom, form the central focus of community development programmes that determine the success in reaching the goals of community development. Thus community development programmes need to be understood with dimensions of their context, creation and culmination. The context factors relate to the issues, problems, concerns of the community, the background of the community and the strengths and weaknesses of the community.

The United Nations defines **community development** as "a process where community members come together to take collective action and generate solutions to common problems." It is a broad term given to the practices of civic leaders, activists, involved citizens and professionals to improve various aspects of communities, typically aiming to build stronger and more resilient local communities.

Community development is also understood as a professional discipline, and is defined by the International Association for Community Development (www.iacdglobal.org), the global network of community development practitioners and scholars, as "a practice-based profession and an academic discipline that promotes participative democracy, sustainable development, rights, economic opportunity, equality and social justice, through the organisation, education and empowerment of people within their communities, whether these be of locality, identity or interest, in urban and rural settings".

Community development seeks to empower individuals and groups of people with the skills they need to effect change within their communities. These skills are often created through the formation of social groups working for a common agenda. Community developers must understand both how to work with individuals and how to affect communities' positions within the context of larger social institutions.

***Approaches used in community development:***

(1) **External Agent Approaches:** The appointment of an external agent for the development of community programme is the best approach. He convinces the people through his personal skills and experience and motivate them to work for the development of community. He identifies various problems and seek suitable solutions for it. He organize the people discuss the situation, arrange meetings, forms committee and village councils to highlight the hinders in the developmental procedures. At last this person presents a policy for the community and the whole society adopt it for development. The external agent approach is also called managerial approach.

(2) **Multiple Approaches:** In this approach the community development experts try to provide various facilities including health, education, sanitation, recreation etc to control the causative factors in the way of community development. The basic philosophy of multiple approaches is to convert centuries into decades. The adaptation process must be kept in mind and the values, traditions, beliefs, and norms should be care. Slowly and gradually development must be given to the community.

In this approach some members are selected from the whole community. They try to make a combined policy for the improvement and betterment of the people. This approach is also called Representative approach because these people work in community as representatives of the whole locality.

(3) **Inner Resource Approach:** In this approach the local people are encouraged and motivated to use their resources for the improvement of the areas. These people are guided by the representatives of the community through various programs working internally. They arrange meetings discussions, give suggestions and agreements in the community. So, the people should motivate to improve the living standard of the whole community by using their internal resources.

**Community Development Values:** Community development has certain inherent values. These can be termed as:

**(1) Co-operation:** Working together to identify and implement action, based on mutual respect of diverse cultures and contributions.

**(2) Equality:** Challenging the attitudes of individuals, and the practices of institutions and society, which discriminate against and marginalize people.

**(3) Participation:** Facilitating democratic involvement by people in the issues, which affect their lives, based on full citizenship, autonomy, and shared power, skills, knowledge and experience.

**(4) Social Justice:** Enabling people to claim their human rights, meet their needs and have greater control over the decision-making processes, which affect their lives.

**(5) Learning:** Recognizing the skills, knowledge and expertise that people contribute and develop by taking action to tackle social, economic, political and environmental problems.

***Assumptions in community development:***

- Individuals, groups and local institutions within community areas share common interests that bind them together.
- This commonness also propels them to work together.
- The interests of the various groups are not conflicting.
- The state is a supra body that is impartial in the allocation of resources and that through its policies it does not further inequalities.
- People's initiatives are possible in the communities because of their common interests.

**Q30. Explain community development programmes and accountability.**

**Ans.** Community development programmes base themselves on the involvement of people in formulating and executing programmes. It also means the development and use of large number of local institutions and voluntary groups local and voluntary groups, use of group work techniques and the development of local leadership, development of administration which is development oriented rather than bureaucratic in approach.

Thus community development programmes aim at achieving certain goals such as collectively working to bring about social change and justice, by working with communities to identify their needs, opportunities, rights and responsibilities:

- Plan, organise and take action;
- Evaluate the effectiveness and impact of the action;
- And to do all these in ways which challenge oppression and tackle inequalities.

**Accountability in Community Development Programmes:** In all community development programmes the key lies in the implementation of the programmes for reaching the goals in such a way that the accountability issues are taken care of. Any community development programme has to have inbuilt components of monitoring and evaluation and transparent accountability procedures. The concept of accountability needs to be understood before we proceed any further.

**Concept of Accountability:** The concept of accountability includes two elements: 'answerability' of those who hold power to citizens and 'enforceability' of penalties in the event of failure to do so (Goetz and Jenkins 2001).

Accountability is seen as political and managerial accountability the former referring to accountability of decisions (social) the latter referring to accountability in carrying out tasks of according to agreed performance criteria (input, output, financial etc) In another case, some authors speak of political accountability, community accountability and bureaucratic accountability.

Accountability requires that one group or individual provides a professional or financial account (or justification) of it activities to another stake holding group or individual. It presupposes that an organisation or institution has a clear policy on who is accountable to whom and for what. It involves the expectation that the group held accountable, will be willing to accept advice or criticism and to modify its practices in the light of that advice and criticism.

***Characteristics and Principles of Accountability:***

- Accountability is personal: authority can only be delegated to one person.
- Accountability is vertical: from top to bottom, responsibilities and authority is delegated from supervisor to subordinate (supervisor holds subordinate accountable).
- Accountability is neutral: It is neither a positive nor a negative concept Excellent results are recognized, but failure may involve sanctions, including the withdrawal or modifications of working systems.

***The Four Principles of Accountability:***

- Specify responsibility and authority
- Provide guidance and support
- Objective comparison of results against targets and standard
- Take appropriate action

**Q31. What is the history of community development programmes?**

**Ans.** The **Community development** is a rural area earmarked for rural development administration in India. The area is administered by a Block Development Officer, supported by several technical specialists and village level workers. A community development block covers several gram panchayats, local administrative unit at the village level.

Currently, they are administrative units of 3rd level in some states of India (equal to tehsils in other states). For example, Bihar has 38 districts, 101 sub-division (sub-districts) and 534 C.D. Blocks. West Bengal has 18 districts and 341 development blocks. The concept of the community development block was first suggested by Grow More Food (GMF) Inquiry Committee in 1952 to address the challenge of multiple rural development agencies working without a sense of common objectives. Based on the GMF Inquiry Committee's recommendations, the community development programme was launched on a pilot basis in 1952 to provide for a substantial increase in the country's agricultural programme, and for improvements in systems of communication, in rural health and hygiene, and in rural education and also to initiate and direct a process of integrated culture change aimed at transforming the social and economic life of villagers. The community development programme was rapidly implemented. In 1956, by the end of the first five-year plan period, there were 248 blocks, covering around a fifth of the population in the country. By the end the second five-year plan period, there were 3,000 blocks covering 70 per cent of the rural population. By 1964, the entire country was covered.

**Q32. Explain community development programmes in rural, tribal and urban areas.**

***Or***

**Describe some of the community development programmes in rural areas. [June-2019, Q.No.-1]**

***Or***

**Write the short note on Kubumbashree Programme.**
**[Dec-2017, Q.No.-5(f)] [Dec-2018, Q.No.-5(h)]**

**Ans.** Rural community development encompasses a range of approaches and activities that aim to improve the welfare and livelihoods of people living in rural areas. As a branch of community development, these approaches pay attention to social issues particularly community organizing. This is in contrast to other forms of rural development that focus on public works (e.g. rural roads and electrification) and technology (e.g. tools and techniques for improving agricultural production).

Rural community development is important in developing countries where a large part of the population is engaged in farming. Consequently, a range of community development methods have been created and used by organisations involved in international development. Most of these efforts to promote rural community development are led by 'experts' from outside the community such as government officials, staff of non-governmental organisations and foreign advisers. This has led to a long debate about the issue of participation, in which questions have been raised about the sustainability of these efforts and the extent to which rural people are – or are not – being empowered to make decisions for themselves.

**Development actions:** Rural development actions are intended to further the social and economic development of rural communities.

Rural development programs have historically been top-down from local or regional authorities, regional development agencies, NGOs, national governments or international development organisations. Local populations can also bring about endogenous initiatives for development. The term is not limited to issues of developing countries. In fact many developed countries have very active rural development programs.

Rural development aims at finding ways to improve rural lives with participation of rural people themselves, so as to meet the required needs of rural communities. The outsider may not understand the setting, culture, language and other things prevalent in the local area. As such, rural people themselves have to participate in their sustainable rural development. In developing countries like Nepal, Pakistan, India, Bangladesh, integrated development approaches are being followed up. In this context, many approaches and ideas have been developed and implemented, for instance, bottom-up approach, PRA- Participatory Rural Appraisal, RRA- Rapid Rural Appraisal, etc.

**Programmes:**

- To secure total development of the material and the human resources in rural areas.
- To develop local leadership and self-governing institutions.
- To raise the living standards of the rural people by means of rapid increase in food and agricultural produce.
- To ensure a change in the mind-set of people instilling in them a mission of higher standards.
- A project are was divided into three development blocks, each comprising about 100 villages and a population of about 65,000 people. In areas where a full project was not considered feasible one or two development blocks were started to begin with. Subsequently CDP became a national programme that covered all the rural areas of the country.

**In tribal areas:** Tribe is a human social group. Exact definitions of what constitutes a tribe vary among anthropologists, and the term is itself considered controversial in academic circles in part due to its association with colonialism. In general use, the term may refer to people perceived by a population to be primitive and may have negative connotations. The concept is often contrasted with other social groups concepts, such as nations, states, and forms of kinship.

In some places, such as India and North America, tribes are polities that have been granted legal recognition and limited autonomy by the national government.

**Programmes:** A number of employment oriented and developmental programmes for tribals have been introduced by the government of India. The major programmes are Integrated Rural Development Programme ( IRDP), Jawahar Rozgar Yojana (JRY), Prime Ministers Rozgar Yojana (PMRY) and Training For Self Employment For Rural youth (TRYSEM). IRDP scheme is absolutely for rural people those belong to below poverty line and others are for both rural as well as urban youth. All there schemes are implemented in the state by District Rural Development Agencies (DRDA's) in collaboration with Commercial and Cooperative Banks. PMRY was initiated in October 1993 to tackle the burning problem of educated unemployment. PMRY relates to setting up of self employment ventures through industries and services. Any unemployed youth who is metric failed/passed or above or passed, is eligible for the benefits of the scheme subject to the condition that if he is between the age group of 18 to 35 years and his family income does not exceed ₹24,000 per annum. The youth should also be the permanent resident of the areas for at least three years and he should not be defaulter to any bank or financial institution. The scheme envisages 22.5% reservation for Scheduled Caste, Scheduled Tribe and 27% for OBC. A maximum loan of ₹1 lakh per candidate is provided under this scheme, at an interest rate of 12.5% to 15.5%. The entrepreneur has to contribute 5% of project cost as margin money. No collateral security guarantee is asked on such loans. Period of repayment starts after a moratorium of six to eighteen months and range over 3 to 7 years. The government provides subsidy to the extent of 15% of the total loan imbursed with a ceiling of ₹7,500 per entrepreneur. In case of joint venture each partner may be provided a loan of ₹1 lakh subsidy. In such cases the interest is calculated for each partner separately at a rate of 15% of his share in the project cost limited to ₹7,500 for each partner.

The Employment Programme on the other hand aims at providing employment through public works during the adverse agricultural season. The employment programme asserts that poverty persists because of the lack of employment opportunities. The earlier employment schemes were adhoc in nature but the employment programme launched from Oct 1980, popularly known as National Rural Employment Programme (NREP) is considered as a permanent plan programme. The travails of tribal development need to be understood properly. The programmes should be related to the specific needs of the tribal community. Also, tribal development programmes should be integrated with the ongoing rural development programmes meant for poverty alleviation. A pragmatic and holistic approach to tribal development alone can produce good results.

**In urban areas:** Urban community development programmes can also be promoted by government or by voluntary organisations. Such community initiatives have been reported in the work of urban sanitation, urban housing and urban health. All of this requires an external element of support or initiative coming from a few individuals or groups. Organisations like the slum Jagathu of Bangalore have also played an important role in raising community consciousness and invoking moral responsibility among those who govern including bureaucracy and legislature.

**Programmes:**

- Swarna Jayanti Shahari Rozgar Yojana (SJSRY) in India is a Centrally Sponsored Scheme which came into effect on 1 December 1997. The scheme strives to provide gainful employment to the urban unemployed and underemployed poor, through encouraging the setting up of self-employment ventures or provision of wage employment.

  The SJSRY scheme is being implemented on a cost-sharing basis between the Centre and the States in the ratio of 75:25. Given the low allocations for the scheme, only about 2 lakh urban poor under skill development and 50,000 under self-employment are being benefitted under SJSRY annually. The target under skill development of the urban poor is very small considering that the number of urban poor was estimated at 81 million in 2004-05 and that nationally a target of 500 million persons to be skill-trained by 2022 has been fixed by the National Council on Skill Development.
- Kudumbashree is the women empowerment and poverty eradication program, framed and enforced by the State Poverty Eradication Mission (SPEM) of the Government of Kerala. The Mission aims to eradicate absolute poverty within a definite time frame of 10 years under the leadership of Local Self Governments formed and empowered by the 73rd and 74th Amendments of the Constitution of India. The Mission launched by the State Government with the active support of Government of India and NABARD has adopted a different methodology in addressing poverty by organizing the poor in to community-based organisations. The Mission follows a process approach rather than a project approach. The mission was officially inaugurated by the then Prime Minister Atal Bihari Vajpayee in 1998 as requested by the State Government.

  Kudumbashree, a community organisation of Self Help Groups (SHG's) of women in Kerala, has been recognized as an effective strategy for the empowerment of women in rural as well as urban areas: bringing women together from all spheres of life to fight for their rights or for empowerment. The overall empowerment of women is closely linked to economic empowerment. Women through these NHGs work on a range of issues such as health, nutrition, agriculture, etc. besides income generation activities and seeking micro credit.

**Q33. Briefly present the main features of tribal community.**
**[Dec-2017, Q.No.-4(e)]**

***Or***

**Highlight the salient features of tribal community.**
**[Dec-2018, Q.No.-4(b)]**

***Or***

**Trace the historical evolution of the concept of a tribe.**
**[Dec-2019, Q.No.-1]**

**Ans.** Tribes are always understood in comparison to mainstream civilisations –that it may fight, serve, mimic, or adopt but cannot ignore. In India it has been found that tribes have been transforming themselves into larger entity of the caste system; others have become Christians or Muslims. There is further a change in their economic life – that is a change in the livelihoods from hunting and gathering to peasantry, and in modern times become wage labourers in plantations, mining, and other industries. There is a changing notion of tribe- which has to be the frame work for understanding tribes.

Robert Redfield considers tribe to be a small community and possessing characteristic features as:

- **Distinctiveness:** where the community begins and where it ends is apparent. This is expressed in the group consciousness of the people of the community,
- **Smallness:** a compact community with a small population,
- **Homogeneity:** all the persons do similar activities and have similar state of mind. All persons have similar livelihood strategies, which continue over generations,
- **Self sufficiency**: The community is self-sufficient and provides for most of the activities and needs of its people.

Mandelbaum (1956) mentions the following characteristics of Indian tribes:

- Kinship as an instrument of social bonds.
- A lack of hierarchy among men and groups.
- Absence of strong, complex and formal organisation.
- Communitarian basis of land holding.
- Segmentary character.

- Little value on surplus accumulation on the use of capital and on market trading Lack of distinction between form and substance of religion.

In this way we can see that a tribe is a social group of people associated with:

- homogeneity,
- isolation and non-assimilation,
- territorial-integrity,
- consciousness of unique identity and common culture,
- animism (now defunct) as an all-pervasive religion,
- the existence of distinctive social and political systems with an absence of exploiting classes and organised state structure,
- multi-functionalist kinship relations,
- segmentary nature of the socio-economic unit,
- frequent cooperation for common goals,
- self-sufficiency in their distinct economy, and
- a common dialect, and many other attributes that seem to have remained unchanged over centuries.

The concept of homogeneity and equality among the tribes has been challenged by social scientists. It has been found that there is considerable inequality in term of economic and political rights related to the control of marriage, exchange of allied goods and the redistribution process. There is enormous diversity within the tribes of India.

The tribes are said to live in exclusion and isolation of other communities but the historical relations of the tribes and non-tribes from time immemorial is often forgotten.

Many of the definitions of tribes are thus problematic; hence social scientists have conveniently used the officially recognised Scheduled Tribes to categorize tribes. The constitution of India in its article 342 (i) provides that the President of India with due consultation with the governors of the states may designate the tribe and tribal communities or parts of groups within tribes or tribal communities to be Scheduled Tribes for each state. This juridical terminology has received uncritical acceptance. Hence both for social workers and social scientists the term is practically synonymous with the list of those communities listed in the Scheduled Tribes.

The definitions of tribes continue to characterize certain categories of pre-literate cultures covering a wide range of forms of social organisational and levels of techno-economic development. In under standing tribes, social workers draw upon a variety of contributions drawn from sociology, anthropology, history and political economy.

**Q34. Difference between Community development and community work.**

***Or***

**Write the short note on Difference between community development and community work. [June-2018, Q.No.-5(b)]**

**Ans.** Community development is best used to refer to a process, or a way of doing something, which entails the mobilisation, participation and involvement of local people on common issues important to them.

Community work, on the other hand, is often used as a general term and refers to initiatives or activities that are delivered at a local level that may not actively involve members of the community as participants but merely as users of services.

Within India, we might say all forms of community practice go together- that is provision of basic services, campaigning for the rights of people and fostering community based approaches for self- development and increasing their stake in the developmental processes.

There is an increasing use of professional approaches, techniques and strategies to build the capacities of communities to undertake community development programmes which aim to bring in self-reliance, freedom and dignity.

❑❑

# 2 COMMUNITY ORGANISATION FOR COMMUNITY DEVELOPMENT

## INTRODUCTION

Community organisation may be more effective in addressing need as well as in achieving short-term and long-term goals than larger, more bureaucratic organisations. Community organisation may often lead to greater understanding of community contexts. It is characterized by community building, community planning, direct action and mobilisation, the promotion of community change, and, ultimately, changes within larger social systems and power structures along with localized ones. Community development practitioners work alongside people in communities to help build relationships with key people and organisations and to identify common concerns. They create opportunities for: the community to learn new skills and, by enabling people to act together, community development practitioners help to foster social inclusion and equality.

**Q1. Define community organisation.**

**Ans.** In a more contemporary context, Murpshy and Cunningham (2003) have defined community organizing as "the systematic process for mobilizing and advocating by using communal power". They opine that "Organizing for Community Controlled Development (OCCD) combines community organisations's mobilisation and advocacy power with neighbourhood investment strategies to build a strengthened and revitalized community". They stress on community organizing as it relates to the small place communities. Further, they characterize 'place based community organising' as "a process in which local people, united by concern for renewing their own small territory, plan and act together to form an organisational base that they control. It is a practice that involves collective human effort centred on mobilisation, advocating, planning and the negotiation of resources". In this practice, 'mobilisation' includes the building and maintenance of an organisational base, 'planning' includes fact gathering, assessment and strategic and tactical thinking and 'negotiation' refers to persistent pressure and bargaining for sufficient resources to achieve goals.

According to this perception, community organizing as a process of change continuously operates on two tracks, the first being the path of pursuit of agree-upon programme goals, and the second is the path of building, maintaining and continually renewing an organisational base. The ultimate aim of this process is to build 'strengthened' and 'revitalised' communities, where strengthening pertains to the unifying and educating initiatives of the residents to meet their social, civic and economic responsibilities and 'revitalizing' refers to making the place livable, democratic, equitable and tolerant, thereby helping its residents to live with dignity and moral integrity.

Marie Weil has been instrumental in popularizing the broader term 'community practice' to instead of community organisation. Community practice includes "work to improve the quality of life and increase social justice through social and economic development, community organizing, social planning and progressive social change". She visualized it to be "a cooperative effort between practitioners and affected individuals, groups, organisations, communities and coalitions". It is also interesting to delve a little deeper into the four central processes of: (1) Development, which focuses on empowering citizens to work in united ways to change their lives and environments in relation to their living conditions, economic conditions, and social, employment and opportunity structures; (2) Organizing which includes the processes of community organizing that engage citizens in projects to change social, economic and political conditions. It includes neighbourhood organizing, development of local leadership and coalition development; (3) Planning, which relates to social planning engaged in by citizens, advocacy groups, public and voluntary sector planners to design programmes and services that are appropriate to given communities or regions. It also involves design of more effective services and the reform of human service systems; and (4) Progressive change, encompassing the actions taken by groups to effect positive social, economic and political change.

Scholars and practitioners like Rubin and Rubin, in 2005, added another dimension to the definition of contemporary community organising. Their definition as also other definitions based on the consensus models of community organizing have sought theoretical grounding and support from scholars like Putnam who have studied social networks and 'social capital'. Putnam studied associational behaviour and proposed that "joining enabled people to build social capital, which was much like economic capital. People could rely on social relationships and use them as an exchange for support and assistance". Putnam's work was quickly adopted by, those working with communities, and 'social capital' has subsequently been as the core of community organizing.

Rubin and Rubin incorporated this core element in their definition of contemporary community organisation. The process of community organisation has been described by them as "the process of helping people understand the shared problems they face while encouraging them to join together to fight back". According to them, "organizing builds on the social linkages and networks that bring people together to create firm bonds for collective action. It creates a durable capacity to bring about change". In a similar vein, Loffer defines community organisation as "the process of building trusting relationships, mutual understanding and shared actions that bring together individuals, communities and institutions. This process enables cooperative action that generates opportunity and/or resources realized through networks, shared norms, and social agency".

Similarly, Staples (2004) focuses on a definition that includes "dual emphasis on participatory process and successful outcomes" and the establishment of disciplined and structured organisations as vehicles for change. This conception of community organisation includes both community or social development in which people use cooperative strategies to create improvements, opportunities, structures, goods and services that increase the quality of community life, and social action in which people convince, pressurise, or coerce decision makers to meet predetermined goals. Therefore, according to contemporary practitioners like Staples, community building models that encourage consensus and social action models that promote conflict can be used simultaneously or sequentially.

There are several definitions available in literature. These have evolved at different times and in differing contexts. Let us look at some of the more widely accepted definitions of community organisation.

**(1) Lindeman:** Lindeman's book in the year 1921 was the first to appear on what became known in North America as Community Organisation. He defined community organisation as "those phases of social organisation which constitute a conscious effort on the part of a community to control its affairs democratically, and to secure the highest services from its specialists, organisations, agencies and the institutions by means of recognized interrelations."

**(2)** **Murray G. Ross:** In the second half of 1940s, a number of works on community organisation appeared, perhaps the best of which was that by Murray G. Ross in 1955. His work contributed to the immense popularisation of the practice of community organisation in the U.S. He saw community organisation as "a process by which a community identifies its needs or objectives, develops the confidence and will do work at these needs or objectives, finds the resources (external and internal) to deal with these needs and objectives, takes action in respect of them, and in doing so, extends and develops cooperative and collaborative attitudes and practices in the community". He goes further to identify three main approaches to community organisation: (a) the 'specific content' approach, whereby a worker or an organisation identifies a problem or set of problems and launches a programme to meet them; (b) the 'general content' approach, whereby a group, association or council attempts a coordinated and orderly development of services in a particular area; (c) the 'process' approach, where the objective is not the content (facilities or services), but initiation and sustenance of a process which will involve people within the community in identifying and taking action in respect of their own needs and problems. All these three components related to 'content' and 'process' find a place in his definition.

**(3)** **Harper:** Harper (1959) perceived community organisation as an effort to "bring about and maintain progressively a more effective adjustment between social welfare resources and social needs". It is concerned with: (a) the discovery and definition of need; (b) the elimination and prevention of social needs and disabilities; (c) the articulation of resources and needs; and (d) the constant readjustment of resources in order to meet the changing needs better. On a similar note Arthur Dunham who was another important contributor to the practice of community organisation felt that social work methodology most commonly associated with society, as opposed to individual change is community work, alternatively defined as community development or the new community organisation. This was "a process of bringing about and maintaining adjustment between social welfare needs and social welfare resources in a geographical area or a functional field".

(4) **Younghusband:** In 1973, Younghusband defined community organisation as "primarily aimed at helping people within a local community to identify social needs, to consider the most effective ways of meeting them and to set about doing so, in so far as their available resources permit".

(5) **Peter Baldock:** Peter Baldock's (1974) concept of community work was very close to the definition of community organisation given by Ross and Younghusband. Baldock opined that community work "is a type of activity practiced by people to identify problems and opportunities and to come to realistic decisions to take collective action to meet these problems and opportunities in ways that they determine for themselves. The community worker also supports them in the process of putting decisions, to help them develop their abilities and independence".

(6) **Kramer and Specht:** Another definition by Kramer and Specht in 1975, referred to community organisation as "a method of intervention, whereby a professional change agent helps a community action system, composed of individuals, groups, or organisations to engage in planned collective action in order to deal with social problems within a democratic system of values". Further, according to them, this method of intervention involves two interrelated concerns: (a) the interaction process, which includes identifying, recruiting and working with members and developing organisational and interpersonal relationships among them, which facilitates their efforts; and (b) the technical tasks involved in identifying problem areas, analyzing causes, formulating plans, developing strategies and mobilizing the resources necessary to have effective action.

(7) **Mc Millan:** Mc Millan also contributed to the understanding of the concept of community organisation by describing it in a generic sense as "deliberately directed efforts to assist groups in attaining a unity of purpose and action". He further elaborates its character by specifying that "it is practiced, though often without recognition of its character, whenever the objective is to achieve or maintain a pooling of talents and resources of two or more groups on behalf of either general or specific objectives".

**Q2. What are the elements of the community organisation?**

**Ans.** An examination of the aforementioned definitions of community organisation reveals certain important elements. These are:

(1) Community organisation has been perceived both as a 'process' and a 'method'. The use of the word 'process' brings into focus the movement from the identification of an objective or a set of

objectives to the attainment of the same. It also signifies the capacity of the community to function as an integrated unit, as it deals with one or more common problems. Moreover, this process may be conscious or unconscious, voluntary or involuntary, short or of long duration. The use of the word 'process' to describe community organisation also connotes a course of action aimed at preparing the members of the community for developmental action. This course of action includes a number of inter-related steps including: (a) Identification of needs, problems and objectives; (b) Prioritisation or ranking of the needs, problems and objectives according to their relative importance and urgency; (c) Developing confidence and determination among community members to meet their needs and solve their problems; (d) Helping them to take appropriate decisions in all these regards; (e) Mobilising resources, in the form of men, money and materials from within the community and outside, necessary to deal with their decisions and plans; (f) Executing their plan of action with proper monitoring of the activities, and taking corrective measures, if required; and (g) Educating others on the strength of collective action, collaborative attitudes and processes of self help.

(2) 'Community practice' and 'community work' are more broad-based terms which find a greater usage in contemporary context. They are used to describe the cooperative effort between the practitioners and the community system. They include work to achieve social and economic development of the community, community organizing, social planning and progressive social change. Thus, community organizing, which encompasses neighbourhood organizing, local leadership development and coalition development is one core component of community practice

(3) Community organisation involves working with the community system, and thus entails working at the level of individuals, groups, organisations, community and coalitions.

(4) Community organisation as a conception has been shown to include both community or social development and social action. In other words, community building models that encourage consensus, and social action models that promote conflict often co exist and can be used simultaneously or sequentially. While the community building model is also the prevailing model used in many international settings, endeavors to bring about large scale systemic changes are also increasingly being undertaken and they represent the social action approach.

(5) The process of community organisation may not always be a natural, spontaneous process. It may also be a deliberative and engineered one. While it may sometimes evolve without the assistance of the professional change agent, it often has to be initiated, nourished and developed by a professional worker, who has the requisite skill and the experience to help people to plan and progressively move towards achieving their agreed on goals.

(6) Community organisation is not value free, as it adopts democratic values; accepts the cultural fabric of the community and aims at creating equitable, tolerant and socially and economically just communities. It operates on the basis of building consensus and self help and simultaneously directs the community towards a positive change through appreciation of this value system.

(7) Social capital has been recognized as a core ingredient in community organizing. It refers to the connections among individuals and the norms of reciprocity and trust worthiness that facilitate civic engagement, social solidarity and cooperation for mutual benefit. It is therefore the fundamental source of strength for the community. In communities with strong social capital, the community organisation process is fostered. On the other hand, in communities with weak social capital, people find it difficult to cooperate, collaborate and join together for collective action.

(8) Community organisation has also been viewed as a process of change which concurrently operates at two levels, the first being the pursuit for achievement of certain programme/service oriented goals, the second being the path of building, maintaining and continually renewing an organisational base. Thus, community organisation as a concept focuses both on development oriented goals as also the ultimate goal of "getting organized". Organizing is the process by which people develop some sort of structure for joining together over time.

**Q3. Briefly discuss the community work and community organisation in social work.**

***Or***

**What is the position of community work in social work?**

**Ans.** Although community residents have always worked collaboratively on common needs and concerns, the evolution of formal practice interventions for community work has its origins in the United Kingdom and the United States in the late 19th century. With the formalization of social work as a profession, community organisation came to be recognized as a method of social work practice. As a result, an increasing number of professionals began working in communities.

During the initial phase, community work was primarily aimed at trying to help community members to enhance their social adjustment, and viewed in this context it was recognized as a method of social work. It was also viewed as a means to coordinate the work of voluntary agencies.

In India, the experience of working with a slum community in the city of Mumbai led to the establishment of the first institution of social work in the year 1936. Community work, as a method of social work in the Indian context has been largely seen as a process of developing local initiatives, especially in the area of education, health and agricultural development.

The focus of work has been, to encourage people to articulate their needs and facilitate them to avail the existing resources to meet their needs. Further, in the situation where there exists a gap between needs and resources, further efforts are made to initiate new services/ programmes. Although community residents have always worked collaboratively on common needs and concerns, the evolution of formal practice interventions for community work has its origins in the United Kingdom and the United States in the late 19th century. With the formalization of social work as a profession, community organisation came to be recognized as a method of social work practice. As a result, an increasing number of professionals began working in communities. During the initial phase, community work was primarily aimed at trying to help community members to enhance their social adjustment, and viewed in this context it was recognized as a method of social work. It was also viewed as a means to coordinate the work of voluntary agencies.

Ross has identified three approaches to community organisation: (1) the 'specific content' approach; (2) the 'general content' approach; and (3) the 'process' approach (which have been elaborated in the previous section). However, while he has included all these elements in his definition of community organisation, he describes community organisation as essentially a "process by which the community identifies its needs or objectives and develops cooperative and collaborative attitudes and practices in the community". In essence, when engagement with the community takes the form of a "process", comprising of a series of interrelated steps or stages, it can be characterized as community organisation.

Authors like Marie Weil have popularized the usage of the term "community practice". According to her "communities are the context of all social work practice, and community practice emphasises working mutually with citizen groups, cultural and multicultural groups and organisations, and human service organisations to improve life options and opportunities in community". Additionally, she describes it as "work to improve the quality of life and enhancement of social justice for the community through social and economic development, community organising, social planning and progressive social change". In other words community practice relies on community organising as a means to achieve its goals.

**Q4. Enlist the guiding purpose of community organisation.**
**[June-2018, Q.No.-3(c)]**

**Ans.** Weil and Gamble have provided a set of eight purposes which provide the basis for most community practice engagement. (Weil and Gamble 2004). These purposes are:

(1) Improving the quality of life of the members of the community.

(2) Extending human rights by developing participatory structures and opportunities and deepening democracy for citizens who are excluded and feel powerless to influence policies that have an effect on their lives.

(3) Advocacy for a community of interest, such as children; for a specific issues such as political and social rights for women and marginalized populations.

(4) Human social and economic development to assure social support, economic viability and sustainability by expanding participation and building grassroots leadership; building economic, social and political assets for the poor in impoverished urban and rural areas.

(5) Service and programme planning for a newly recognized or re-conceptualized need or to serve an emerging population.

(6) Service integration developing local to national and international means of coordinating human services for populations in need.

(7) Political and social action to build political power for the economically and socially marginalized, protect the weak and the poor, foster institutional change for inclusion and equity, and increase participatory democracy and equality of access and opportunity in local, regional and international efforts.

(8) Social Justice to build towards human equality and opportunity across race, ethnicity, gender and nationality.

In conclusion, the community worker who has a focus on values and purpose, and who makes those explicit with community groups, will have a greater capacity to develop mutually respectful relationships with the group members and to work as a facilitator to find sufficient common ground for collaborative action.

**Q5. Briefly describe value orientation of community organisation.**

***Or***

**Value orientation in community organisation is a prerequisite for social work practice. Do comment.**

***Or***

**Write the short note on Value orientation in community organisation. [Dec-2019, Q.No.-5(c)]**

**Ans.** Community organisation derives from a unique frame of reference, the nature of which is based on a particular value orientation. As in social work, the focus of community organisation practice is also guided by a system of personal and professional values.

Values are beliefs that delineate preferences about how one ought or ought not to behave. Such formulations of values obviously have some subjective element. We seek a position or an objective we prefer; we value what we think embraces human dignity. There may not be any data to prove that this is "right", "better" or "desirable". It is largely a matter of choice based upon preference for a particular position or objective. There may be a combination of wisdom, experiences and facts that may support this position, but ultimately it is a matter of choice and preference.

The value orientation of community organisation as of all social work methods derives from acceptance of certain basic concepts and principles as a foundation for work with people. These core values which are now increasingly being reflected in the professional code of ethics in many countries are also reaffirmed in the international definition of social work, given by the International Federation of Social Workers (IFSW) in the year 2000. This is as follows:

"The social work profession promotes social change, problem solving in human relationships, and the empowerment and liberation of people to enhance well being. Utilising theories of human behaviour and social systems, social work intervenes at the points where people interact with their environments. Principles of human rights and social justice are fundamental to social work".

The core values reflected in the aforementioned definition of social work as also those which find a place in the code of ethics adopted by professional associations of social workers include: dignity and worth of the person, importance of human relationships, social justice, human rights and human dignity, integrity and competence, and professional conduct.

Ross has provided certain articles of faith which represent the value orientation to community organisation (and, indeed all of social work). Among these are: (1) the essential dignity and ethical worth of the individual; (2) the possession of potentialities and resources in each person for managing his own life; (3) the importance of freedom of expression of one's individuality; (4) the great capacity for growth within all social beings; (5) the right of the individual to basic physical necessities; (6) the need for the individual to struggle and strive to improve his own life and environment; (7) the right of the individual to help in time of need and crisis; (8) the need of a social climate which encourages individual growth and development; (9) the right and the responsibility of the individual to participate in the affairs of the community; (10) the practicability and importance of discussion, conference, and consultation as methods for the solution of individual and social problems; (11) the importance of a social organisation for which the individual feels responsible and which is responsive to individual feeling; and (12) "self help" as the essential base of any programme of aid. Ross refers to these and other orientations as constituting the "bias" of social work, which condition its goals and precludes certain types of action as being more useful (Ross, 1967).

**Q6. What are the major assumptions that influence the method of community organisation? [June-2018, Q.No.-3 (b)]**

***Or***

**Highlight the various assumptions regarding community organisation as a method of social work practice.**

**[Dec-2017, Q.No.-3 (a)]**

***Or***

**Explain the assumptions regarding Community Organisation as a method of social practice.**

**[Dec-2018, Q.No.-3 (b)]**

**Ans.** According to Ross, community organisation derives from a unique frame of reference, which assumes a distinct form due to a particular value orientation which stems from traditional religious values which have been expanded to form the basis of social work philosophy; a particular conception of the problems confronting modern man in the community and certain assumptions that influence the method (Ross, 1955). While we have covered the first component in the previous section, and we will cover the second component in another unit, let us look at the assumptions that influence the method of community organisation, which derive in part from the value orientation of, and in part from experiences in social work. Some of these are as follows:

(1) Communities of people can develop capacity to deal with their own problems. This implies that the community people may confront situations in which they feel disenchanted and hopeless, but they can nevertheless develop attitudes and skills which permit them to work towards shaping their community appropriately to meet their needs.

(2) People want change and can change. This implies that communities of people constantly change their ways of life and are interested in making their lives better. The will to change is often paralysed by challenging social forces, but if blocks to free thinking and feeling are removed, all people will participate in changes which aim to meet their needs more adequately.

(3) People should participate in making, adjusting, or controlling the major changes taking place in their communities. This

assumption implies that people should have the opportunity to organize to achieve their own common goals, plan the adjustments which must be made in response to certain changes which are beyond their control, and to regulate their own communities as far as possible.

(4) Changes in community living which are self-imposed or self-developed have a meaning and permanence that imposed changes do not have In the community, people as they strive towards achievement of their goals, modify and develop capacities consistent with these goals. In the process the culture as a whole adjusts to the changes that are taking place. Changes such as these are self-imposed and determined last longer than those that are externally imposed, because in the latter situation, the community does not feel any sense of participation or conscious planning for adjustment to such changes.

(5) A "holistic approach" can deal successfully with problems with which a "fragmented approach" cannot cope. This implies that social problems can be dealt with by adopting more coordinated approaches rather than piecemeal initiatives by the separate social agencies working apart from each other. Most of the problems have multiple causation and a single specialized approach to the problem will have limited value.

(6) Democracy requires cooperative participation and action in the affairs. Of the community, and that people must learn the skills which make this possible. There must be active participation in the development and use of an effective communication process, which facilitates the identification of common objectives and implementation of collective action. People may require practice and the help of experts to establish and maintain democratic community institutions.

(7) Frequently, communities of people need help in organising to deal with their needs. This help may be of diverse types, ranging from advice, to resources/inputs, or programme designing etc. While people may possess their own resources and capacities, they may often require professional help in mobilising them effectively.

**Q7. Discuss the historical perspective of community organisation in the United Kingdom.**

**Ans.** During this period between the end of the Civil War and the beginning of World War I, a number of social issues emerged in the US and these had a strong impact on the welfare practices. These included the rapid industrialization of the country, the urbanization of its population, problems emerging out of immigration and changes in oppressed populations. These issues highlighted the need for the emergence of community organisation practice. Immediately after the Civil War there were organisations that sought to support and sustain the newly won civil rights. The black community, the Chicanos, the Native American community and the Asian American Community were all confronted with problems related to poverty, race relations, cultural conflicts and marginalization.

Community organisation activities during this period can be divided into two categories: the first being those which were carried out by institutions related to present day social welfare activities and the second category of activities were those conducted by those with no direct connection to contemporary community organisation programmes, but which nevertheless have been of interest for community practitioners. The latter include the organisation of political, racial and other action groups.

A number of factors had contributed to the development of the Charity Organisation Societies in England in 1869 and by 1873 in the United States. These Societies initially came into existence to coordinate the work of the private agencies which provided for the needs of the poor. Soon they began to offer direct relief and other services. A number of social factors contributed to this development. These included the movement of large populations into cities like those defended from Mexicans, large scale immigration to meet the manpower needs of growing industries and the emergence of many social problems associated in the wake of these, like poverty, inadequate housing, declining health status and exploitation. This led to the development of agencies directed to ameliorating these conditions. Separate efforts were also made by groups associated with different neighbourhoods, as also ethnic and religious groups.

A number of other influential reports were also published which had impact on the development of community work in the country. One of these was the Seebohm Committee Report, 1968, which recommended the expansion of community work especially through social service provision and the Skeffington Report, 1969, which recommended increased public participation in urban planning.

The British Community Development Projects were launched in 1969 as one among a series of initiatives designed to deal with urban deprivation. The projects aimed at evolving cost effective welfare measures to tackle the high concentration of deprivation and adopted a variety of strategies to work with the communities. While some projects operated on 'dialogue model' of social change, and focussed largely on ameliorative activities, some rejected such approaches, as they only provided 'support for the status quo'. By and large, the projects rejected conflict-based community action as a means of achieving their goals, as it was felt that such action was sporadic, alienated the decision-makers and led to group instability. In their view the way to achieve change at the local level was to increase access to, and democratic control over the resources that were already available. Its goal was to radically change the organisation of resources within the local area, and not to act as an outside pressure group.

In the period since 1968 a substantial number of those professionally engaged in community work became advocates of 'community action', a form of community work whose main features included a support of disadvantaged groups in conflict with authority and an accompanying reformist or Marxist perspective on society. There were a number of reasons for this development. The impulse of urban community action was encouraged to some extent by the example of urban action among the blacks in the U.S. from Martin Luther.

Secondly, developments in community work practice in the form of the Urban Programme in 1968 and the Twelve Community Development projects which emerged from this programme in 1969 also impacted the emergence of community action. The Projects which focussed on twelve poor communities, closely reflected on the impact of poverty on people's lives and advocated that it was the radical/structural Marxist analyses of discrimination which was responsible for the continued existence of poverty and the plight of the urban poor.

Thirdly, the work of community organisers like Gramsci, Paulo Freire and Saul Alinsky started impacting the community work practice in the subsequent phase. They were strong advocates of the radical tradition of community action were largely instrumental in popularising the radical stance in community work.

Fourthly, the early seventies had witnessed an increasing recognition and expansion of community work, both through the voluntary and government sectors. However as the decade progressed, there was a greater emphasis on state sponsorship of community work. This resulted in some inherent contradictions. While community workers were working with the local people to organize them and to facilitate them to demand better public services, they were employed by the very state which was responsible for the provision or the 'non'-provision of these services.

As a result of all of the aforementioned developments, two spilt/ distinct approaches to community work arose. The first approach believed that there is a multiplicity of competing power bases in society which are mediated by the state and that community work is only capable of ameliorative small scale neighbourhood organising and small scale reforms. This approach was conservative, with an emphasis on consensus and cooperation. On the other hand, the alternate approach strongly proposed community work as the locus of change within the struggle for transformation of the structures of society that were recognized to be the root cause of all oppression. This approach, also known as the radical approach to community work, took on the 'hard issues' of social justice and sustainability, while the former 'consensus' approach focussed on the local 'soft issues' such as provision of services and interagency work.

**Q8. Discuss the history of community organisation in the United States of America.**

**Ans.** The movements in England also impacted the turn of events in the United States. In 1880, he Charities Organisation was set up to put rational order in the realm of charity and relief. The development of community organisation within American communities since 1865 was concerned both with community activities in which professionals were engaged and also with indigenous community efforts, especially within oppressed groups.

For the purpose of analysis American history can be divided into five phases (Gavin and Cox, 2001). These are as follows:

**1865 to 1914:** During this period between the end of the Civil War and the beginning of World War I, a number of social issues emerged in the US and these had a strong impact on the welfare practices. These included the rapid industrialization of the country, the urbanization of its population, problems emerging out of immigration and changes in oppressed populations.

These issues highlighted the need for the emergence of community organisation practice. Immediately after the Civil War there were organisations that sought to support and sustain the newly won civil rights. The black community, the Chicanos*, the Native American community and the Asian American Community were all confronted with problems related to poverty, race relations, cultural conflicts and marginalization.

Community organisation activities during this period can be divided into two categories: the first being those which were carried out by institutions related to present day social welfare activities and the second category of activities were those conducted by those with no direct connection to contemporary community organisation programmes, but which nevertheless have been of interest for community practitioners. The latter include the organisation of political, racial and other action groups.

**1915 to 1929:** After World War I, several new conditions emerged that had a significant impact on community organisation practice. The development of community organisation institutions like the Community Chest and United Fund was one such condition. This period saw an increase in the number of welfare institutions, which generated demands for coordination, and better fund raising methods. While the philanthropists established the Community Chests or United Funds to supply aid, the professionals supported the community welfare council to dispense this aid. Community Chests were initiated by large contributors and most of the work was handled by volunteers. World War I gave great impetus to the development of chests like war chests.

The Council of Social Agencies and the Community Welfare Council developed as a result of the increasing professionalism among those who helped the poor. The friendly visitor was replaced by the paid agent. The COSs founded schools of philanthropy, which became graduate schools of social work. A growing cadre of welfare professionals with the support of many volunteers were interested in organising a rational, systematic approach to the welfare needs of communities. They formed councils which were often assigned the responsibility of distributing the money raised by community chests.

**1929 to 1954:** Social Work in this period was deeply affected by the depression and the World War II. There was a vast increase in unemployment, as also bank and stock market failures. The expansion of government programmes was a direct result of the depression. The government became the most significant planner and promoter of welfare prgrammes through the enactment of legislations and social security and minimum wages.

The Federal government through its agencies became the main impetus for social planning. While this was not really a period of innovation in community organisation, it was a time during which efforts were made to conceptualise the nature of community organisation practice. The relation between community organisation and social work was examined, the objectives of community organisation were reflected upon and the role of the community practitioner was deliberated upon.

As far as development of the profession was concerned, this was a time during which intensive efforts were made to conceptualise the nature of community organisation practice. There were three overriding concerns. These were:

(1) The relation between community organisation and social work. While one school of thought contended that community organisation was not really a legitimate form of social work practice, the other school made efforts to establish community organisations affinity to the basic values and concerns of social work.

(2) An interest in the objectives of community organisation, ranging from strengthening community cohesion to prevention/ amelioration of a wide ranging set of social problems, and

(3) The appropriate role for the practitioner, which was envisaged to "strike a balance between giving help and fostering self determination of the community".

**1955 to 1968:** The growth of the Civil Rights Movement, the end of legal school segregation and the rising dissatisfaction of the black Americans gave birth to a number of organisations which sought to end the inequality of opportunity for the black people. Martin Luther King, Jr emerged as a leader in this struggle.

As these organisations fought for black pride, they also demanded autonomy in black affairs including neighbourhoods. Subsequently, other minority groups also started asserting themselves, claiming their rights and their special identity. Thus, there was a growing effort to create ethnic minority institutions, including neighbourhood control of schools, business, professional societies, labour unions, interest groups and rights organisations.

**1969 and After:** The year 1969 marked the beginning of the Nixon administration, followed by the Carter and Reagan administrations. The thrust of these administrations was on reducing the role of the government, particularly the national government in social welfare. Three main developments during the period, specifically in the eighties and thereafter shaped the social conditions and the trends in social work practice at the community and societal levels. These were:

(1) The emergence of an information society, characterized by "high technology" in every sphere of life;

(2) The growth of a world economy, leading to vast shifts in investment patterns and inter organisational relationships on a global scale; and

(3) Decentralisation, leading to the increased role that state as opposed to national government started playing in the U.S., and the vast increase in neighbourhood organisations and the shift of population to rural areas and small towns (Naisbitt, 1982).

The most important development with the most impact on the current phase of community organising is the belief in the value of self-help activities. Hundreds of organisations have arisen for mutual aid in the last many years and continue to be created on almost a daily basis in the U.S. The move towards participation has grown, together with a rise in initiatives, activism and a greater say of people in determining their own affairs. Another important trend which has emerged according to Naisbitt is "networking", particularly that enabled by computer utilization, in which people seek ways of locating that American society has moved towards becoming a society of even more diversity. This is reflected in the many forms that the family is taking.

**Q9. Trace the history of community organisation in India.**
**[Dec-2017, Q.No.-2] [June-2019, Q.No.-1]**

**Ans.** Community work in India was largely seen as a process of developing local initiatives, particularly in the areas of education, health and agricultural development. This was to be undertaken by liasoning needs with available resources. The major thrust was on motivating people to express their needs, and to avail themselves of existing resources.

From 1937 to about 1952, community work in India was fairly dormant. This was the time when the social work profession was in its infancy and trainees were primarily absorbed as case workers in different settings.

While community organisation was being taught as a method of social work, there were hardly any job opportunities which provided avenues for community practice. Some opportunities only emerged with the launching of the Community Development Programme in India in 1952.

In this initial phase a prominent advocate of community development in India, was Mukherji. He described community development as "a movement designed to promote better living for the whole community, with the active participation and if possible at the initiative of the community". Further, he emphasized that "whenever the initiative is not forth-coming, efforts should be made to arouse and stimulate this initiative". Mukherji contributed significantly to the development of community work in India. He perceived community development as an amalgamation of two processes: 'extension education' and 'community organisation'. 'Extension education' was expected to improve the knowledge and skill base of people; and to change their attitudes to make them progressive and desirous of improving their living conditions.

'Community organisation', on the other hand entailed setting up of three institutions in the village. These were: the village panchayat, the village cooperative and the village school. Other associated organisations such as women's organisations, youth groups, farmers and artisans associations were also sought to be developed to assist the three main institutions in achieving the overall development of the community.

In the 1970s, the nature of community work largely remained ameliorative, and not radical or conflict oriented. Social workers started working in urban slums in sizeable number. This was primarily on account of the fact that a large number of voluntary organisations started undertaking work in the realm of literacy, provision of basic amenities of life, women and children's development etc. Many other organisations, previously confined to institutional work started adopting a community focus. This led to a wider practice of community work, where 'community' mainly implied target population in a defined geographical area or neighbourhood.

**Q10. "Community organisation is considered as a macro method of practice in social work." Do comment.**

***Or***

**Discuss briefly community organisation as a macro method of practice in social work.**

**Ans.** Community organisation is considered as a Macro method of practice in social work or macro level social work, as it is used to address the broader social problems that affect a large group of people. The term 'macro' is used because of ability of this method to involve a large number of people in solving the social problems collectively. This method thus enables us to enhance the scope/degree of intervention. Unlike case work, which deals with only one individual at a time or group work, which deals with a limited number of participants, community organisation deals with a large number of people at any given time.

Individual approach is not practical in a context where the magnitude of problems faced is alarming. In such cases we have to use a method which can concurrently help a large number of people. This is especially true in case of developing countries where the magnitude of several problems faced by people is immense and so there is an urgent need to work with larger constituencies. In such a context, the community becomes an important level of social work intervention and community organisation emerges as an effective method of social work practice to ameliorate the widespread economic and social problems faced by these countries.

Community organisation is also characterised as a macro method because it can be successfully implemented at the local level or at state level or even at the regional or international level.

**Q11. Briefly discuss the community organisation as a problem solving method.**

***Or***

**Explain community organisation as a problem solving method. [Dec-2019, Q.No.-4(b)]**

**Ans.** Community organisation also strives to solve the problems and fulfil the needs of its 'client', which is the community. It is also concerned with:

(1) The release of its latent potentialities;
(2) The optimalised use of its indigenous resources;
(3) The development of its capacity to manage its own life; and
(4) The enhancement of its ability to function as an integrated unit.

The end goal is the development of self confidence and self help; the emergence of cooperative and collaborative attitudes, skills and behaviour, which then form the basis of sustainable action and change in the client system.

Like the other methods, community organisation also relies on similar assumptions, namely the dignity and worth of the client, the resources possessed by the client to deal with its own problems; the inherent capacity that the 'client' possesses for growth and development; and the ability to choose wisely in the management of its own affairs. A case worker assumes that often individuals become overwhelmed by the complexities of life and thereby become psychosocially paralysed, which in turn curtails their own capacity for response by way of action. But with appropriate facilitation, this stage can be overcome, and the normal process of growth can be resumed for the individual concerned. Moreover, like the case worker who accepts the client as he/she is; develops a professional relationship with the client; starts from where the client is; and helps the client to become functional and autonomous, the community organiser also has the same general orientation and relies on a similar approach in working with the community, which is the client for him/her. Community organisation therefore shares a common base, and a common core of philosophy and method with case work and group work. It is also committed towards solving problems and facilitating change in the client system. The nature of problems dealt with in the context of Indian communities relate to poverty, unemployment, exploitation, lack of access to basic services and denial of social justice/rights. The problems may also be more group specific i.e. as they relate to particular groups like women, children, youth, elderly or the backward classes.

Since the worker in community organisation works on a larger canvas, he/she is (a) concerned with the different sub-groups and sub-cultures within the same; (b) has to develop insights about the value systems, behaviour patterns, social organisation, formal and informal leadership as they pertain to the diverse groups; (c) understand the interests and problems that these groups have in common; and (d) assess the degree of cooperation and competition that exist in them. The methods of understanding and operation used will therefore be different from that of the case worker or the group worker.

In any process of problem solving there are three basic steps viz. study, diagnosis and intervention/treatment.

First, the problem has to be studied by collecting information. From this information, the main causes leading to the problem have to be identified. This step is referred to as 'diagnosis'. Based on the diagnosis, a solution or intervention is evolved called 'treatment'. In any context, problems can be solved only after following this three step procedure.

**Q12. What is the relationship between community organisation and other methods of social work?**

***Or***

**Discuss the relationship between community organisation and other primary methods of social work.**

**[June-2019, Q.No.-3(b)]**

**Ans.** The relationship between community organisation and other methods of social work can be viewed as:

**(1) Community Organisation and Case Work:** Case work forms an integral part of community organisation. When the community organiser enters the community, he/she interacts with people on an individual basis, identities their needs and works towards their mobilization into groups and organisations. In other words, work with individuals and families become the beginning point for community mobilization. Individual contact strategy is also used to create awareness on relevant issues/problems.

The community organiser also has to deal with a number of significant individuals in the community. These may be (a) individuals who may be expected to oppose and resist change; (b) individuals in special positions like leaders, power holders; (c) individuals belonging to weaker/marginalized sections, who may be lacking the will and the capacity for participation. It is in such instances that knowledge and skills related to case work become an absolute must for successful community work.

**(2) Community Organisation and Group Work:** The community can be understood as a collectivity of groups, existing in a web of interlinked social chains. In the course of community organisation, the organiser's most prominent preoccupation is to deal with the small and large groups and subgroups. Community organisation therefore is also described as inter-group practice. An understanding of group work helps the community organiser to strengthen inter group relationships and facilitate their convergence on a common platform. He/she often identifies small groups where a beginning can be made and then strives to develop inter-group linkages to achieve wider participation on commonly perceived needs. In such a context, dealing with groups and group processes becomes an integral part of community organisation.

It is therefore clear that, a community organiser has to work with individuals, families and groups to achieve community goals, and should possess case work and group work skills, apart from community organisation skills.

**(3) Community Organisation and Social Work Rcsearch:** During the process of engagement with communities, the community organiser has to also rely on research knowledge and skill sets. Community organisation as a process has to start with fact finding. Use of research is inevitable in locating, identifying and understanding the community. It is also relied upon to undertake need/problem assessment, which requires an objective and systematic gathering of quantitative and qualitative data. Research also furnishes important qualitative data on priorities and preferences of people, their attitudes and perceptions towards an issue or a problem. It may also be used for specific purposes like conduction of epidemiological studies or for the study of social indicators. Monitoring and evaluation also requires an ongoing use of research through the conduction of baseline and end line surveys.

In contemporary context, participatory research techniques are increasingly relied upon to elicit community participation in assessing and prioritising needs, as also in drawing up preferred community interventions.

**Q13. Briefly discuss the relevance of community organisation for community development.**

***Or***

**Write a short note on community organisation and community development.**

***Or***

**Explain the relevance of community organisation for community development.**

**Ans.** Community organisation and community development are interrelated. The community organisation method is used to achieve the goals of community development. According to the United Nations, community development deals with total development of a community, that is in its economic, physical, and social aspects. For achieving total development, community organisation is used as a means. In community development the following aspects are considered as important:

(1) Democratic procedures
(2) Voluntary cooperation
(3) Self-help
(4) Development of leadership
(5) Educational aspects

All the above aspects are relevant from the perspective of community organisation. (a) Democratic procedures deal with allowing all the community members to participate in decision-making. It is possible to achieve this through community organisation. The selected or elected members or representatives are helped to take decisions. Thus democratic procedures help people to take part in achieving the community development goals. The community organisation method also values democratic procedures for enlisting people's participation. (b) Voluntary cooperation means that the people volunteer their participation. For this they have to be first convinced. They should feel that they need to involve themselves in the process of development without inhibitions. This attitude is supported by the community organisation method. People's emotional involvement is necessary for successful community organisation. If discontentment about their conditions is created, then people will volunteer for participation. Community organisation emphasizes the discontentment aspect only to make them initiate participation. (c) Self-help is the basis for community development. It deals with the capacity of people to mobilize internal resources. Self-help is the basis for self-sufficiency and sustainable development. Even in the context of community organisation, self-help is emphasized and promoted. (d) Development of leadership is an important aspect in community development. Leadership deals with influencing and enabling people to achieve the stipulated goals. Community organisation also places great emphasis on leadership development. It is only with the help of leaders that people are motivated to participate in action. (e) Educational aspects in community development imply helping people to know, learn, and accept the concepts of democracy, cooperation, unity, skill development, effective functioning etc.

**Q14. What are the differences between community organisation and community development? Discuss.**

***Or***

**Differentiate between community organisations and community development.**

**Ans.** There are many similarities between community organisation and community development. But for theoretical purpose it is possible to differentiate between community organisation and community development.

(1) Community organisation is a method of social work while community development is a programme for a planned change send development.

(2) Community organisation emphasizes the process, but community development emphasizes the end or goals.

(3) Community organisers are mostly social workers and social change agents. But community development personnel can be from other professions including agricultural experts, veterinary experts, and other technical experts.

(4) Community organisation is not time bound. It is achieved step by step according to the pace of the people. But community development is time bound and time is specified for achieving the development objectives.

(5) In community organisation people's participation is important. But in community development people's development is more important.

(6) In community organisation the assistance provided by the government and external agencies is not a critical factor. But in community development external assistance from the government or other agencies is considered important.

(7) Community organisation is a method of social work and this method is used in many fields. But unlike community organisation, community development is considered as a process, a method, a programme, and a movement for planned change.

(8) Community organisation is used in all the fields but community development is mostly relied upon in context of economic development and for enhancing the living standards of the people.

(9) In community organisation planning is undertaken by the people but community development planning is mainly carried out by an external agency mostly belonging to the government.

(10) In community organisation people are organized to solve their problems, but in community development goals have to be achieved and it is for this purpose that people are organized.

(11) Community organisation is universal to all communities, but community development programmes differ from people to people depending upon whether the area is rural, urban or tribal, as also other characteristics of the area.

Thus, it is observed that even though there are differences, both community development and community organisation are interrelated. The ideal community development takes places where community organisation method and its various steps and principles are effectively put into practice.

**Q15. Discuss principles of community organisation.**

**Ans.** Principles of community organisation, in the sense in which the term is used here, are generalized guiding rules for sound practice. Principles are expressions of value judgements. The principles of community organisation, which are being discussed here, are within the frame of reference, and in harmony with the spirit and purpose of social work in a democratic society. We are concerned with the dignity and worth, the freedom, the security, the participation, and the wholesome and abundant life of every individual. This implies practice of following principles of democracy, such as betterment of the marginalized, transparency, honesty, sustainability, self-reliance, partnerships, cooperation, etc.

In the literature on community work, we find various sets of principles. Dunham, in 1958 suggested a set of twenty eight principles of community organisation, broadly categorized under seven headings:

(1) Democracy and social welfare.
(2) Community roots for community programmes.
(3) Citizen understanding, support, participation and professional service.
(4) Cooperation.
(5) Social welfare programmes.
(6) Adequacy, distribution, and organisation of social welfare services, and
(7) Prevention.

**Ross** (1967) outlined specific principles – the elementary or fundamental ideas regarding initiation and continuation of community organisation processes. These principles have been discussed in terms of the nature of the organisation or association and the role of the professional worker. The twelve principles identified by Ross are:

(1) Discontent with existing conditions in the community must initiate and/or nourish development of the association.
(2) Discontent must be focussed and channeled into organisation, planning, and action in respect to specific problems.
(3) Discontent which initiates or sustains community organisation must be widely shared in the community.
(4) The association must involve leaders (both formal and informal) identified with, and accepted by, major sub-groups in the community.
(5) The association must have goals and methods and procedures of high acceptability.
(6) The programmes of the association should include some activities with an emotional content.
(7) The association should seek to utilize the manifest and latent goodwill which exists in the community.
(8) The association must develop active and effective lines of communication both within the association and between the association and the community.
(9) The association should seek to support and strengthen groups which it brings together in cooperative work.
(10) The association should develop a pace of work in line with existing conditions in the community.
(11) The association should seek to develop effective leaders.

(12) The association must develop strength, stability and prestige in the community.

Keeping in mind the actual practice situations in India Siddiqui (1997) has worked out a set of 8 principles.

(1) The Principle of Specific Objectives.
(2) The Principle of Planning.
(3) The Principle of People's Participation.
(4) The Principle of Inter-group Approach.
(5) The Principle of Democratic Functioning.
(6) The Principle of Flexible Organisation.
(7) The Principle of Optimum Utilisation of Indigenous Resources.
(8) The Principle of Cultural orientation.

We are trying to interpret some of the principles from the available sets of principles for guiding our practice community organisation in Indian context.

- **Community Organisation is means and not an end:** The community organisation is a process by which the capacity of the community to function as an integrated unit is being enhanced. In this sense it is a method or a means to enable people to live a happy and fully developed life. It refers to a method of intervention whereby a community consisting of individuals, groups or organisations are helped to engage in planned collective action in order to deal with their needs and problems.
- **Community Organisation is to promote community solidarity and the practice of democracy:** It should seek to overcome disruptive influences, which threaten the well being of the community and the vitality of democratic institutions. In community organisation discrimination and segregation or exclusion should be avoided and integration and mutual acceptance should be promoted.
- **The clear identification of the Community:** Since the community is the client of the community organisation worker, it must be clearly identified. It is likely that there are several communities with which he/she deals at the same time. Further it is important that once the community is identified the entire community must be the concern of the practitioner. No programme can be isolated from the social welfare needs and resources of the community as a whole. The welfare of the whole community is always more important than the interest or the well being of any one agency/group in the community.
- **Fact-finding and needs assessment:** Community organisation programmes should have its roots in the community. Proper fact-finding and assessment of the

community needs is the prerequisite for starting any programme in the community. It is generally desirable for local community services to be indigenous, grass-roots developments rather than imported from outside. Whenever possible, then, community organisation should have its origin in a need felt by the community or by substantial number of persons in the community. There should be vital community participation, and essential community control, of its development.

- **Identification, mobilization and utilization of the available resources:** The fullest possible use should be made of existing social welfare resources, before creating new resources or services. In the absence of resources/services the worker has to mobilize the resources from various sources such as community, government, non-government agencies, etc. While utilising the indigenous resources it must be recognized that these resources may sometimes need extensive overhauling before they will meet certain needs. Apart from mobilising physical resources, indigenous human resources should be put to optimum use.
- **Participatory planning:** The community organisation worker must accept the need for participatory planning throughout the process of community organisation. It is important that the practitioner prepares a blue print in the beginning of what he/she intends to do with the community. This is done with the community taking into consideration the needs of the community, available resources, agency objectives, etc. Planning in community organisation is a continuous process as it follows the cycle of implementation and evaluation. The planning should be on the basis of ascertained facts, rather than an expression of guesswork, "hunches," or mere trial and error methods.
- **Active and vital participation:** The concept of self-help is the core of community organisation. The community members' participation throughout the process of community organisation should be encouraged from the standpoint both of democratic principle and of feasibility– that is, the direct involvement in the programme of those who have the primary stake in it's results. "Selfhelp" by citizen or clientele groups should be encouraged and fostered.
- **Community right of self determination should be respected:** The Role of the community organisation worker is to provide professional skill, assistance, and creative leadership in enabling people's groups and organisations to achieve social welfare objectives. The community members should make basic

decisions regarding programme and policy. While the community organisation worker plays a variety of roles in different situations, he is basically concerned with enabling people's expression and leadership to achieve community organisation goals, and not try to have control, domination, or manipulation.

- **Voluntary cooperation:** Community organisation must be based upon mutual understanding, voluntary acceptance, and mutual agreement. Community organisation, if it is to be in harmony with democratic principles, cannot be through regimentation. It should not be imposed from above or outside, but must be derived from the inner freedom and will to unite all those who practice it.
- **The spirit of cooperation rather than competition, and the practice of coordination of effort:** Community organisation practice should be based on the spirit of cooperation rather than competition. The community organisation practice has proved that the most effective advances are made through cooperative effort. It is by the coordinated and sustained programmes attacking major problems rather than through sporadic efforts by different groups.
- **Recognition and involvement of indigenous leadership:** Community organisation as it has been described requires the participation of the people belonging to the community. However everyone in the community cannot be involved in face-to-face contact with all others in the community; therefore it is important to identify and recognize the leaders (both formal and informal) accepted by various groups and subgroups in the community.
- **Limited use of authority or compulsion:** Invoking the application of authority or compulsion may sometimes be necessary in community organisation. But it should be used as little as possible, for as short a time as possible, and only as a last resort. When compulsion must be applied, it should be followed as soon as possible, by resumption of the cooperative process.
- **The dynamic and flexible nature of programmes and services:** This principle is basic to sound community organisation. Social welfare agencies and programmes must be responsive to the changing conditions, problems, and needs of community life. Community is a dynamic phenomenon, which constantly changes and thus the needs and problems also keep

changing. Therefore it is necessary that the programmes and services are flexible enough.

- **Continuing participatory evaluation:** As programmes are developed to meet community needs, some time must be set aside for evaluation of the process. Regular feedback from the community is important. Criteria must be set up for evaluation of the programmes, to see how effective the action has been and what has been accomplished.

**Q16. What are the steps of community organisation?**

***Or***

**Enlist various component of needs assessment.**

**[June-2018, Q.NO.-4 (e)]**

***Or***

**Describe the steps in the process of community organisation.** **[June-2018, Q.No.-2]**

**Ans.** These important steps or stages in the community organisation process are presented below:

**(1) Role Searching:** The first step in the community organisation process is an analysis of the proposed goals that the worker or the implementing agency proposes to pursue. In practice this decision is usually influenced by the objectives of the parental organisation which employs the worker directly or which funds the organisation which employs him.

**(2) Enlisting People's Participation:** The organiser is expected to develop a positive and purposeful rapport with the people in the community. He may either adopt a formal way of introducing himself directly or through a known community contact like a leader, school teacher, or anganwadi worker, or utilize an informal approach, wherein he may simply start visiting the community and meeting people. The basic purpose is to acquaint himself with the community and to explain his presence.

**(3) Developing a Community Profile:** A community profile is information about the community and its members. It is necessary to include a variety of information to provide a good description of the community. The knowledge should be acquired in partnership with the community. The knowledge should be acquired in partnership with the community members and its key persons.

**(4) Needs Assessment:** The community organiser has to assess and understand the needs and problems faced by the community people. The needs could range from:

(a) Basic needs such as housing, electricity supply, water supply, sanitation etc.

(b) Economic needs such as need for employment, increase in agricultural productivity, procurement of credit etc.

(c) Educational needs, such as needs for non formal education, remedial coaching, improvement in quality of education, available/infrastructure, need for vocational courses etc.

(d) Health needs, such as need for health facilities/staff. Recreational needs such as need for sports facilities, community centre, reading room, playground, park etc.

(e) Information needs, with regard to available resource centres, services, schemes/programmes being implemented.

**(5) Ordering/Prioritising Needs:** All the identified needs and problems of the community are first listed by the community with the help of the community organiser. This is a process which makes the people understand their own situation. This involvement of the community in listing their needs and problems will ultimately lead to their participation in the solving of the problems or fulfilment of the needs.

**(6) Problem Analysis and Redefinition:** The selected need/problem has to be examined, analysed and stated in order to be fully understood in its multiple dimensions by the people. This step is also imperative in order to undertake purposeful planning and action.

Need/problem analysis involves: (a) making a statement of the need or problem, in a way that it most clearly express the difficulty experienced by the affected people; (b) identifying the direct causes and direct effects of the core problem and (c) stakeholder analysis.

**(7) Formulation of Achievable Objectives:** The redefined need/problem is converted into achievable objectives for further action. At times the objectives/goals will have to be split into many parts, so that they could be converted into specific programmes and activities oriented towards fulfilling the needs and solving problems.

**(8) Development of Community Confidence and Willpower:** Many communities identify needs and problems which they feel incompetent to achieve or deal with. This is particularly true of those communities in which apathy, indifference, and complacency has set in. In such circumstances, identifying, analysing and stating the needs/ problems is of little use if the people do not find the will and confidence for action. Communities lacking these will find it difficult to mobilize for action.

**(9) Work Out the Alternatives:** Based on the objectives, different options are explored by the community through brain storming. In order to solve the selected problem the community has to generate a number of alternatives to address the problem. For example, the problem of a high drop out rate from the school in the community may be directly related to the defective functioning of the school.

**(10) Selection of an Appropriate Alternative:** Among the proposed alternatives, the best alternative or set of alternatives is selected for dealing with the selected problem. Often one starts with exercising a mild option, and gradually going on to other more strong measures. If nothing works out the use of the radical social action method also offers a possibility.

**(11) Work Out a Plan of Action:** To meet the selected need or deal with the selected problem, an action plan is proposed in which responsibilities are assigned and a tentative organisational structure is prepared. The time frame, resources required and personnel involved are decided at this stage. Suppose the drop out problem considered earlier is to be tackled, it may be decided to first meet the school authorities and present a petition. This has to be planned in terms of date, time, who, how many, where, etc.

**(12) Mobilisation of Resources:** To implement the proposed plan of action, requisite resources are to be assessed, identified and mobilized. These resources may be in the form of money, time, manpower and material. An estimate is made and the sources are identified for mobilization.

**(13) Implementation of Action:** Taking action is the most vital component of the community organisation process. While implementing the plan of action, the active participation of people through acceptance of responsibilities has to be ensured. The people have to be prepared and guided to hold responsibilities and become partners in the problem solving process. There has to be a gradual taking over by the community and a simultaneous withdrawal of the agency/ worker to facilitate sustainability of the process.

**(14) Evaluation of Action:** The implemented plan is evaluated to assess the success implementation. Maintenance of accurate records of all work done and development of a framework for analysis are necessary pre-requisites for objective evaluation.

The positive and desirable results need to be appreciated and the shortfalls/undesired results need to be identified, analysed and discussed.

(15) **Modification:** Based on the evaluation, necessary modifications are planned and incorporated. The learning derived through the evaluation process enables the community to identify the strong points and the weak points of its action plan.

In order to enhance the effectiveness of the intervention and to bring about a permanent solution of the selected problem, modifications are imperative. These modifications facilitate a more effective response to the need/problem taken up for collective action.

(16) **Development of Cooperative and Collaborative Attitudes:** While all the aforementioned stages are important and in fact inseparable, certainly none is more important than the final one viz. the development of cooperative and collaborative attitudes and practices in the community. What is implied here is that as the process of community organisation evolves and progresses, people in the community come together to understand, accept and work with one another. In the process of fulfilling a common need or dealing with a common problem/s, the diverse sub groups and their leaders become aware and inclined towards cooperation with other sub groups in similar endeavors.This process may not necessarily lead to the eradication of all differences between the subgroups and subcultures within the community or the achievement of complete homogeneity, but it often leads to an increased ability of the groups to understand this diversity and accept the same. They will be more inclined to develop the skills of overcoming the conflicts which may arise from time to time. At the same time it may also lead to the development of a common frame of reference within which all can work together for common ends.

**Q17. What are the models of community organisation?**

***Or***

**Describe the various models of Community Organisation.**

**[Dec-2017, Q.No.-1]**

***Or***

**Write the short note on Social planning.**

**[June-2018, Q.No.-5(a)]**

***Or***

**Discuss the three modes of intervention to Purposive Community Change as developed by Rothman.**

**[Dec-2018, Q.No.-1]**

**Ans.** In the year 1968, Jack Rothman introduced three models of community organisation.

***These were:***

(1) Locality Development

(2) Social Planning

(3) Social Action

These three models construct were revised and refined by him in the year 2001 (Rothman, 2001), taking into account the changes in practices and conditions in communities. Instead of referring to the three approaches as the 'Models', he preferred referring to them as the 'Core Modes of Community Intervention'.

Moreover, these three approaches or modes are described as ideal-type constructs, which to a very large extent do not exist in pristine, full blown form in the real world, but are useful mental tools to describe and analyse reality.

**Mode A: Locality Development:** This approach presupposes that community change should be pursued through broad participation by a wide spectrum of people at the local community level in determining goals and taking civic action. It is a community building endeavour with a strong emphasis on the notions of mutuality, plurality, participation and autonomy. It fosters community building by promoting process goals: community competency (the ability to solve problems on a self help basis) and social integration (harmonious inter-relationships among different ethnic and social class groups). The approach is humanistic and strongly people-oriented, with the aim of "helping people to help themselves". Leadership is drawn from within and direction and control are in the hands of the local people. "Enabling" techniques are emphasised. Some examples of locality development include neighbourhood work programmes conducted by community based agencies, and village level work in community development programmes.

**Mode B: Social Planning/Policy:** This approach emphasises a technical process of problem solving regarding substantive social problems, such as housing, education, health, women's development etc. This particular orientation to planning is data-driven and conceives of carefully calibrated change being rooted in social science thinking and empirical objectivity. The style is technocratic and rationality is a dominant ideal.

Community participation is not a core ingredient and may vary from much to little depending on the problem and the circumstances. The approach presupposes that change in a complex modern environment requires expert planners who can gather and analyse quantitative data and manoeure large bureaucratic organisers in order to improve social conditions. There is heavy reliance on needs assessment, decision analysis, evaluation research, and other sophisticated statistical tools.

By and large the concern here is with task goals: conceptualising, selecting, arranging and delivering goods and services to people who need them. In addition fostering coordination among agencies, avoiding duplication and filling gaps in services are important concerns here. Planning and policy are grouped together because both involve assembling and analysing data for solving social problems.

Two important contemporary constraints impacting this mode, according to Rothman are: (1) Planning has become highly interactive and diverse interest groups rightfully go into the defining of goals and setting the community agenda. It involves value choices that go beyond the purview of the expert or bureaucrat; and (2) Impact of reduced governmental spending on social programmes, due to economic constraints, leading to a lower reliance on the elaborate, data driven planning approach.

**Mode C: Social Action:** This approach presupposes the existence of an aggrieved or disadvantaged segment of the population that needs to be organised in order to make demands on the larger community for increased resources or equal treatment.

This approach aims at making fundamental changes in the community, including the redistribution of power and resources and gaining access to decision making for marginal groups. Practitioners in the social action domain aim to empower and benefit the poor and the oppressed. The style is primarily one in which social justice is a dominant ideal.

**Q18. Explain various approaches to community organisation.**

***Or***

**Describe the approaches to community organisation.**

**Ans.** A model can be understood as a medium through which a person looks at the complex realities. It serves as a reference for the work undertaken and gives a clearer understanding of what could be expected. A model can also be understood as a strategy or an approach for accomplishing a vision, and the appropriate steps to be followed to get there. Some models have evolved out of the specific ideologies of change, while some have arisen in response to certain concrete situations or experiences.

A number of persons have attempted to develop a classification of models of community organisation. A. Murray. G. Ross (1955) preferred to use the term 'approach'. He identified three main approaches to community organisation.

***These are:***

(1) **The General Content Approach:** The focus of this approach is on the coordinated and orderly development of services in the community. This approach incorporates two sub-approaches

viz: (a) the strengthening of the existing services and (b) initiating new services. The general objective is effective planning and organisation of a group of services in the community.

(2) **The Specific Content Approach:** This approach comes into operation when an individual organisation or the community itself becomes concerned with some specific issue of concern or some requisite reforms, and consciously launches a programme to achieve the stipulated goal/s or objective/s. Thus, this approach involves specific issue oriented organisation of services.

(3) **The Process Approach:** This approach does not focus so much on the 'content', as on the initiation and sustenance of a 'process' in which all the people of the community are involved, either directly or through their representatives. It involves identification of problems and taking purposeful action with regard to the same. The emphasis is more on building the capacity of the community for self-help initiatives and collaborative enterprise. Four factors are very important for this approach. These are: (a) Self determination of the community; (b) Indigenous plans; (c) People's willingness to change; and (d) Community pace.

**Q19. Describe the models of practice has been given by siddiqui.**

**Ans.** There are three models which are outlined below:

(1) **Neighbourhood Development Model:** The general assumption underlying this model is that people living in a community (neighbourhood) have the basic and inherent capacity of meeting their needs/problems through their own initiative and resources. The worker is expected to induce a process which will make the community realise this and consequently make efforts to achieve a greater degree of satisfaction for its members, individually and collectively. Recent changes in this model of community work lay more emphasis on the development of a self sustaining, indigenous organisation within the community to take over this role from the worker or the agency as soon as possible. Thus, the role of the worker is seen as unleashing developmental energies within thc community, rathcr than as a providcr of scrviccs.

Contrary to its name, the model's application is not limited to generating services to cater to people's needs or improving the physical/resource infrastructure of the neighbourhood. The model can be employed to develop new ideas too. The emphasis is to encourage thinking on the part of people themselves, to adopt progressive attitudes, rather than doing things for them.

***The specific steps involved in this model are:***

(a) Identification, local and demarcation of the physical area
(b) Entry into the community
(c) Identifying the needs of different sections
(d) Programme Planning
(e) Resource Planning
(f) Developing an organisational network in the community
(g) Partial withdrawal within a time frame

**(2) System Change Model:** This model presupposes the existence of various arrangements in society to cater to the basic needs of education, health, housing, employment etc. These are considered as independent systems, which in turn are comprised of sub systems. The ultimate rationale for the existence of these systems is social production and social consumption.

These systems can become dysfunctional due to a variety of factors, which in turn create strain and pressure on the system. The system may become dysfunctional either because what it is producing is not relevant for people, or because many people do not have access to what is being produced, on account of disparities between different socio-economic or spatial segments of the population. Symptoms of this dysfunction appear within the community as a problem or a set of problems. For these to be tackled, first the system and its sub systems need to be understood in order to arrive at a useful framework for understanding what one finds at the grass roots level. Subsequently, the worker attempts a strategy of either restructuring or modifying the system. This is termed as a "system change" approach/model to community work.

***The specific tasks associated with this model are:***

(a) Collecting relevant facts about the specific deficiencies in the system, e.g. urban bias; disparity in access to services; lack of trained functionaries, inadequate delivery structure; lack of funding etc. leading to inadequacy.
(b) Sharing of the findings within the community/communities.
(c) Selecting an appropriate strategy to influence decision making bodies or to focus attention on the issue.

(d) Mobilising community and outside support to put the plan into action.

(e) Developing an organisation in the community and linking it to similar organisations in other communities and other agencies which can help them in demanding change.

**(3) Structural Change Model:** This model visualises the community as a small cell within the larger body of society. In other words, various tiny communities constitute the bigger whole i.e. the society or a nation state. The model assumes that the manner in which the relationship between different sections of the population is structured, formally (constitutional framework, law, policies etc.) or informally (customs, public opinion etc.) determines the social rights of individuals. This also determines the relationship of the state vis-à-vis the individual or a community, as also the intra-community and inter community relations.

In the structural change model, the worker analyses the link between the macro structuring of social relationships and the micro-reality (the latter could be the problem of unemployment in the community, or lack of access of large sections of the people to education or health facilities or credit/other resources). The worker tries to mobilise the community to participate in the radical alteration of the macro structure so as to impact the micro reality.

***The specific tasks involved in the model are:***

(a) To develop an understanding of the link between micro and macro social realities.

(b) To make a conscious decision about an alternative political ideology.

(c) To share this understanding with the community, to enable it to make its own decisions.

(d) To help the community identify a plan of action to pursue its goal by locating specific issues and consequent action to launch a long struggle.

(e) To help the community sustain its interest, enthusiasm and capacity to meet the strain which is likely to arise out of an inevitable conflict with the existing power structure.

**(4) The Inter-Community Model of Community Work:** The scope of this model is wider than the neighbourhood model. There are certain problems/needs in the community which may not be tackled, either within the community or through community resources. For example, the problem of unemployment or lack of training facilities or health facilities cannot be tackled within a community. Low income levels and resource base of the community make it difficult to initiate and sustain a programme which aims to meet some such needs within the single community context. This calls for an inter-community approach.

The worker locates the programme in a place where people from different communities can come and participate. The worker visits various communities, to make people aware of the programme and motivates them to participate. A community nucleus is usually established, comprising of beneficiaries and other influential persons, to dispense information about the initiative. In such efforts, the representatives of the different communities participate in deciding the programme, its location and the mode of sharing resources and responsibilities for its management. This model can lead to the establishment of an organisation or council to provide specific services in different communities.

The inter community work model is different from the neighbourhood model, as the scope of its coverage is wider. It differs from the other two models since its goal is to meet local needs, rather than change the system or structure.

**Q20. Discuss the other strategies and approaches of community organising.**

**Ans.** Other strategies and approaches of community organising are as follows:

**Peter Dreiver (1996),** another writer has given a typology that confines itself to locality, but in the small community world he finds the same tripartite division by dimensions: social, political, and economic. Dreiver (1996) called his typology "Community Empowerment Strategies" and identified the following alternative directions:

(1) **Community Organising:** Mobilising people to combat common problems and to increase their voice in institutions and decisions that affect their lives and communities (a direction with political emphasis).

(2) **Community Based Development:** Neighbourhood based efforts to improve an area's physical and financial condition such as new construction or rehabilitation of housing (a direction with economic emphasis).

(3) **Community-Based Service Provision:** Involves neighbourhood-level efforts to deliver social services (e.g. child care vocational training, maternal and child health etc.) and is

called “building human capital”. (a direction with social emphasis).

**Robert Fisher (1984)** presented a much broader perspective of approaches. He identified “three dominant approaches”, to neighbourhood organising. These are as follows:

**(1) Social Work Approach:** In this approach, the society is viewed as a social organism and all efforts are oriented towards building a sense of community. The community organiser plays the role of an enabler, an advocate, a planner and a coordinator, who helps the community to identity a problem in the neighbourhood, attempts to procure the requisite resources by gathering the existing social services and by lobbying with those in power to meet the needs of the neighbourhood. This approach is consensual and gradualist in nature. The goals was the Social Settlement Movement in the US and the War on Poverty Programme of the Johnson administration in the sixties.

**(2) The Political Activist Approach:** This approach is characterised by militant confrontation and heavy pressure on the power institutions of society. Power sharing is a major goal. This method is based on advocacy, conflict and negotiation and is used by mass based organisations such as those initiated by Saul Alinsky, who is also considered to be the founder of this approach. The organiser is a mobiliser and leadership developer, and the problem condition is social and economic oppression arising out of powerlessness. The ultimate goal is the elimination of social, economic and political disparities (a direction with political emphasis).

**(3) Neighbourhood Maintenance Approach:** This approach arose out of both the previous approaches, and is characterised by middle-class residents and their small business and institutional allies who seek to “defend” their community against change and perceived threats to property values. The “problem conditions may include decline in municipal services, deterioration in neighbourhood sanitation, water supply, or increased crime. The organiser might be a volunteer community leader or a trained specialist in urban planning, community development etc.

**Saul Alinsky (1945)** one of the founders of modern neighbourhood organising reflected deeper into the different approaches of community organising. According to him social change and community organisation could either be primarily reformist or revolutionary, depending on how fundamental the changes are, which are sought.

Saul Alinsky presented two distinct approaches or traditions to organising. These are:

(1) **The Social Mobilisation Tradition:** Here the core strategic goal is to get people to act together; to gain power through the numbers of people involved. This is based on the assumption that such pressure will make those in power comply with the demands that are made.

(2) **Social Production Tradition:** In this tradition, the strategic goal is to acquire services, material goods and resources for the people in need. The core emphasis is on achieving the outcome i.e. helping those in need with the problems they face. In order to achieve the core goal of acquiring goods/services for the target group/s or to attempt redistribution of resources/ benefits, supporters of this tradition are more likely to work with those in power. People are encouraged to learn to participate in the political system and to manage relationships with agencies that provide services. The social production initiatives are usually labeled as "projects" as they are primarily endeavors to create services that benefit those in need.

**Hanna and Robinson (1994)** also advocated the relevance of the transformative model, as opposed to the more traditional approaches. Like Alinsky, their typology also sprung out of the soul of the oppressed resident, and included the following three strategies:

(1) Traditional Politics, which involves elite, non participative efforts that bend the status quo just enough to preserve it. It involves rational problem solving, but income, resource, and status gaps remain.

(2) Direct Action Community Organising, which involves mass-based organising, sometimes using confrontation. It is power oriented and aims to empower non elites to negotiate with the elites for a share in power.

(3) Transformative Social Change, which involves small groups, intensive study and reflection, and people becoming acutely aware and knowledgeable about the oppressive forces. Emphasis is on self-directed learning and a fully collective approach to group awareness, decision making and social action, which liberates participants from the mind set of dependency and oppression.

**Q21. Explain the working of Indian communities with the community power structure.**

**Ans.** Power is the ability to influence others, their beliefs and behaviour. It is the ability to make things happen. It also implies political or social ascendancy or control. Floyd Hunter explained the nature of power and power structure. Power appears in many forms and in a variety of combinations. It flows from many sources like money; votes; law; possession of information, expertise or skills; group support; links and contacts; charisma, social roles, access to rewards and resources; position, titles, ability to gratify important needs; monopoly of essential resources, alliances, conviction, courage etc. Power often accumulates in a person or a constituency and this is usually referred to as a power centre. Every society is characterised by a power structure. Power is not confined within a single or specific power centre. Every level or organisation of society is characterised by the presence of some power. Even the so called 'powerless' persons and constituencies within society possess power, only it is latent and yet to be discovered and developed.

In Indian communities a multiplicity of power sources exist. In other words, power is usually dispersed across many persons and groups. There is often a flexibility in the power structure that is noticed. The primary aim of some community groups is to gain or extend their power. While those in power are concerned with maintaining or even enlarging their power base, those with relatively less power strive to bring about a redistribution of power and exerting an influence on the decisions taken by people in power. All community groups are likely to come up against, and have to recon with the exercise of power in their locality.

The perspective of the community as a centre for power and conflict places power and politics front and centre in our understanding of the community. It assumes that communities are composed of competing groups and power centres, which are constantly engaged in expanding their power base and control over scarce resources. Some groups, based on social class or caste have less access to power and must constantly challenge those with power to acquire access to community resources, such as education, employment opportunities, healthcare, housing, police protection etc.

The idea of class conflict has its origins in the work of the 19th century German economist and philosopher Karl Marx, who argued that society is divided into two groups-those who have access to wealth and power and who control the means of production, and those who have little or no power and are exploited by the small privileged group.

In the Indian context, the social structure becomes important to locate power centres and leaders in society. In rural India, power centres are found in various contexts, such as caste, lineage, and territorial groups. There are mainly two primary sources of power in the rural communities. First, are those who derive power from traditional sources like caste and kinship. As caste and kinship still form the core of village social organisation, they go a long way in defining the power structure and decision making process in rural India.

The second category comprises of those who derive power by occupying positions in the organisations introduced in the context of developmental activities like panchayat sarpanch/members, functionaries of voluntary organisations/community based organisations, chairpersons of mahila mandals/nav yuvak mandals etc. In certain cases, some persons may acquire power due to their personal qualities and abilities, as also their commitment/past experience at handling or solving community problems.

Power is often dispered and there are usually several power centres. Beginning with the joint family, the power and authority in the joint family centres around the senior male member of the family, who is considered as the head or 'karta' of the family. His authority is unquestionable and his decisions are binding on all members. Heads of large and important households enjoy a dominant position and exert great influence in community matters. The senior member of the lineage group (i.e. the kunba) also weilds significant power and authority on account of his seniority and heriditory rights. He is the leader and the representative of the kunba, and solves the inter-kunba problems. He attends all village meetings and is the spokesperson for his kunba. His decisions are binding on the members/constituents of his group. The family, lineage and kinship groups merge into caste, which is all pervasive. The principle of seniority in age, inherited privileges and economic power determine the position of individuals or groups of individuals as caste leaders. The members of the dominant caste wield great power and influence in the village. The headman or the lambardar usually comes from the dominant caste.

The village temple and priest/maulvi also hold positions of power. They are not merely religious heads but are also consulted on a number of other issues affecting the community, like settling disputes. Besides these sources of power, age is another factor which has considerable significance in determining village leadership. Seniority in age is respected and revered.

External sources of power and outside leaders derive power from their specialised knowledge, skills and ideas they bear. Besides, their position or designation may also facilitate them to acquire a position of power within the community. They may unwillingly compete with established leaders. They gain their position of power and prestige and influence established groups. They may also create new groups. School teachers, village health workers, doctors, heads of local NGOs and block officials comprise this category of leaders/power holders.

**Q22. Explain the relevance of power and leadership in community organisation. [June-2018, Q.No.-4(f)]**

**Ans.** Development is influenced by the power structure of the community. People who are influential can mobilise a major segment of the community. There are two models of community power structure. These are the Stratification Model and the Pluralist Model. The Stratification Model suggests that social class principally determines the distribution of community power. According to this model, the power structure in the community is composed of the stable upper class elite whose interest and outlook on community affairs are relatively homogeneous. The Pluralist Model, rejects the idea that a small homogeneous group dominates community decision-making. It states that there are numerous small special interest groups that cut across class lines, which are represented in the community decision-making process/system. These are interest groups with overlapping memberships, and widely differing power bases. Community decisions are the result of the interactions of these different interest groups. Their theoretical orientation can help the community organiser in his action.

The organiser has to identify the members of the power structure. He can rely on the Reputation Approach to locate the community elites. According to this approach, the basic procedure is to ask a group of informants who are knowledgeable about the community to list the people they believe to be most influential in the community affairs. There may be variations in this procedure with regard to how informants are selected, and how questions are put up. By tallying those people most frequently named as influential leaders, he can identify the core of the community power structure.

The Position approach is another method of locating the members of the power structure based on the assumption of the Stratification Model. This approach assumes that people holding the highest office in the community are at the top of the power structure. By scanning the executive lists of the important social, political and economic organisations in the community, one can compile a list of members occupying the power structure. This approach requires fewer efforts than the Reputation Approach.

Locating the power structure and the leaders, who may be both formal and informal and who can influence the thinking and behaviour of the community members thus assumes primary importance. These power holders are involved to induce peoples' participation in order to achieve the organisational objectives. If the existing power centres are not in line with the community organisational objectives, then a new centre of power is identified and developed to get peoples' commitment and participation, and thereby facilitate purposeful community change.

The community organiser must therefore concern himself with the identification of those leaders who will encourage the participation of the other members of their groups. Some specific advantages of working with leaders are: (1) Leaders contribute by bringing the different factions in closer contact with the larger community and thereby integrating groups into a more cohesive whole. (2) By working with the power centres and leaders of the different factions and groups, the organiser is indirectly able to work with the whole community. It is not possible for him to work with each and every member of the community. However, leaders being representatives of their respective groups facilitate participation from members of these groups. (3) Leaders can also be used as a leverage point for initiating a process of change, which may eventually spread throughout the whole system. (4) Leaders provide readymade communication channels to reach the community. If the organiser is able to reach the leaders, his message is sure to reach the people. (5) In a similar vein, leaders also provide readymade cooperative groups for self help projects and thereby obviate the greater amount of work that would be necessary in a less organised and more individualistic type of society. If the leaders are convinced about the desirability and utility of a proposed community initiative, then they can be instrumental in influencing/ convincing the members of their group, thereby rendering the task of the organiser much simpler than it would otherwise be. Thus, leadership from within the community can facilitate mobilization, organisation and participation of the community in community initiatives and is therefore the key to enlisting peoples participation.

**Q23. What is Gender Sensitive Community Organisation practice?**

***Or***

**Explain the gender and gender injustice.**

***Or***

**Describe the concept of caste and class and their functions.**

***Or***

**Write a short note on sex and gender.**

***Or***

**Write a short note on Gender inequalities.**

**Ans.** The gender system gives different values to men and women. Society is organised around specific parameters, the functionality of which is ensured by developing a set of systems and institutions. The system of patriarchy provides basis to male – female differentiation and the unfavourable conditions that girls and women face. The practice of male female differentiation is created and fostered by the adoption of differential norms, codes of conduct, life styles and discriminatory practices for males and females. The biological differences between males and females are extended to become the criteria for the economic and social positioning of the two sexes.

Allocation of differential roles in a certain manner is a core aspect of the gender system. Roles are allocated not only in accordance with the biological function of procreation, but are misappropriated according to the values prescribed to males and females. Patriarchy prescribes 'dominating and controlling' social functions to males, while 'supportive' functions are in the domain of females. Right from birth, males are attributed to be superior, as they are the inheritors of resources, and the carriers of the family name and lineage. The function of the main earner is also attributed to the male, scaling his position of importance. The females are expected to be the 'family caretakers' and perform secondary functions of child nurturing and running the households.

Along with role allocation, certain norms, beliefs, values, as well as practices reinforce this male female hierarchy. Males therefore procure access to economic resources like land and property, inheritance, education, skills, productive employment and the associated high status.

On the other hand, women are deprived of all such privileges, including nutrition, medical care, education, skill development and opportunities for productive employment. Multiple social handicaps and atrocities keep them in a position of subjugation. The declining sex ratio and increasing incidence of female foeticide and infanticide are grim reminders of this unfortunate reality. The practice of male-female differentiation results in deprivation and oppression for the female at all stages and in all spheres of life.

The community organisation initiatives must ensure that they do not reinforce the different forms of structural oppression, against women, and preferably counter them in whatever way or ways are appropriate within the specific context.

**Q24. Explain practice of community with the help of marginalised group.**

***Or***

**Explain community organisation practice with the marginalised groups. [Dec-2019, Q.No.-3(b)]**

**Ans.** Caste groups are hereditary groups with fixed status, classes are defined in terms of the relations of production. The members of a class have a similar socio-economic status in relation to other classes in the society, while the members of a caste have either a high or a low social status in relationship to other castes.

**Caste:** Caste is understood to be both a structural and cultural phenomenon. As a unit, it can be defined as a 'closed rank status group', that is, a group in which the status of the members, their occupation, the field of mate selection and interaction with others are all fixed. As a system, it refers to interrelated status and patterned interaction among castes characterised by an aggregation of restrictions like restrictions on change of membership, occupational mobility, marriage and communal relations.

**Class:** A social class is "one of two or more broad groups of individuals who are ranked by the members of the community in socially superior and inferior positions" (Ginsberg, Morris, 1961). Thus, the social class is characterised by (a) a feeling of equality in relation to members of one's own class; (b) a consciousness that one's mode of behaviour will be in harmony with the behaviour of those with similar standards of life; (c) a choice of occupations within a limited range; (d) a feeling of inferiority in relation to those who stand above in the social ranking; and (e) a feeling a superiority in relation to those falling below in the social hierarchy.

**The Notion of Empowerment:** The notion of empowerment is itself a complex one and is central to a social justice strategy. It is central to community work and many community organisers choose to define their role in terms of an empowerment process. Simply stated, empowerment aims to increase the power of the disadvantaged. It involves giving power to individuals or groups, allowing them to take power into their own hands and redistributing power from the 'haves' to the 'have nots' (Ife, 1995).

There still remains the important question as to what sort of power is involved in the term 'empowerment', i.e. what kind of power is it that we as community organisers wish to enhance? While this is primarily a value question, we can identify certain parameters of power, as they obtain in community based empowerment strategies. Jim Ife (1995) identifies seven main categories of power.

***These are:***

(1) **Power over personal choices and life chances:** Many disadvantaged groups have little power to determine the course of their lives and make decisions about their lifestyle and occupation. This may arise out of consequences of poverty, patriarchal structures and values, caste based restrictions or oppression against indigenous people and minorities. Cultural norms and values can also restrict people's options. An empowerment strategy will therefore seek to maximise people's choices, to increase their power over decisions involving their lives.

(2) **Power over the definition of need:** 'Dictatorship over needs' implying that needs often tend to be determined and defined not by the person who is experiencing them but by others (the state, professionals etc.). This is disempowering, and an empowerment perspective would require that people be given the power of defining and prioritising their own needs. This may require education and access to information.

(3) **Power over ideas:** Empowerment should necessarily entail the power to think autonomously, and not have one's world

view dictated by force or by being denied access to alternative frames of reference. It should legitimise the expression of these ideas in a public forum and the capacity of people to enter into dialogue with each other. This approach emphasises the educational aspect of empowerment.

(4) **Power over institutions:** A good deal of disempowerment comes from the effect of social institutions, such as the education system, the health system, the family, etc. An empowerment strategy should therefore aim to increase people's power over these institutions and by changing these institutions to make them more accessible, responsive and accountable to all the people.

(5) **Power over resources:** Many people have little access to resources and little discretion over how these resources will be utilised. This applies to both economic and non-economic resources such as education, opportunities for personal growth, recreation, health etc. An empowerment strategy to maximise the effective power of all people over the distribution and use of resources and to redress the inequality of access to resources is necessary.

(6) **Power over economic activity:** The basic mechanisms of production, distribution and exchange are vital in any society, and to have power, one must be able to have some control over and access to, these mechanisms. This power is unequally distributed, and is a cause of significant disempowerment. An empowerment process would, therefore, seek to ensure that power over economic activity be more evenly distributed.

(7) **Power over reproduction:** Control over the process of reproduction has been a significant issue for feminist critique. It not only includes the process of birth, but also child rearing, education and socialization: all the mechanisms by which the social, economic and political order is reproduced in succeeding generations.

**Achieving Empowerment:** The various strategies which can be adopted by the community organiser to achieve the empowerment of the marginalised and disadvantaged groups can be broadly classified under the following headings:

(1) **Policy and Planning:** Empowerment through policy and planning is achieved by developing or changing structures and institutions to bring about more equitable access to resources, services and opportunities to participate in the life of the community. Apart from facilitating people to use existing policy provisions, programmes and services, through widespread

awareness generation, and helping in setting up of appropriate mechanisms for redressal of problems pertaining to lack of access, the community organisers can focus on pressing for more progressive policies of affirmative action or positive discrimination to redress the existing disadvantages faced by the specific groups.

(2) **Social and Political Action:** This approach emphasises the importance of political struggle and change in increasing effective power. It emphasises the activist approach and seeks to enable people to increase their power through some form of direct action.

(3) **Education and Consciousness Raising:** Empowerment through this approach emphasises the importance of an educative process adopted to equip people to increase their power. This incorporates notions of consciousness raising: helping people to understand the society and the structures of oppression and giving them the vocabulary and skills to work towards effective change. These forms of empowerment provide the basis for an empowerment model of community work practice.

**Q25. What is globalization and discuss its impacts on community practice?**

*or*

**Discuss globalisation and its impact on community practice.**

**[Dec-2018, Q.No.-3 (c)]**

**Ans.** Globalization is the process of interaction and integration between people, companies, and governments worldwide. Globalization has grown due to advances in transportation and communication technology. With increased global interactions comes the growth of international trade, ideas, and culture. Globalization is primarily an economic process of interaction and integration that's associated with social and cultural aspects. However, conflicts and diplomacy are also large parts of the history of globalization, and modern globalization.

**Impacts on community practice**: The spread of privatization and the concentration of transnational corporate power, as also the influence of such organisations as the World Bank, the International Monetary Fund (IMF), and the World Trade Organisation (WTO) is impacting the local, national and regional frameworks. The emergence of the well integrated global market is leading to a number of changes including the shift of manufacturing and service industries to those areas of the world which have the cheapest labour and least restrictive regulations; the increasing use of technology; the need for fewer workers with high skills; a decline in the gender distinction of work with its resultant impact on family and work relations, and a widening gap in income, wealth, education, skills and status between different groups. Many of the changes that underlie globalization are particularly damaging to the poor nations and to the low-income or disadvantaged communities.

Governments of poor nations like India have been forced to divert human resources and funds away from the more urgent development priorities, such as education, public health, and the social service sector. The choice of the development strategy is increasingly being influenced by the powerful nations and international organisations and is therefore moving away from public debate. Removal of subsidies in agriculture, removal of import restrictions, dilution of the Public Distribution System, unrestricted entry of foreign MNCs into the country, acceptance of intellectual property rights and many such changes are already having serious implications on both rural and urban communities. While on the one hand, the public sector is forced to effect funding cuts on social programmes, the private sector is quite naturally concerned with lowering the costs of production, especially wages and benefits. All this will ultimately result in the destabilization of long standing institutions and communities, particularly in the subsistence model economies like India. Globalization is also leading to environmental degradation and commercialization of the natural resources, which often form the basis of livelihood sustenance for the poor and marginalised communities.

Thus, community organisers will have to assume responsibility to influence the direction of major economic and political trends by combining long standing principles of self determination, social justice, and democratic participation with updated skills and knowledge that reflect new social and technological realities.

**Q26. Discuss the roles of community organiser.**

***Or***

**Mention the role community organiser.**

**[June-2019, Q.No.-4 (c)]**

***Or***

**Briefly enumerate the role of a community organiser.**

**[June-2018, Q.No.-3 (d)]**

**Ans.** The community organiser having the essential characteristics and skills as also knowledge about the principles, process and steps of community organisation, will be in a position to apply the same in the community setting through the assumption of appropriate roles.

The diverse roles of a community organiser are discussed here. These roles are neither exhaustive nor mutually exclusive.

**(1) Guide:** The primary role of the community organiser is that of a guide who helps the community to discover the ways and means of achieving its own goals. As a guide, he helps the community to move effectively in the direction which it sets for itself. While the organiser has some responsibility to help the community choose this direction wisely, based on the many factors which may operate in the given context, the choice of direction and method of movement must ultimately be that of the community. Thus, he is not a person to shoulder the responsibility or solve problems of the people. Instead, he provides the various options or avenues, and shows different ways of dealing with the community problem. As a guide, he is required to provide the much needed information and ideas which the community may initially lack. For example, in a community facing the problem of unemployment, he should be able to provide information about the various employment schemes, options for self employment, the terms, conditions and sources of availing credit, and other relevant information to those seeking employment. The ultimate choice and means of deriving employment/income generation rests with the community.

In a situation where the community organiser perceives the need and relevance of a particular project for community development, he may stimulate a need with respect to this project. He may encourage discussion on the project and may suggest the advantages of action on the same. But his role as a guide does not permit him the liberty of launching action on this project unless the community is ready and is desirous for such common action.

**(2) Communicator:** The community organiser transfers or transmits information and knowledge to the community. Often community members demonstrate an ignorance of information and ideas. Sharing of information enables the community to use this information to meet its needs or resolve its problems. Thus, the organiser being an essential link between the community and the outside world is expected to play the role of an effective communicator. The communication between him and the community may be handled through diverse forums, including individual contacts, group meetings, group discussions, public meetings, written material etc.

The community organiser can also rely on the use of different techniques like skits, role plays, street theatre, and audio-visual shows to disseminate the requisite information. A greater reliance on the locally accepted and indigenous channels of communication is desirable, as it leads to more effective communication. Local leaders, and local groups like women's groups, youth groups, children's clubs etc. are some such options.

The ability of the community organiser to play this role effectively will, to a very large extent, determine the quality and the intensity of the community organisation process.

(3) **Enabler:** The community organiser plays the role of an enabler by facilitating the community organisation process. As mentioned earlier, he is not expected to carryout the work by himself but is expected to enable the community to plan and execute work related to achievement of its needs/problems autonomously. It is through the performance of this particular role that the community organiser is able to facilitate a process of capacity building and empowerment of the community.

Within the ambit of his role as an enabler, the community organiser enables by first awakening and focussing discontent about some community conditions, followed by facilitating members to verbalise their discontent.

Thereafter, he helps them to see the commonality of their feelings and nourishes the hope that something can be collectively done about the same. He further enables the community to organize to act. The role of the enabler requires judgement about how much of encouragement can be given, how much anxiety relieved, how much support provided at different stages so that the community is able to move at a comfortable pace and with sufficient self confidence. Enabling the community to maintain good interpersonal relations, cooperative and collaborative attitudes and practices, and to deal with inter-group tensions, conflicts and other blocks also fall in the domain of the community organiser.

(4) **Expert:** As an expert, the organiser's role is to provide information, knowledge and advice in a number of areas about which he has specialized expertise. Often, the organiser has to provide research data, technical experience, and resource material, advice on methods which the community may need and require in the process of achieving its goals.

The organiser may serve as an "expert" in community diagnosis and analysis and may help the community to understand its own structure, dynamics, potentialities and constraints. He is expected to be skilled in research methods, able to conduct studies and formulate research policy. He may also have expert knowledge of organisation and procedure. He should also be well informed and able to provide information about programmes, policies, legislation as also resources provided by government departments, private agencies, international organisations, and ways of securing the same. He should be able to facilitate the bridging of gaps between community's needs and available resources.

The worker as an expert does not superimpose or insist on the acceptance of his "expert knowledge". This is only offered for consideration and discussion, to be used as effectively as the community is able to adopt it.

**(5) Counsellor:** The community organiser initiates work by developing an intensive understanding of the community. Often he is expected to enable the community to understand itself in terms of its multiple dimensions. It may entail diagnosis and treatment of the community as a whole.

He may help the community to face its underlying forces and attitudes which may be creating tension and conflict among the groups in the community. Further, after enabling the community to recognize these deep rooted ideas and practices, verbalise about them, and begin to cope with them, the community is helped to develop a capacity to function more effectively as an integrated unit. Thus, as a counselor and social therapist, the organiser deals with the deep-lying and often latent forces which threaten to disrupt the community organisation process.

**(6) Animator:** In the process of community organisation, the organiser encourages and provides direction to the community to carry out collective, self help initiatives. In developing societies like India, people are often victims of a chronic 'dependency syndrome' and therefore fail to spontaneously mobilize of action or even take crucial decisions on their own. In such a context, the organiser as an animator helps the people to come forward and participate in all phases of the process, from planning to evaluation. By raising suitable questions/issues, he assists in conscientising the community and stimulating people to overcome their attitudes and blocks to participation.

**(7) Collaborator:** The community organiser collaborates with his colleagues, co-professionals and other organisations working in the community. In contemporary context, the importance of maintaining collaborative partnerships with other organisations is well recognized.

In the situation where there are also other organisations working towards similar problems, a collaborative effort is not only more desirable but also more productive and feasible. Therefore, the community organiser is expected to network with such other organisations to establish effective linkages and collaborations.

**(8) Consultant:** The community organiser enjoys the trust and confidence of the people and is often relied upon to advise them about matters of vital importance to them. His expertise and experience is relied upon by the people, who often seek his guidance and expert advice. As a consultant, he makes himself available to people, who are in need of his inputs. He is also able to furnish his expertise to community groups and community organisations.

(9) **Model:** The community organiser is often perceived as a role model and a source of inspiration by the people. He needs to be conscious of the influence that he is able to exert on the community. His behaviour and approach are often emulated by the people who look up to him for his knowledge, skills and expertise. He also sets innovative models of working on community issues which could be replicated in other communities facing similar circumstances/problems. By proper planning in approaching a problem and executing the plan and documenting the whole process will be of great help to others. The problem solving process sets a model for others to follow.

(10) **Innovator:** The community organiser innovates, performs and constantly strives to improve upon the techniques through the process of community organisation. This gives a lead to the people of the community and enables them to try out new ways and means to find solutions to their needs and problems. Community organisation is not merely for solving problems, but the broader goals of capacity building of individuals, groups and the community as a whole have to be meaningfully achieved.
Innovative ways of improving the capacity of the people, introducing new and more effective ways of community building, as also reviving the traditional and indigenous systems from within the community form an integral part of the role expected from the organiser.

(11) **Motivator:** The community organiser stimulates and sustains active interest among the people for reaching a solution to their needs and problems. The community organiser encourages the community to take up a minor task and complete it successfully. This in turn enables the people to take up more difficult tasks. In such a process, the people at times may not take any initiative or may be content to live with the existing situation. In such a context, the organiser motivates the people by making them observe, analyse, understand and respond to the situation. When people are discouraged, because they are not able to achieve what they wanted or there is resistance and opposition, in such situations the organiser plays the role of a motivator to help them continue efforts in spite of difficulties.

**(12) Catalyst:** In the process of community organisation, the community organiser enables the people to become empowered by gaining accessibility and control over resources and acquiring skills in decision-making. He/she accelerates the actions and reactions of people so that they are able to achieve the desired results. As a catalyst, the organiser is able to increase the response level of the people. The catalyst role further enables the people to become independent and become better equipped in responding to their own needs and problems.

**(13) Advocate:** The role of the advocate is to represent or persuade the members of the community and prepare them to represent their issues to the concerned authorities in order to bring about an effective solution to their unmet needs. The advocacy role is an important one in the present context of community work. The needs and problems of the people have to be presented at appropriate forums and the required support and networking obtained in order to increase the pressure on the oppressive forces. In the role performance of the advocate, the community organiser champions the rights of community groups. He/she speaks on behalf of the community to gain access to services or to improve the quality of services provided. Thus, as an advocate, the community organiser argues, debates, bargains, negotiates, and confronts the forces working against the interest of the community.

**(14) Facilitator:** The community organiser helps the community to articulate its needs, clarify and identify its problems, explore appropriate strategies, select and apply intervention strategies, and develop people's capacities to deal with their own problems more effectively. A facilitator provides support, encouragement, and suggestions to the community so that people may proceed more easily and skillfully in completing tasks or solving problems. A facilitator assists the community in finding coping strategies, strengths and resources to produce changes necessary for realising goals and objectives. A facilitator helps client systems to alter their environment in the desired direction.

**(15) Mediator:** The community organiser intervenes in disputes between parties to help them find compromises, reconcile differences, or reach mutually satisfying agreements.

The mediator takes a neutral stance between the involved parties. A mediator is involved in resolving disputes between members or between the community and other persons in the broader environment.

**(16) Educator:** The community organiser as an educator conveys information to the community and those in the broader environment. The organiser provides information necessary for coping with problem situations, assists the community in practicing new behaviour patterns or skills, and teaches through presentation of role models.

The community organiser makes available information necessary for decision making.

Community organisation is a macro method in social work. The community organiser, with the required qualities and skills will be able to work with the people.

While working with people of different backgrounds or from different geographical settings, the different roles can be applied. All the roles need not be, or cannot be, applied in all the settings or in dealing with all the problems. Moreover, there is no one role which is superior or inferior and while dealing with any problem the organiser has to play more than one role. Therefore, depending upon the situation and the needs and problems of the community appropriate roles have to be performed.

**Q27. What are the skills used in community work?**

***or***

**Write the short note on Skills in community work.**

**[Dec-2019, Q.No.-5(d)]**

***or***

**List out the skills required for community practice.**

**[Dec-2017, Q.No.-4(d)]**

**Ans.** Community organisation, like any other method, or intervention strategy of working with people, requires specific skills. These skills help the worker in carrying out specific tasks with precision and with minimum effort. "Skill" means the worker's capacity to apply knowledge and understanding to a given situation (Trecker, 1948). However, to identify the different types of skills needed for community work practice is difficult for a variety of reasons. Firstly, as is evident from the discussion on models, the scope of community work is vast. Secondly, working with a community entails working with groups and individuals. And lastly, there is no consensus on what constitutes "skill" (Siddiqui, 1987) in social work literature. A closer analysis of the attempts made so far to identify helping skills reveals that usually the author trics to conceptualize the various steps in the helping process, and accordingly identifies skills around these steps.

McMohan (1996) has identified the following skills for social workers and refers to them as the 'Foundation Skills for Social Work'. These hold relevance for the practice of community organisation:

**(I) Relationship skills**

| | |
|---|---|
| Listening | Responding |
| Feeling/sensing | Paraphrasing |
| Clarifying | Information giving |
| Referring | |

**(II) Problem solving skills**

| | |
|---|---|
| Problem identifying | Data Collecting |
| Assessing/goal setting | Planning/task defining |
| Selecting and implementing intervention | Evaluating |
| Terminating | |

**(III) Political skills**

| | |
|---|---|
| Advocating | Taking legal action |
| Providing evidence | Bargaining |
| Organising | Publicising |
| Demonstrating | |

**(IV) Professional Skills**

| | |
|---|---|
| Recording | Research |
| Time-management | Teamwork |

**Rivera & Erlich (1995)** have identified some skills along with values and attitudes, the community organiser is expected to possess:

(1) Similar cultural and racial identification.
(2) Familiarity with customs and traditions, social networks, and values.
(3) An intimate knowledge of language and subgroup slang.
(4) Leadership styles and development.
(5) An analytical framework for political and economic analysis.
(6) Knowledge of past organising strategies, their strengths, and limitations.
(7) Skills in conscientization and empowerment.
(8) Skills in assessing community psychology.
(9) Knowledge of organisational behaviour and decision-making.
(10) Skills in evaluative and participatory research.
(11) Skills in programme planning and development and administration.
(12) An awareness of self and personal strengths and limitations.

**Siddiqui (1997)** categorized skills in the following eleven categories:

**(I) Skills in Rapport Building Include:**

(a) Skill in developing professional relationships with the community.

(b) Skill in developing rapport with funding organisations.
(c) Skill in developing relationship with colleagues.

**(II) Skills in Identification of Needs include:**

(a) Skill in identifying the needs of different communities.
(b) Skill in classifying needs and fixing priorities.
(c) Skill in helping people arrive at a consensus about the community needs.

**(III) Skills in resource mobilization include:**

(a) Skill in identifying sources which can be harnessed for resources.
(b) Skill in preparing a project proposal.
(c) Skill in locating indigenous resources.

**(IV) Skills in Programme Planning include:**

(a) Skill in developing a programme in accordance with the needs of the community.
(b) Skill in keeping the programme in harmony with the cultural needs and traditional practices of the community.
(c) Skill in achieving self sustainability with minimum resources.

**(V) Skills in Programme Management include:**

(a) Skill in developing a blueprint for a division of roles.
(b) Skill in finding the right person for the job.
(c) Skill in developing an adequate system of monitoring and supervision.

**(VI) Skills in Evaluation include:**

(a) Skill in identifying a specific set of indicators.
(b) Skill in data collection.
(c) Skill in analysis of the data.

**(VII) Skills in Recording include:**

(a) Skill in process recording.
(b) Skill in maintaining proper records.
(c) Skill in keeping personal records.

**(VIII) Skills in encouraging community participation include:**

(a) Skill in identifying ways to involve people in decision-making at every stage in community work.
(b) Skill in developing suitable structures to institutionalize peoples participation.
(c) Skill in a gradual transfer of programme management to people to achieve self sustainability of the programme.

**(IX) Skills in working with groups include:**

(a) Skill in analysing the group situation.

(b) Skill in dealing with group feelings.
(c) Skill in developing inter-group relationship.

**(X) Skills in working with individuals include:**

(a) Skill in identifying and accepting individual cases.
(b) Skill in assessing the problem.
(c) Skill in using referral.

**(XI) Skills in mobilising community action include:**

(a) Skill in identifying a suitable issue.
(b) Skill in using multiple strategies.
(c) Skill in using the mass media.

**Weil (2005)** has identified the following range of specialized skills relevant to community practice in the 21st century:

***Practice Skills***

- Policy practice
- Lobbying
- Advocacy
- Programme design, implementation and management
- Financial management
- Management
- Organising
- Non-profit development
- Social marketing
- Fund raising
- Facilitation
- Citizen participation
- Leadership development
- Volunteer management
- Proposal development
- Contract management
- Human resources management
- Grassroots planning
- Sectorial planning
- Cross-sector planning
- Campaigns
- Public education
- Contest skills
- Confrontation tactics
- Negotiating
- Mediation
- Position-taking and writing
- Group and intergroup development
- Economic and social development
- Social planning
- Political and social action

- Coalition/network development

***Research Skills***

- Programme evaluation
- Participatory research
- Use of administrative data
- GIS
- MIS
- Community assessments
- Community mapping and asset mapping
- Neighbourhood analysis
- Policy and poverty research
- Cost benefit/cost-effectiveness analyses
- Community analysis
- Empowerment research
- Action research
- Statistics
- Use of social indicators

**Q28. Elaborate on the neighbourhood model as given by siddique. [Dec-2018, Q.No.-3(a)]**

**Ans.** The general assumption underlying this model is that people living in a community (neighbourhood) have the basic and inherent capacity of meeting their needs/problems through their own initiative and resources.

The worker is expected to induce a process which will make the community realize this and consequently make efforts to achieve a greater degree of satisfaction for its members, individually and collectively. Recent changes in this model of community work lay more emphasis on the development of a self sustaining, indigenous organisation within the community to take over this role from the worker or the agency as soon as possible.

Thus, the role of the worker is seen as unleashing developmental energies within the community, rather than as a provider of services.

The model's application is not limited to generating services to cater to people's needs or improving the physical/resource infrastructure of the neighbourhood. The model can be employed to develop new ideas too. The emphasis is to encourage thinking on the part of people themselves, to adopt progressive attitudes, rather than doing things for them.

This model of effecting change has the limitation of being confined to the micro perspective only. It does not look at linkages of the micro with the macro realities, and the impact of the latter on the community. However, in spite of this limitation, this model has continued to be practiced in India and other third world countries more commonly than the other models.

The experience of community work in India has shown that a complete withdrawal of workers/agency, even in the best planned neighbourhood model is not possible.

A long term involvement of the social worker/agency due to the change process being a long drawn and gradual one is required. The specific steps involved in this model are:

(1) Identification, local and demarcation of the physical area.
(2) Entry into the community.
(3) Identifying the needs of different sections.
(4) Programme Planning.
(5) Resource Planning.
(6) Developing an organisational network in the community.
(7) Partial withdrawal within a time frame.

❑❑

# 3 SOCIAL ACTION FOR COMMUNITY DEVELOPMENT

## INTRODUCTION

Social Action has been used to signify a wide range of primarily voluntary initiative to bring out change in social systems, processes and even structure. Social workers, more often than not, have divergent opinion about the scope and relevance of social action. This ambiguity has even accelerated the debate whether to recognize social action as a method of professional social work.

Social workers advocate for the rights of the marginalized sections of the society. They may have to employ strategies like hunger strike, sit-ins, protests and such other ways to demonstrate their discontent. It is the usage of such strategies that have made social action a debatable issue and a controversial method of social work.

**Q1. Discuss the concept of social action.**

**Ans.** Social action is considered an auxiliary method of professional social work. As one of the methods of working with people, it has remained a debatable issue among the social work professionals. Social action is a method of social work used for mobilising masses in order to bring about structural changes in the social system or to prevent adverse changes. It is an organised effort to change or improve social and economic institutions. Some of the social problems like dowry system, destruction of natural resources, alcoholism, poor housing, health, etc. can be tackled through social action.

As a method of professional social work, social action has remained an issue with wide ranging of opinions regarding its scope, strategies and tactics to be used, its status as a method and its relevance to social work practice. Mary Richmond was the first social worker to use the word 'social action' in 1922. She defines social action as "mass betterment through propaganda and social legislation". However, Sydney Maslin (1947) limits the scope of social action by considering it as a process of social work mainly concerned with securing legislation to meet mass problems. Baldwin broadens the scope of social action by emphasising on bringing about structural changes in the social system through social action.

Baldwin (1966) defines social action as "an organised effort to change social and economic institutions as distinguished from social work or social service, the fields which do not characteristically cover essential changes in established institutions. Social action covers movements of political reforms, industrial democracy, social legislation, racial and social justice, religious freedom and civic liberty and its techniques include propaganda, research and lobbying". In the same line Friedlander (1977) defines social action as an individual, group or community effort within the framework of social work philosophy and practice that aims to achieve social progress, to modify social policies and to improve social legislation and health and welfare services. Similar views are expressed by Lee (1937) who says "social action seems to suggest efforts directed towards changes in law or social structure or towards the initiation of new movements for the modification of the current social practices".

According to Coyle (1937) social action is the attempt to change the social environment in ways, which will make life more satisfactory. It aims to affect not individuals but social institutions, laws, customs, communities. Fitch (1940) considers social action as legally permissible action by a group (or by an individual trying to promote group action) for the purpose of furthering objectives that are both legal and socially desirable. A broad outlook has also been given by Hill (1951) who describes social action as "organised group effort to solve mass social problems or to further socially desirable objectives by attempting to influence basic social and economic conditions or practices".

Further, social action is a term applied to that aspect of organised social welfare actively directed towards shaping, modifying or maintaining the social institutions and policies that collectively constitute the social environment. So lender (1957) states that social action in the field of social work is a process of individual, group or inter-group endeavour, within the context of social work philosophy, knowledge and skill. Its objective is to enhance the welfare of society through modifying social policy and the functioning of social structure, working to obtain greater progress and better services. It is, therefore, evident that social action has been viewed as a method of bringing about structural changes along with social legislation.

**Q2. Explain the history of social action.**

***Or***

**Discuss the history of social action in India.**

**[Dec-2019, Q.No.-2]**

**Ans.** India has a long tradition and history of reform movements, voluntary actions and philanthropic initiatives with the aim to seek welfare of masses, which you have read in your other blocks covering history and philosophy of social work.

In India, problems were of different nature — illiteracy, poverty, exploitation of lower caste people, untouchability, abuse and exploitation of women and inherent practices of gender discrimination and the like. These social evils prevented a large section of the society from getting equitable distribution of resources and opportunities for development and thereby enjoying a dignified life. Social reform movement led by Raja Ram Mohan Roy, Iswarchandar Vidhyasagar resulted in abolition of sati pratha, measures for permitting widow remarriage among Hindus, entry of women in the formal education system and so on. Dwarkanath Tagore, Debendranath Tagore, Keshab Chandra Sen and others worked for founding educational institutions for women and emancipation of women in West Bangal. In western part of the country like Maharashtra, Prarthana Samaj established in 1867 in Bombay clamoured for caste reform.

Freedom movement, especially led by Mahatma Gandhi laid foundation of a strong culture of social action. It may be noted that the legacy of the Gandhian social action has played a crucial role in laying the foundation of social action in India. Gandhian social action includes a combination of samrachana (that is, reconstruction) and satyagraha (insistence on truth). He practiced and preached for imbibing values of non-violence, stressed on ideas of swadeshi (of one's own country) and swaraj (self-rule). Gandhian ideology of peaceful protest in the freedom struggle has made the whole world bow down in front of his ideology, conviction and belief.

Gandhian activism to protect the rights of peasants in Champaran and Kheda and the rights of mill workers in Ahemdabad demonstrated the effectiveness of micro-level social action in influencing the larger political arenas and action. The Gandhian praxis of grassroots political struggle along with macro-level policy initiatives and broader interventions for social reform further set the guidelines for social action. The ideas of satyagrah and swadeshi served both as ethical principles as well as political strategies.

After 1920, for about three decades, many other instances of social action emerged at the center-stage. Prominent ones are communist movements, Dalit movement initiated by Dr. Ambedkar, the Hindutva movement propounded by Hindu Mahasabha and Rashtriya Swayam Sevak Sangh. In consonance, the social reform movement against the hegemonical Brahmanism, led by Mahatma Phule in Maharashtra, Narayana Guru in Kerala and Periyar Ramaswamy Naykkar in Tamil Nadu were other important social justice initiatives. The reformist initiatives for the welfare and equality of women by Pandita Ramabai and Savitribai Phule also played significant role in the endeavours of political freedom. Likewise, Ramakrishna Mission initiated a number of charitable, reformist, educational, welfare and development activities.

All these small scale and large, regional and national level social action initiatives propagated mass mobilization, mass awareness and action, provided ample opportunity to practice skills, techniques of social action, encouraged leadership among few and ability to question surroundings among the masses that hamper their social functioning. This in turn, strengthened the historical background of social action in India and courage and confidence to fight for freedom against colonialism.

After Independence, many young idealists expressed their dissent to the apathy of the state and to the cynical manipulation by the dominant political parties. Social action by JaiPrakash Narayan, social movement led by Medha Patekar, Aruna Roy and Arvind Kejriwal's initiatives for Right to Information Act and many more are some fine examples of relatively recent social action interventions.

Likewise, the world history is also full of examples of social action that were expressed in the form of Civil Rights Movement, Student Unrest in the USA against the Vietnam War, the revolt in Prague against the authoritarian State, the Naxalite movement in India and the neo-left movements in different parts of the world. Many of these movements were a reaction to an increasingly authoritarian and oppressive state and associated insensitive socio-political processes. Emergence of Liberation theology was an expression of dissent to the oppressive power structures of the state. Feminist movement sought to question the structure of patriarchy. The two aspects common in various kinds of movement were the sense of dissent (to traditional state, power structures, culture and ideologies) and a mass mobilization to bring about change in the existing structure and system. These social movements, reform initiatives and social action activities formed the background for social action as a method of social work practice.

**Q3. What is the scope and relevance of social action?**

**Ans.** The scope of social action is very vast and it is one of the most apt methods of social work practice even in today's context. The innovative approaches, participatory techniques, outreach, and holistic thinking are critically important in creating a better world, which is indeed the vision of social work profession.

Poverty levels continue to be high even though every year newer schemes and approaches for poverty alleviation are designed and implemented. Even after nearly 60 years of Independence, there are places like Kalahandi where still people die of hunger. At many places like in Orissa, people sell off their offspring for 10-20 rupees because of poverty. Crores and crores of rupees are allocated for combating poverty, and statistics reflect that numbers of people below poverty line are increasing every year.

Further, Female literacy rate in the country is still nearly 50%. According to one estimate, close to 50% of students in the age group of 6-11 years are not able to read, write and do simple arithmetic. Similarly with respect to health, the situation is very bleak if not worse – 80% people opt for private healthcare system when need arises as government healthcare system lays behind both in quality and quantity. It is estimated that about 3% of the population are pushed below poverty line every year because of health expenditure. Social security system in the country lags behind even those nations that are economically quite poor off compared to us.

Nonetheless, taking the broader and optimistic view of India's fast progress and booming economy would not let us (the social work professionals) to pay attention to problems like poverty, illiteracy, unemployment, gender discrimination, female foeticide, child labour, accessibility and affordability of adequate healthcare system, provision of social security system and so on and so forth. Social action is meant to bring about necessary changes in the policy and legislation for well-being of disadvantaged sections of society. Further, if policies and social legislations are in place, then focus should be shifted to implementation stage. Social workers may have to deal with problems like corruption, red-tapism, insincerity, lack of accountability and transparency that hamper formation of egalitarian social structure.

Thus, social action is a powerful tool that becomes much more effective if the primary stakeholders (beneficiaries) are mobilized to create the pressure. Nowadays, even media is playing a vital and pro-active role – justice in Jussica Lal Murder case, Priadarshini Mattoo case were resolved after media's social action. Even Indian cinema has projected potential of social action in excellent manner through movies like Lage Raho Munna Bhai, Rang De Basanti that have triggered successful social action and advocacy in different parts of the country. In this and other units of the block, you would come across many examples of social action that have been carried out in recent past in various parts of the country that would again project the scope of relevance of this method of social work.

**Q4. Describe the reflections of social action.**

**Ans.** The radical social work approach could not gain ground strongly, despite a rich historical and cultural background because of several reasons. One, fieldwork training, in majority of educational institutions, is not designed in such a way that trainee students spend substantial time in the community and develop a rapport strong enough to mobilize resources. Such restrictions often drive students not to take up hardcore issues. Therefore, skills needed for social action are not inculcated adequately among the trainees. Second, many of the voluntary agencies have to depend for funds either on government or international agencies. They were coming in conflict with the system that comprise of government control. International agencies or foreign funding too have their own guidelines and they may not fund for the hard pressing issues requiring social action. Third, social work professionals may not feel motivated enough to contribute required time and energy resources in the community, which may not be part of their job (employment). Voluntarism has its own limitations, which is, at times, internally driven.

In most of the Third World countries, welfaristic approach dominates due to charity and religious obligations being the starting point of social work. In that context, adopting an empowerment perspective, largely through consensus, is not an easy task. Facilitating increased access for maximum number of people to the essential social service needed for their development, obviously, would call for social action as a primary method of social work. Unfortunately enough literature is not developed on social action. The use of the process of social action requires far greater clarity on the part of trained social workers of its goals and objectives, conceptual framework, ideological and belief system.

The process of social action is often moulded by the larger socio-political contexts and cultural ethos. Social action encompasses both moral and political undercurrents. Unfortunately, social work practice in India has not depicted any significant changes in the social structure or in major problems like poverty, child labour, women exploitation, illiteracy, unemployment, etc., and to a large extent, social work professionals have confined themselves to service delivery roles. Becoming a change agent was taken up by a handful of social work professionals.

Stated otherwise, social action was done by various people in many parts of the country and most of them never had social work background, understanding of theoretical frameworks and professional skills and expertise. It just required commitment, understanding of the issue at hand and conviction and courage. In the next unit, you would be able to understand various facets of social action in a better way when we will deal with principles, values and ethical considerations in social action as a method of social work.

**Q5. Describe the understanding of various systems in social work.**

**Ans.** Social work practice based on system's approach primarily focuses on the interaction between people and various systems in social environment. People are dependent on systems (say, ethnic and cultural system, economic system, health system, workplace system) for obtaining the material and non-material resources, services and opportunities to growth and development.

Inadequacies at informal resource system may be lack of informal helping system (there may be no friends or neighbours, people of a particular social group not included in social intercourse) or reluctance to turn to informal system (hesitation to ask for help from friends, relatives, etc., past experience, fear of loss of face may add to these inhibitions) or inability of the system to meet the needs of the people. For instance, in a village in India, a particular socially marginalized group, may be geographically staying at secluded place or may be shy in putting their needs across to people in the neighbourhood. Further, informal system may be responsive but not well-equipped to solve the problems of the people in distress.

The purpose of social work, in above mentioned cases, is to enhance the problem solving or coping capabilities of people and link people with systems that provide them with resources, services and opportunities. The aim of social work is also to promote the effectiveness of operative systems through improvement of social policy about which you would study at length in subsequent sections. The systems can be understood from the perspective of social work intervention.

From the viewpoint of social work intervention, four basic systems have been laid down – Change Agent System, Client System, Target System and Action System. Detailed description of these systems is as follows:

(1) **Change Agent System:** Change Agent may be any person or group, professional or non-professional, inside or outside a system, who is attempting to bring about change in that system. A change agent is a helper who is specifically employed for the purpose of creating planned change. It may be an agency, NGO or social worker.

(2) **Client System:** It is the 'specific system that is being helped'. Client system may be the individual, family, group, organisation or community which, in addition to being the expected beneficiary of services, is a system that asks for help and engages the services of social worker as a change agent.

(3) **Target System:** This system includes the people the change agent needs to change or influence in order to accomplish his/her goals from the target system.

(4) **Action System:** It is used to describe those with whom social worker deals in his efforts to accomplish the tasks and achieve the goals of the change efforts. An action system can be used to obtain sanctions and a working agreement or contract, in order to identify and study a problem, establish goals for change or influence the major targets of change.

The intervention by change agent may include working at various levels – state to ensure Income generating programmes, shops selling alcohol in the community to be banned, creating awareness about harmful effects of alcoholism, knowledge creation about Prevention of Domestic Violence Act. In this case, target system would be the state (reluctance on the part of administrators to run income generating programmes, red tapism, corruption), shops selling alcohol, all alcoholics in the community and all the people believing that alcoholism is associated with masculinity and it is right on the part of men to 'drink'.

An important diagnostic task of the social worker, usually in collaboration with the client system, is to establish the goals for change and then determine the specific people- the targets–that will have to be changed if the goals are to be reached. Let us look at the process of intervention under integrated social work approach.

**Q6. What is the process of changing effort?**

**Ans.** The process of intervention in social work can be categorized in eight phases, details of which are as follows:

(1) **Assessing Problem:** In first phase, the social worker (change agent) identifies the problem area (say, news reports of weavers committing suicide in Banaras of Uttar Pradesh) and collects more information about the nature of problem, social situation, life-style of people, contingent and precipitating factors causing the problem at hand [community of Julahe (weavers) in Banaras are traditionally involved in making famous hand woven Banarasi saris as a small scale family enterprise. Since, hand weaving consumes lots of time and in the advent of technological advancement, industrialization and globalization, people have options for cheaper electronic machine made banarasi sarees.

(2) **Collecting Data:** It is the second phase, where the social worker collects data about the problem at hand in an objective, scientific manner. She (let us assume social worker is female) may use research tools like questioning (direct verbal, direct written, projective verbal, projective written), observations (participative, non participative) and analyses in order to find the root cause of the problem. In the situation discussed above,

the change agent collects all the details of number of weavers, their proportion, their family background, their work details like time taken in weaving a sari, designs adopted, knowledge about government's schemes for loans, options of selling to co-operatives, coping patterns and so on.

(3) **Making initial contacts:** In this third phase, the change agent gathers information about the systems (other than client system) and tries to develop initial contacts. Stated differently, the social worker gains more insight about the functioning and transactions of other systems in the social environment vis-à-vis client system. It is stakeholders' analysis that you have read in previous units of this block. With the information collected about various systems, the change agent develops action plan for intervention. This would answer the questions as to which part of the system to contact, and method of initiating contact that may include direct approach or asking somebody to influence target system, one to one or group approach and usage of mass media.

(4) **Negotiating contracts (means joint agreement on action system):** In this fourth phase, operating procedures are laid down with respect to client system, action system and target system. More clarity is gained in terms of tasks performed by each party to achieve the goals. In this strategies are explicitly laid down in terms of dealing with resistance to change in relation to various systems in the social environment. These would include involvement of other systems or replacing the services of one system from the other, upsetting equilibrium, providing hope, motivating, negotiating with the system on behalf of or with client system (see the similarity with social action).

(5) **Forming Action System:** In this fifth phase, the change agent concretizes the action system by chalking out all the details of who all would constitute action system, what roles they would perform and what would be their entry points and period of exit, duration of their intervention and the probable impact. In any one change effort, the worker may form many different action systems to collect data, assess the problem, make an initial contact, negotiate a contract, or influence the major targets to help achieve the outcome goal.

(6) **Maintaining and coordinating an action system:** It is the sixth phase, when focus is on the coordination between various components of action system. It would also involve looking at the problems in the development of relationships between members of action system, if any, may, differ in levels of motivation, commitment among members, job turnover,

knowledge and skill enhancement, etc. Likewise, there may be problems in functioning that may result from absence of clarity about role distribution, communication gaps, rapport formation by action system, conflicting values and attitudes. The worker or change agent is required to deal with conflicts within the action system and finally prepare the system for ACTION.

(7) **Exercising influence:** In the seventh phase, the actual intervention to bring about desired change is put into action. The change agent, through the use of relevant knowledge, expertise, and legitimate or charismatic authority, status and reputation, personal attractiveness, control over flow of information and established relationship with the client group brings out desired changes. The process, specifically includes change in behaviour, attitude, belief in target system by providing positive or negative inducement, (influencing a target system by providing rewards for complying, with an influence effort, or punishing it for not complying), persuasion and use of relationships to achieve desired goals.

(8) **Terminating the change effort:** This eighth phase is the last one in the process of intervention. It necessarily does not merely indicate a point reached at the end of planned change, rather is the integral part of the whole process. Specifically, it includes – evaluation of the change effect (means assessment of success-failure in terms of planned change and foresight gained for future action which is self-sustained) and disengaging from relationships (means that formal separation from client system so that they are no more dependent on change agent system for 'help' and dealing with reactions like denial, regression, expression of needs, flight and so on) and lastly, stabilization of change effort (creating systems, institutionalising people's participation, developing coping skills towards self-reliance).

**Q7. What is the role of social worker?**

**Ans.** Following are the roles of social worker:

- **Broker:** The social worker is involved in the process of making referrals to link a family or person to needed resources. Social work professionals do not simply provide information. They also follow up to be sure the needed resources are attained. This requires knowing resources, eligibility requirements, fees and the location of services.
- **Advocate:** In this role, social workers fight for the rights of others and work to obtain needed resources by convincing others of the legitimate needs and rights of members of society. Social workers are particularly concerned for those who are vulnerable or are unable to speak up for themselves. Advocacy

can occur on the local, county, state or national level. Some social workers are involved in international human rights and advocacy for those in need.

- **Case Manager:** Case managers are involved in locating services and assisting their clients to access those services. Case management is especially important for complex situations and for those who are homeless or elderly, have chronic physical or mental health issues, are disabled, victims of domestic or other violent crimes, or are vulnerable children.
- **Educator:** Social Workers are often involved in teaching people about resources and how to develop particular skills such as budgeting, the caring discipline of children, effective communication, the meaning of a medical diagnosis, and the prevention of violence.
- **Facilitator:** In this role, social workers are involved in gathering groups of people together for a variety of purposes including community development, self advocacy, political organisation, and policy change. Social workers are involved as group therapists and task group leaders.
- **Organiser:** Social Workers are involved in many levels of community organisation and action including economic development, union organisation, and research and policy specialists.
- **Manager:** Social Workers, because of their expertise in a wide variety of applications, are well suited to work as managers and supervisors in almost any setting. As managers, they are better able to influence policy change and/or development, and to advocate, on a larger scale, for all underprivileged people.

**Q8. Explain the relation of social action to the community work.**

**Ans.** The term 'community development' refers to a process aimed at economic and social progress of the whole community with active participation of the community people.

Social action shares many similarities with community organisation. Sometimes there is a debate whether social action is a part of community organisation or is completely a different entity. Some believe that it is a part of community organisation. The problem of confusing social action with community organisation arises mainly on account of lack of agreement as to what the term community stands for in social work. While community organisation is meant for a limited geographical area – the 'community', social action has larger context. It signifies the society, say, nation-state. Social action definitely has a larger scope and impact. Some of the techniques used by both the methods (social action and community organisation) may be common but they differ in their approach. Community organisation is a process of effective coordination of different agencies within a particular area and involves cooperative planning and implementation of social policy relating to the area. However, social action as a process is used for tackling issues, which are of a much wider nature than issues affecting a particular area. Community organisation is an integral part of social action. It is the precursor or pre-requirement to social action. In fact, many of the social work professionals consider social action as an extension of community organisation.

Community organisation, is defined by Ross (1955), is a process by which a community identifies its needs or objectives, orders or ranks these needs or objectives, develops the confidence and will to work at those needs or objectives, finds the resources (internal and/or external) to deal with these needs or objectives, takes action in respect of them, and in doing so extends and develops cooperative and collaborative attitudes and practices in the community. Social action is a conflictual process of varying intensity to bring about or prevent changes in the social system through the process of making people aware of the socio-political and economic realities conditioning their lives and by mobilising them to organise themselves for bringing about the desired change, or to prevent the change that adversely affects them, through the use of whatever strategies they may find workable, with the exception of violence.

Thus, we see that 'organising people or community or target population' is the common thread between community organisation and social change. In both the methods of social work, people are helped to realize their needs or problems and in finding out the solution of their felt needs. People organise themselves, collaborate and cooperate and work together for a commonly accepted goal. In both the processes, that is, community organisation and social action, need or problem identification is the first step. It is followed by making the people aware of their pressing need or problem, that is, prioritizing the problems. An environment is created in which the community people feel confidence and gain faith that together they would be able to solve their pressing problems or meet their needs. Emotional impulse to meet the need and to take required action quickly is inherent in both the processes.

However, in social action, change of authority and power structure is involved which invariably requires some degree of conflictual process. It is the redistribution of resources and power. So, we see that social action is community organisation with the aim of bringing about or preventing long lasting social change where confrontation with the existing authority is involved. The strategies and tactics involved in social action like, propaganda, picketing, strike, boycott, sit-in, fast, etc. make social action different from community organisation.

**Q9. Explain the model of Elitist social action.**

***Or***

**Explain the elitist social action model.**

**[Dec-2019, Q.No.-4(c)]**

**Ans.** Elitist Social Action: It is the action initiated and conducted by the elites for the benefit of the masses. In this model of social action, general public or the target group is not involved. The three sub-models of elitist social action are:

(1) **Legislative Social Action Model:** It is a process in which elite groups conduct studies on the gravity, extent and urgency of the problems, create public opinion and lobby to try to modify the social policy. Here, the general population or the target group is not involved directly in the process. Some elites either themselves or along with like-minded individuals take-up the social issues, which they think can be related to the pressing problem. Social legislations like 'Child Labour (Prohibition and Prevention) Act 1986; Dowry Prohibition Act, 1961; Sati Prevention Act (revised) 1987; Immoral Traffic (Prevention) Act 1956; Juvenile Justice Act, 1986; Maternity Benefit Act, 1961 are the results of the legislative social action carried out by the elites.

(2) **Economic Sanction Model:** In this type of social action, the elites, by gaining control over some economic, social, political or religious weapon try to obtain benefits for the society. In this process, the elites gain control over some economic resources and use it as a threat to obtain benefits for their clientele. For example, labour officer in a shoe making industry was sensitive enough towards the felt needs of the female labourers who wanted some time off to feed their infants. The authority of the industry put their stand clearly that if any female worker takes the time off, her pay would be deducted. There were fifteen such females out of 90 female staff who wanted the time off. The labour officer held a meeting with the female staff and asked the opinion of all on this issue. He said that tomorrow any other female might be in the position of these 15 lactating mothers. After a series of meetings, all the females agreed to stand united for special privileges given to them. The authorities first disagreed. However, later, when the whole staff threatened to go on indefinite strike and persuasion from the labour officer giving the reference of Maternity Benefit Act 1961, they agreed to give in to the demands of the female staff. Not only this, a small creche was also opened for the infants and children of the female staff.

(3) **Direct Physical Model:** It is a process where elites take the law in their own hands and punish those responsible for the

cause of injustice and thus try to bring about benefits to their clientele. The NGOs working for the welfare and development of the child labour got united and initiated a Campaign Against Child Labour (CACL) throughout the country. It was realized that mere formulation of Child Labour (Prohibition and Regulation) Act is not enough to provide security and justice to the children working in formal and informal sectors. So a campaign was initiated in 1992 at the national level to work for eradication of child labour and ensuring the fundamental right to education for them. The NGO workers carried out rallies, morchas, dharnas and did sit-ins against the apathy of the government as well as the greed of employers who ruin the lives of millions of children for their profits and selfish motives.

**Q10. Explain the model of popular social action.**

***or***

**Discuss Britto's social action model with the help of field examples.**

***or***

**Write the short note on Conscientisation model.**

**[June-2019, Q.No.-5(c)]**

**Ans.** It is the second type of social action model given by Britto. In the popular social action model, a large section of people with or without elite participation is involved. They aim their confrontational/conflictive action against the unjust and dehumanizing structures, agencies, policies, procedures or oppressive agents. Direct mobilization model, dialectical model and the conscientisation models are the sub-types of social action. These models differ from each other in some respects and they have some common features, as mentioned below:

(1) **Conscientisation Model:** It is based on Paulo Friere's concept of creating awareness among masses through education. Paulo Friere developed the concept of conscientization, which means educating the people about the oppression, oppressed and the oppressor (their own position in the two groups), their inter-relationship, the power structure and ways to liberate from the oppressed or oppressor class. Friere maintains that the situation when the oppressed and/oroppressor are conscientized, there exists motivating possibilities for the true liberation of mankind as well as for the most efficient domestication of man. He believed that education can be a tool for re-education and social action. Conscientization process results not merely in learning of literary skills, but it is intended to assist the participants to liberate themselves from all structures, which inhibit the realization of their full humanity through action-reflection-

action. This form of social action involves maximum participation of the concerned population.

***Field example:*** An NGO working in a resettlement colony in Kolkata has taken up the issue of discriminatory treatment done against the girl child at the familial, community and society level. The gender prejudices and biases in our patriarchal social structure have most often given lesser share than due in the distribution of family resources, be it nutrition, education or other opportunities for development. The NGO made use of street plays, emotional speeches, debates, documentary films, etc., to conscientize the people towards the vulnerability and exploitation of female children. Issues of female infanticide/foeticide, poor health and malnutrition, school dropouts, low wages, torture of dowry victims, rape, molestation and so on were taken up. With the usage of conscientization model of social action, the NGO was able to make a little difference in the negative and indifferent attitudes of general public towards girl child.

(2) **Dialectical Mobilization Model:** It helps in promoting conflict to exploit the contradictions in a system, with the belief that a better alternative system will emerge as a result. Dialectic means the art of logical disputation. This process involves an initial proposition (thesis), which is inadequate and generates a counter proposition (antithesis) and the rational context of both are taken up into the synthesis. In other words when individuals or groups take up extreme positions and argue, the position of one may be taken as the thesis and that of the other as antithesis. The result of their argumentation, a certain conclusion acceptable to both, may be termed synthesis. Thus, the posing of contradictory positions and arriving at a better conclusion is termed dialectics in logic. Actionists who follow a dialectical process take the logical to the ontological. They assume that all forces in nature and human institutions, clash and develop.

***Field Examples:*** A group of human rights activists have organized 'Jan Sunwai' with the aim of raising voice against torture by police on innocent people in Bihar where the local SHO and higher rank officials of police department, representatives from Nation Human Rights Commission and district magistrate were called and police were questioned about the custodial deaths of two minors who were in lock up for petty theft and many other such cases were taken up. Both the parties (perpetrators, here, the police and the victims, families of accused) presented their point of view.

(3) **Direct Mobilization Model of Popular Social Action:** In direct mobilization model, specific issues are taken up by the social actionists and the masses are mobilized to resort to protests and strikes to achieve the objectives. In this process, the leaders or elites pick up specific grievances or issues that are affecting the people at large. They analyse the causal factors, which are at the root of the injustice. They formulate the alternative policies and procedures and mobilize the masses for protest activities for the purpose of achieving the set objectives.

***Field Examples:*** One fine example of this model would be the fishermen's movement. During post independence period, a large number of trawlers and mechanized boats entered in the fishing sector. This led to massive over fishing to capture lucrative foreign markets. Their fishing method destroyed several species of fish. The imbalance, thus created in the eco-system, led to lowering of the stock available for traditional fishermen. Mechanization in the fishing sector had put poor fishermen at the mercy of moneylenders, merchants, exporters and multinationals. The government was apathetic.

**Q11. Describe institutional and non-institutional models.**

**Ans.** Singh (1984) has delineated certain other models of social action based on the locus of action and the initiators. He has described two models — Institutional and Non-institutional or Social, with sub models. In Institutional models, social action is initiated either by State or non-government organisations while in non-institutional or social or populist model, common people or the disadvantaged sections of the society make the first move. It may, however, be noted that the approaches taken in all these models of social action might be overlapping.

**Institutional (state) model of social action:** It is the social action initiated by the state or government. Social action by the state generally takes an indirect form, and its aim is to benefit the people with or without their participation. The approach is commonly parliamentary, representational, bureaucratic and elitist. The action is organized or sponsored within the framework of law, or may be legalized subsequently. For instance, government passing orders for regularization of unauthorized settlements of poor in urban settings and also implementing programmes for community reconstruction, say, proper sewage, availability of safe drinking water, free immunization and health check-ups. Especially, in the context of India, the State has, through the Constitution, committed itself to be a 'welfare-state' and therefore, is obligatory to provide all the services needed for the development and well-being of all sections of the population.

**Institutional-social model of social action:** In this type of model social action is initiated by voluntary organisations, whether or not getting financial support from the government. In this model, action is initiated either directly or with the support of the people. People's participation may be sought at the beginning or in between the process. Stated otherwise, in the beginning the action may be initiated by leaders of the voluntary organisation for the disadvantaged section of population group but subsequently it progresses with and through them (the marginalized group). The inherent theme behind such type of social action is primarily 'welfarist' or providing relief and services to the needy. The action often takes place within the framework of law. To exemplify, social action taken up by NGOs, say, fixing the allocating sweepers by the municipal corporation of that area during sanitation drive in the slums or a initiating a movement to re-admit school drop-out girls and boys in a community.

In the above two models, social action is initiated by formal agency like State or NGO and in the second subtype (i.e., institutional-social model), people are involved subsequent to initiation of social action. The next two models – social institutional model and populist model are initiated and carried out by the marginalized groups themselves.

**Social institutional model of social action:** This type of social action may be organized by the citizens, self help groups, elites, the deprived and others for their benefit but in its progression and development may seek support from formal groups and institution(s) which may like to espouse its causes. It may be direct, participatory and even radical. Depending upon its success it may institutionalize itself formally or remain in the character of a spontaneous and sporadic effort with an informed and critically aware social base and power. The nature of such action may be constitutional or extra constitutional. The social institutional model can be distinguished from the institutional social model in that in the latter one action is initiated by the institution, say an NGO, and at some stage people are mobilized to participate. On the other hand, in social institutional model people initiate social action and may collaborate with some institution working for the similar cause.

**Populist/movemental model of social action:** The fourth model rests entirely on popular social base and power, rejects dependency and stresses self-reliance through collective effort, active participation, and continuing education. This is an ideal form of social action in the sense that participants join hands together out of their own experience, take decisions in collaboration and consensus with each other, and while thinking, deciding and working together in helping themselves strengthen their collaborative attitude, mutual trust, shared dreams and aspirations. This type of social action is, indeed, an action of the people, for the people and by the people. This type of action may take of some of the characteristics of a movement and may both be constitutional and extra-constitutional. It may be routinizing or self-terminating.

**Q12. Explain Gandhian model of social action.**

***Or***

**Discuss Gandhian model of social action.**

**[June-2019, Q.NO.-4(d)]**

**Ans.** Social action of the Gandhian tradition emerges as a class by itself because of its emphasis on spirituality, purity of means and ends, non-violence as a creed, austerity (limitation of want), and moral re-armament of people. Constructive thinking, mobilization, organisation and action are the essential ingredients of this model. People's power remains the basis in all the three types of social action of this tradition. This model has three sub-types:

**Militant non-violent tradition:** With non-violence still the base, this tradition or approach calls for political and revolutionary character to the social action. It aims at forceful intervention to bring about radical changes in the social system. It does not rely totally on the peaceful and mere constructive work done at the grassroots level. It believes in redistribution of power and resources and to achieve this aim it intends to mobilize masses to take action. For example, chipko movement emerged out of the protest against rampant deforestation in the Himalayan hills caused by indiscriminate deforestation for commercial consumption.

**Gentle non-violent tradition:** The Satyagraha done by Vinoba Bhave for satyagraha and village and community reconstruction explains gentle non-violent form of Gandhian social action. It blends the components of the social (populist-movemental) and the grassroots-institutional (constructive work). Bhudaan (donation of land) and gram-daan (donation of villages) for reconstruction of the Gandhian socialist community are the fine examples of this tradition.

**Citizenship model of constructive work:** This type of social action concentrates mainly on the grass root level of social action (citizenship) through the means of education. This type of social action relies on constructive work and believes that necessary changes in the social system would take place in due course of time. It rejects coming in conflict with the authorities, protests and boycotts to achieve the desired objective of social change. It prefers to lay stress on consensus (Lok-sammati), citizenships role (model) and through it visualizes a revolution in thought and method (Bichar kranti and paddhati kranti).

Gandhian approach further subscribes to the view that the government depends upon the people and not the people on the government. That all exploitation is based on cooperation-willing or forced– of the exploited and therefore there is a need to generate social power – a capacity to control the behaviour of others, directly and indirectly, through action by groups of people which impinges on other groups. Non-violent action is not only a policy for a true Gandhian worker but also a creed, and the constructive programme is considered to be the core of such action.

In all the three traditions of Gandhian social action, people's base is considered primary; a parliamentary approach is regarded as inadequate; and while the last two types concentrate on the solution of social and economic problems, through people building and action, militant non-violent tradition model also adds political dimensions to them. The role of institutions is considered enabling, people-based and supportive in all the three forms–which aims towards the creation of a caring and welfare society as contrasted with welfare state.

**Q13. Explain the strategies and tactics in the social action.**
**[Dec-2019, Q.No.-3(c)]**

**Ans.** Strategies and tactics provide dynamism to the process of social action. Therefore, forming a consensus on the strategies that are possible and available is quite difficult as newer strategies and tactics are being used with changing times in various stages of social action. Lees has described following main strategies:

**(1)** **Collaboration:** In this, the underlying assumption is that to bring about change in power equation, resorting to conflictive strategies are not always necessary. The authority may be responsive and bring out necessary changes to provide equitable resource sharing to the marginalized groups too. In this, social workers collaborate with the local authority and other authorities or agencies with the aim to bring about needed improvements in the existing social policy. This strategy is based on homogeneity of values and interests, through which substantive agreement on proposed interventions is obtainable. In collaborative strategy, the change in the social structure or institution is brought through peaceful means. Such means are education, persuasion, demonstration, and experimentation.

**(2)** **Competition or bargaining, negotiation, advocacy:** The second set of strategies are based on the premise that one anticipates some resistance to change, and the activity of the change agent may have to be accompanied by tactics which are not exclusively persuasive but rather seek to affect change through pressure. In this strategy, contending parties utilize commonly accepted campaign tactics to persuade, to negotiate and to bargain, with the willingness to arrive at a working agreement.

**(3)** **Disruption or conflict/confrontation:** Third set of techniques are based on the premise that in the struggle between those who are pro status quo and those who are pro change, resistance is an aspect of the change effort and therefore the dynamic of conflict is inherent in the social action effort. This strategy signifies a more militant approach and it may include strikes, boycotts, fasts, tax-refusal, 'sit-ins' etc. Lees also includes riots and guerilla warfare though these may be omitted by many other social workers as any use of violence will be unacceptable to values and ethics of professional social work.

**Q14. What are the strategies of planning?**

**Ans.** Planning is one of the most crucial aspects of the process of social action. It is developing a blue print of the action to be taken. It is often said that good planning is half the work accomplished.

**Situational analysis:** This strategy gives a clear and comprehensive view of problematic environment and justifies social action. Depending upon the problem at hand, through research or other objective methods, information is collected about political factors (favourable/unfavourable national and regional policies and programmes; political decision-makers and decision-making mechanisms; relevant local reform policies and strategies; and related legislations and regulations), Institutional factors (responsible administrative system and their efficacy related to handling the 'problem'), economic and financial resources and factors (economic policy and economic reform and their impact on common people in general and poor in particular; system of micro-credit and loan, etc.), infrastructure and civic amenities (any differential, implicit or explicit service delivery system in civic amenities and infrastructure), social and cultural conditions (social and ethnic groups, linguistic groups, gender roles, religious and caste system, social values and attitudes and their impact), environment factors (natural resources, geographical and climatic conditions and their impact on living conditions of habitants).

**Problem Analysis:** It is more specific and confined approach where not only the root cause of the problem is analysed but also its multifarious effects. Analysis should be based on objectively identified facts and apparent reasoning of the problem. For instance, in a village of Thakurs and dalits, the latter not getting access to safe drinking water, may be due to political rivalry at the panchayat level and seemingly obvious reason of Thakurs oppressing dalits may not be the real case.

**Resource Analysis:** This includes appraising the availability/non-availability of human, material, financial, technical, social and political resources. It also involves identifying stakeholders who have resources which are deficit in the case of marginalized community and strategic planning of redistribution of the same needed for development of disadvantaged group for whom social action is initiated.

**Stakeholder Analysis:** This is a dominant strategy to sharpen the intervention focus and design appropriate strategies ahead for action. Stakeholder analysis provides the social actionist/activist with information about all the stakeholder groups like target groups, direct beneficiaries and final beneficiaries and whether they are favourable or unfavourable. The analysis starts with identifying the various players who are affected by the problem (mainly the marginalized group) or who affect the situation (the oppressor group like state, elite, etc.), might become useful partner (like electronic or print media) or might become conflict partners or threats to the intervention (say, administrators or elected representatives at various levels).

**SWOC (Strength, Weakness, Opportunity and Challenges) Analysis:** This goes hand in hand with stakeholders' analysis. It gives an insight into the intervention designed for achieving goals. The main actors/leaders/facilitators analyse what are their strengths and weaknesses and well as that of their opponents', what are the opportunities available to them and what are their challenges or constraints. This is basically cost benefit analysis after which intervention strategies are designed.

After understanding the concept and principles of social action, let us take a look at the skills needed by social workers for social action. These skills are no different from the general skills the social worker possesses by imbibing the ethics and principles of professional social work. A social worker using social action, as a method of social work requires certain skills, main among them are dealt with below in brief.

Planning strategies are quite crucial as they lay foundation for success or failure of the intervention. Chances of successful social action are least, if problem is wrongly identified at the initial stage or real cause is not looked into or strengths and weaknesses of partners and opponents are not realized properly. Objectivity, observation, analytical skills, skills to use strategies like SWOC analysis, stakeholders analysis, skills to analyse and present qualitative and quantitative data, skills in research, skills to help people identify their problems and probable solutions, skills to communicate results of baseline study for problem analysis to the target audience are some of the vital skills needed in the planning stage. Planning helps in setting realistic objectives that in turn would help in monitoring and evaluating the intervention. Let us now pay attention to managerial strategies.

**Q15. Explain the strategies of managerial or mobilization.**

***Or***

**Elaborate advocacy as a key strategy of social action.**

***Or***

**Briefly describe different types of advocacy.**

**[Dec-2019, Q.No.-4(d)]**

**Ans.** Managerial/mobilization strategies would aim at influencing those people who have social, political and economic power so as to facilitate re-distribution of resources and power with the aim of improving the life of disadvantaged sections of society. It includes – lobbying, public mobilization, mediation, civil disobedience, strikes, dharnas, protests, signature campaigns and legislative efforts ways, to mention a few. Mobilization strategies are meant to facilitate marginalized group raise their voice regarding the oppression and exploitation against them.

Advocacy is considered the key strategy in social action, which in fact, is a combination of various strategies aimed at bringing about change in social systems and influence power and political relations between various social agencies.

Advocacy may be done at various levels – personal level (raising issues concerning daily life), family level (gender discrimination, age related issues like child abuse, elderly abuse; not letting a member live life in his/her own terms; unequal distribution of family resources, etc.), community level (issues related to community well-being, any section of community not getting equitable share and discriminated against on account of ethnicity, religious, caste bases), area (basic amenities and services like water, sanitation, health facilities, school, and other infrastructure not made available by the responsible administrative authorities), state (schemes, programmes, implementing policies, political representation, land rights, etc., are not in consonance with equality and social justice), nation (influencing policy intervention, human rights, basic rights, interventional conventions, ties and relations for the benefit of poor and disadvantaged) and International (issues related to world trade treaties, international loan, Arms deals, illegal trade, global warming, etc.)

Mainly three types of advocacy have been identified – Legislative, Bureaucracy and Judiciary advocacy. Legislative advocacy aims to influence the legislative process and recommend new legislations, to amend legislations or raise voice against proposed and accepted ordinance or record dissent against implementation of legislations. Legislative processes are held in parliament or Vidhan Sabha. Policies are passed through legislatures, new legislations are made and amendments are made to older ones. For this legislative procedures like question hour (first one hour of the (Parliament) House, lower or upper, is reserved for asking and answering questions, Zero hour (time period between question hour and parliament's next session), adjournment motion, violation of parliamentary privilege, call attention notice, Half-an-hour discussion, no confidence motion, petition, etc., may be used for advocacy purposes.

**Bureaucracy advocacy:** At times, rigid bureaucratic structure, red-tapism causes much hurdle in the process of implementation of pro-poor policies and programmes, which calls for social action against the system. At present, Right to Information Act has become a strong tool to fight against negative aspects of bureaucratic system and ensure transparency and accountability. There have been many success stories after the advent of this RTI Act.

**Judicial advocacy:** Mainly aims to protect public interest, challenge state's anti-poor policies and programmes, enforcing constitutional and legal rights and bringing forward desired changes in the existing legations. Public interest litigations are filed, participation as Amicus Curie and knocking doors of Supreme Court under Right to Constitutional Remedies are some of the measures advocacy groups can make use of.

**Media advocacy:** It is the most popular strategy in the contemporary scenario. Usage of media for fulfilment of objectives of social action is called media advocacy. Radio, Television, newspapers, street plays, stories, the Internet, and such others, may be used for advocacy. Media advocacy is used not only to create pressure on policy makers and bureaucratic system but also for creating public opinion, mobilizing and involving common man for the cause.

**Q16. What are the skills used in social action?**

***Or***

**Enlist skills required by social workers at various stages of social action. [June-2019, Q.No.-4(e)]**

**Ans.** Specific skills needed by social actionist would be beneficial, especially at the planning stage. These can be broadly identified as follows:

**Relational skills:** Social workers (or social actionists or social activists) should have skills for building rapport with individuals and groups and skills for maintaining these relations. They should be able to develop and maintain professional relationship with the clients. The social workers should have the ability to identify the leadership qualities among the clientele and should be skillful to harness these qualities for social action. Along with this, working harmoniously with the established local leaders is needed. The social workers should identify tension-producing situations and diffuse them before they become serious. Developing and maintaining cordial relations with other agencies and NGOs working in the same geographical area and those working for similar causes is also required.

**Analytical and research skills:** Social workers, engaged in social action, should have the ability to objectively study the socio-cultural and economic characteristics of the community. They should be able to find out the pressing problems and needs of the clientele. They should be able to analyse the social problems, contributing factors and its ramifications on the social, economic, political, ideological, cultural, ecological aspects of life. They should be able to conduct research and/or understand the likely impact of research studies in a functional sense. Added to this, the social workers should be able to facilitate the community people to speak out their own felt needs and prioritize them. They should never try to impose their own understanding of the social situation and problems to the community people.

**Intervention skills:** After need identification, the social workers should have the ability to help the clientele chalk out practical intervention strategies to deal with the problem. They should provide various options to the clientele and help them in analyzing pros and cons of each option for taking up proper steps. Social action requires 'confrontation' with authorities. The social workers must inform the community about the consequences of taking up hard steps like sit-ins, boycotts, strikes, etc. They should be able to maintain the desired level of feeling of discontent and emotional surcharge to bring about the necessary change, enthusiasm and courage among the community people for a fairly long time so as to minimize the scope of failure of mass mobilization before the set objectives are achieved.

**Managerial skills:** The social workers also need the knowledge and ability to handle organisation, which may be the outcome of the institutionalization of people's participation. They should be able to coordinate and collaborate with various groups and local leaders so as to unite the clientele for the required intervention. They should be skillful to make policies and programmes, programme planning, coordinating, recording, budgeting and elementary accounting and maintenance of various records.

**Communication skills:** These skills are highly crucial for social action. The social worker should have the ability to develop effective public relations with local organisations and leaders. They should be able to effectively communicate verbally (including public speaking) and in writing as well. The social workers should be able to deliver or identify adequate people to deliver powerful speeches. They should be able to devise programme media for effectively communicating with the target audiences. The social worker should be able to evaluate and use folk and mass media suited to diverse groups. These skills are used for developing slogans and motivational songs, speeches and IEC materials for mass mobilization.

**Training skills:** The social workers should be able to train local leaders and identified leaders for taking up the charge of mass mobilization and confrontation with the authorities. They should be able to train selected people at the local level aimed at imparting knowledge about the social issue taken up for action and the modalities of carrying out the intervention including the 'confrontation process'. These people should be trained for creating public opinion for or against the social issue taken up and identify and involve people in social action. They should also be trained to utilize social action strategies and tactics (confrontation, persuasion, negotiation, boycott, etc.) without the use of violence.

**Q17. Explain social action as a method of social work.**

**Ans.** Every profession has a tested body of knowledge, which includes principles, techniques, methods, procedures, tools and terminology of its own. The same is true with professional social work. Social work has six methods of working with people (casework, group work, community organisation, social action, social welfare administration and social work research). These methods are the techniques of enabling the people for better social functioning. Social action, as a method of professional social work practice, is an organised effort to change or improve social and economic institutions through organisation and mobilization of the community people. Unlike other social work methods, social action emphasizes on long-term essential changes in established social institutions. Social action covers movements of social, religious and political reform, social legislation, racial and social justice, human rights, freedom and civic liberty. Previously social action was considered as a tool within the field of community organisation, but now it has been considered as a separate technique of social work and as such a fourth process.

As a method of social work, social action adheres to the philosophy of professional social work. It does not blame people for the deficiency or problem. It strongly believes in the worth and dignity of human beings. Social action rejects the doctrine of laissezfaire and survival of the fittest. The unfit person has the same fundamental rights as do the more fit, and the rich or powerful is not necessarily fit, and nor a poor or weak is indeed unfit. It adopts a commitment to the capacity of all the people to take action to improve their life circumstances.

Another aim of social action, which has been mentioned by many social work scholars, is formulation of or change in existing social legislation. Once the legislation comes into force, its implementation at the ground level is another salient task of social actionists or social workers. Thus we see that social action, as a method of social work profession, is a powerful tool of bringing about positive changes in the social system for the betterment of the masses.

**Q18. What are the values and ethics of social action?**

**Ans.** The prime goal of social worker is to reduce suffering and enhance social functioning. Establishing an egalitarian system is also the goal of social action. In fact, social action as a method of social work is used where inequality in terms of resource distribution is seen in the social system that puts a section of population to marginalization. For instance, country is recording high economic growth but at the same time nearly a half of the population is living below poverty line or in poor economic condition. This means that resources and opportunities for development are in the hands of a few and there is hardly any representation from weaker sections of the population in the decision-making process. Enactment of 73rd and 74th Constitutional Amendments that provided one-third reservation to women and proportionate reservation (as per the configuration in general population) to the Scheduled Castes and Scheduled Tribes is one such effort directed to provide equitable share in decision-making process.

Values of social work profession are described as equality, social justice, equity, liberty and dignity of human beings, social action also indeed rests on these values. It addresses inequality that leads to vulnerability, marginalization, destitution, oppression and exploitation. Ensuring human rights in every individual is the basic goal of social action as well as social work (Empowerment perspective). A look at Human Rights as per the Universal Declaration of Human Rights (1948) would be quite beneficial in understanding the value and ideological base of social work in general and social action in particular as these Rights form the backbone of social action and provide conceptual framework for intervention. These include:

- Right to freedom and inequality (no discrimination on the basis of caste, class, race, etc.)
- Right to Live (life, liberty, security)
- Right to Health
- Right to live without being subject to torture
- Right to Marry and Found a family
- Right to Education
- Right to Cultural Practices
- Right to Religion
- Equality and Protection of Law
- Right to Vote, Citizenship
- Right to Expression
- Right to Property
- Right to Work

Social action believes in the inherent worth, dignity and integrity of individuals. It has strong conviction in democratic functioning and equal opportunities for all. Social action is based on the assumption that it is the duty of the state to ensure distributive justice and fairly equitable social change. People and civil society should be united to raise their concerns against violations of human rights. It is the duty of the state to ensure human rights of each and every citizen. General public is not the receptive beneficiary of state's doles and obligations.

Social justice and Human rights form the moral fibre of social action. It commits itself to protect the rights of marginalized sections of the society. Fully believing in democratic values and inherent dignity and rights of each and every individual, it envisages preparing downtrodden to raise voices for their own self. Social Action believes in creating a social environment where common man's political, economic, social and cultural rights are realized. Social action believes in promotion of democracy and empowerment of civil society.

Objectives of social action can be described as :

- To introduce structural changes for equitable redistribution of resources available in society,
- To promote the realization of potentials of the target population,
- To eradicate social evils as against human dignity, l Curb abuse and exploitation,
- Conserve physical, social mental and moral health, and
- Strengthen the existing social institutions conducive for promoting people's well being.

**Q19. What are the principles of social action?**

***Or***

**Elaborate on the principles of social action.**

**[June-2019, Q.No.-3 (d)]**

***Or***

**Write the short note on Principle of dramatisation.**

**[Dec-2019, Q.No.-5 (e)]**

**Ans.** The efforts of desired social change and political action are important ingredients of social action. Social action deals with power equations and decision-making process that results in skewed or equitable resource distribution.

Though social action has a wide canvas and may include entire gamut of activities from relief, charity and welfare to reform, the term has a clear socio-political connotation. After understanding the values and ethics of social action, the principles that act as guidelines in the process of social action can be discussed as propounded by Britto (1984) well grounded to Gandhian ideology of social action. These principles of social action are as follows:

**The Principle of Credibility Building:** Building credibility is most important factor for mobilizing people and initiating social action. It is a very crucial task of creating positive public image regarding the leadership, ability to stand firm for the cause, reliability of worker's efforts and the organisation. Credibility can be built through one or many of the following ways:

(1) **Gestures of goodwill towards the opponent:** For instance, when Gandhiji was in England, World War I broke out. He recruited students for service in a British Ambulance Corps on the Western Front. These gestures of goodwill towards the opponents built up the image of Gandhiji as a true humanitarian personality. His philosophy of non-violence facilitated the credibility-building process among his opponents, the British.

(2) **Example setting:** Example setting is important to show to reference public as well as all the stakeholders that conviction and commitment, values and ethics for which you are raising voice are not utopian and can be practiced in real life. It ensures credibility of your message and action. Gandhiji's entire life was the reflection of what he preached — non-violence, tolerance and insistence on truth.

(3) **Selection of typical, urgently felt problems for struggles:** The leader/social actionist gains credibility if s/he focuses on the felt-needs of the people. Scarcity of water has remained one of the pressing problems for the people of Rajasthan.

(4) **Success:** Successful interventions help in setting up credibility of the leader as well as the philosophy he/she is preaching. Seeing the successful work of Dr. R. Singh in certain villages of Rajasthan, State government also came forward to extend its support. Local leaders from various other villages and NGO professionals also approached him for help.

**Principle of Legitimization:** Legitimization is the process of convincing the target group and the general public that the movement-objectives are morally and ethically right. If leaders present the cause they are fighting for as a moral imperative, it legitimizes the movement or social action initiative. Social actionists may give justification with theological, philosophical, legal-technical base to legitimize the goal of social action. Moral approach to legitimization would be when you, as social actionist, try to create a public opinion that a particular behaviour is morally right or wrong. For instance, people in the Campaign Against Child Labour, have through peaceful rallies, persuasive speeches, media usage, have made efforts in creating an environment in the country where employing children in any occupation is considered morally wrong. Thirdly, Legal-technical approach to legitimization is seen when Ms Aruna Roy and later on Mr. Arvind Kejriwal initiated campaign for Right to Information that resulted in RTI Act of 2005.

**Principle of Dramatization:** Principle of Dramatization is directed for mass mobilization by which the leaders of a movement galvanize the population into action by emotional appeals to heroism, sensational news-management, novel procedures, pungent slogans and such other techniques. Almost every leader mobilizing the masses, uses this principle of dramatization. Gandhiji, Vinoba Bhave, Subhash Chandra Bose, Bal Gangadhar Tilak, and other leaders resorted to this principle.

(1) **Use of songs:** Catchy songs, which put forth the cause of a movement, create a dramatic effect. In a village of West Bengal, child-activists have made parody songs and rhymes giving messages on girl child education, on keeping houses and surroundings clean, anti-alcoholism and the like, which they would collectively sing.

(2) **Slogans:** do boond zindagi ki (for pulse polio campaign) ho HIV avastha ka gyan toh bani rahe muskan (for HIV testing), sab padhen sab badhen (for Sarva Sikhsha Abhiyan), etc., are some of the slogans used to give dramatic effect to various social movements.

(3) **Powerful speeches:** This is also a crucial way of motivating the masses and creating dramatic-effect. Gandhiji's appeal to sacrifice and martyrdom was thrilling and it had a special appeal for the youth to work for the cause.

(4) **Role of women:** Making prominent women lead marchers was a technique, which gave a dramatic effect to the movement. At Rajkot, Kasturba Gandhi herself inaugurated the civil disobedience movement by courting arrest first.

(5) **Boycott:** Boycott is a dramatic way of influencing public opinion both when the effort is successful and when it is crushed. It means excluding a particular group from enjoying the privilege of social interaction, status and social prestige. Picketing and 'hartals'– voluntary closure of shops and other organisations, were used by Gandhiji to dramatize the issue.

**Principle of Multiple Strategies:** Also known as basket principle, this indicates the adoption of a multiple strategy, using combined approaches and also a combination of different types of programmes. Zeltman and Duncan have identified four development strategies from their experience of community development, which are:

(1) **Educational strategy:** As one of the basic requirements of social action, this strategy is used to educate/inform the prospective participants about various relevant dimensions of the issue(s) at hand at the individual, group and mass level. People or target groups are given information about the issue, awareness is created and people are motivated, persuaded to participate in the action/movement.

(2) **Persuasive strategy:** Persuasive strategy is the adoption of a set of actions/procedures to bring about change by reasoning, urging and inducing others to accept a viewpoint. In fact in every rally, protest demonstrations focus is laid on winning new converts by oratory and gentle presentation of arguments.

(3) **Facilitative strategy:** This refers to a set of procedures and activities to facilitate the participation of all sections of society in the mass movement. The programme Gandhians devised was often so simple and devoid of any risk that even illiterate children could do them and participate in the National Liberation Movement.

(4) **Power strategy:** It involves the use of coercion to obtain the objectives of social action. The forms of coercion may vary ranging from social exclusion or ostracism, denial of opportunity to smooth functioning to defaming, protests, moral pressure by hunger strike and sit-ins. Medha Paketar's hunger strike unto death during Narmada Bachao Andolan was one of the techniques of power strategy. Media's role in defaming top-shot personalities and police during Campaign: Justice for Jussica (Jussica Lal Murder Case) is another example of usage of this power strategy.

**Principle of Dual Approach:** In social action, it is important for activist to develop counter-systems or revive some moribund system, meeting some of the felt needs of the reference group. Since, in social action, there is an attempt to destroy the established/maintained system, it is important that simultaneously constructive systems may be developed. Gandhian constructive work programme performed such a function, in a small measure, together with conflictual programmes of satyagrahis.

**Principle of Manifold Programmes:** It denotes developing a variety of programmes with the ultimate objective of mass mobilization. These can be broadly categorized into three parts: Social, Economic and Political programme. Dr. Rajendra Singh has taken up the issue of water conservation as a composite of Manifold Programmes. His conservation helped the villagers, particularly women, who had to go miles to fetch water.

**Q20. Describe the relation of social action with the other methods of social work.**

**Ans.** The importance of social group work can be understood with the fact that a man is considered a group animal. Group experiences are the essential needs of human beings. A human turns from a biological being to a social being through group life. Attention may now be paid to social group work, which is a method through which individuals develop the ability of establishing constructive relationships with each other through group activities. Social group work acts as a building block in the process of social action. Group members learn organisation, cooperation and coordination. They learn interdependence and democratic values. In the group work process, while participating in the activities of the group, the group members learn to live and work together to attain some specific goals. Social group work solves adjustment problems and enhances positive interpersonal relations. It prepares the individuals to learn and share responsibility in working together. All these factors contribute to the success of social action taken up for a social cause influencing a large segment of the population. During the social group work process, the group members learn to respect each other's views and take criticisms positively. They learn emotional control and tolerance, empathy and sympathy, breaking down of prejudices and enhance problem solving capacity. It teaches the individuals to keep their personal likes-dislikes, aspirations, perceptions, ego-hassles aside and work towards the goals planned by the group as a whole. Such a learning opportunity prepares the individuals for a social change and chances of failure of a movement due to internal conflicts are substantially minimized.

Social action shares many similarities with community organisation. Sometimes there is a debate whether social action is a part of community organisation or is completely a different entity. Some believe that it is a part of community organisation. The problem of confusing social action with community organisation arises mainly on account of lack of agreement as to what the term community stands for in social work. While community organisation is meant for a limited geographical area– the 'community', social action has larger context. It signifies the society, say, nation-state. Social action definitely has a larger scope and impact. Some of the techniques used by both the methods (social action and community organisation) may be common but they differ in their approach. Community organisation is a process of effective coordination of different agencies within a particular area and involves cooperative planning and implementation of social policy relating to the area. However, social action as a process is used for tackling issues, which are of a much wider nature than issues affecting a particular area.

**Q21. Describe the relation of social action with the social movement.**

**Ans.** Indian history has a rich heritage of inspiring social movements. It shares strong resemblance with social action, in terms of its goal as well as process. Marginalized communities have mobilized themselves to raise their voice against exploitation and violation of their rights, whenever the state has failed to safeguard their livelihood and rights. Blumer (1957) defines social movement as collective enterprises to establish a new order of life. This definition reflects that social action and social movement, both have similar goal that of bringing change in the existing system/structure to ensure equality and social justice.

Social reform movement made efforts to bring improvement in status of women and downtrodden communities, as they addressed sati abolition, widow remarriage, women's education, caste discrimination, untouchability, rigidity of practicing profession based on caste and many more. Gradually social reform movements, during that period, merged into freedom movement. After Independence too, many social activists have taken up various issues related to injustice and exploitation on specific sections of population and initiated movements. Chipko movement, in 1968, in Tehri Garhwal, the then Uttar Pradesh, was recorded as the first environmental movement in India. There were certain issues like rampant commercial exploitation of timber in that area and state policy seemed to be hostile and indifferent towards the needs of poor hilly habitants whose subsistence was dependent on forest products. Private contractors, individual businessmen, wood merchants and owners of forest based industries exploited forests for decades. This excess deforestation resulted in overflow of Alaknanda river in 1970, washing away of fields, crops, property and human settlements, massive devastation in hills. This led to protests against timber contractors where hill women saved large numbers of trees from felling by physically embracing them with a slogan, 'Chop me before you chop my tree', saving them from the axe of contractors.

Wilkinson (1971) has stated that a social movement is a deliberate collective endeavour to promote change in any direction and by any means, not excluding violence, illegality, revolution or withdrawal into 'utopian' community. This gives the differentiating point between social action and social movement. Social action, strictly denies usage of any illegal, violent means in their strategies. Despite the fact that social action comes in conflict with the existing configuration and functioning of social system/institution/structure, it rejects violence and blood-shed and resorts to peaceful means of expressing protest and dissent.

Personal ego clashes in a disguised way in ideological fights which may hamper social movement as we see in the case of Chipko movement between two leaders, Sunderlal Bahuguna and Chandi Prasad Bhat. Social worker has expertise to mobilize the public and maintain sustainability, which leaders (often non-social work professionals) in social movement do not have.

❑❑

# 4 SOCIAL WELFARE ADMINISTRATION

## INTRODUCTION

Social Welfare Administration translates Social welfare policies and Social legislation into social work practice. It administers the resources and personnel available for Social work practice. It ventilates the many choices open to clients to adjust themselves as well as to recover themselves from problem situations.

Social welfare administration deals with social welfare agencies and helps them to achieve their objectives for the target groups for which they are working. It is specifically concerned with identification of social objectives, the formulation and implementation of proposed programmes to achieve the objectives laid down.

**Q1. Write a note on the following:**

**(a) Social work**

**Ans.** Help the helpless to help themselves'. Social work is a method or process based on scientific knowledge and skill to assist the individuals, group and communities, with the view to enhance their social functioning to grow in accordance with their knowledge, capacities and capabilities. Therefore, social welfare has been used as an end and social work, as a means for the provision of social welfare. It is based on a systematic body of knowledge derived from research and practice, from different fields of social work. Social work acknowledges the complexity of interactions between human beings and their environment, and the capacity of people both to be affected by and to alter the multiple influences upon them including bio-psychosocial factors.

The social work profession is derived from theories of human development and behaviour and social systems and works for individual, organisational, social and cultural changes for the betterment of the society. Social work is committed to the pursuit of social justice, to the improvement of the quality of life and to the development of the full potential of each individual, group and community in the society. It seeks to address and resolve social issues at every level of society and economic status, but especially among the poor and sick. Social workers are concerned with social problems, their causes, their solutions and their human impacts. Social workers work with individuals, families, groups, organisations and communities. Social workers need to equip themselves with social welfare administration to work better in the field of social work.

**(b) Social development**

**Ans.** Is the process of focussed change to meet objectives and goals desired in the society. Development means progressive change in the living conditions and qualities of life of the members of the society. The process of social development is growth in the direction of modernity, nation-building and socio-economic progress. Development has to be a whole, value laden, cultural process, including the natural environment, social relations, education, production, consumption and well being of the whole nation.

When we talk social development we do not mean just the infrastructure development of the country we mean development of the people of the country, all human beings must have a satisfying material, cultural and spiritual life. Thus social development is the transformation of the society. It is very essential that social welfare administration be practiced to bring in the required social development in our country.

**(c) Social welfare**

**Ans.** It is a dynamic process that circles around social problems and ways in which society responds to these problems. Social problems affect individuals and the society at large. Social problems come from unfulfilled individual needs. Individuals have a variety of needs, some more basic like food, clothes and shelter, some more sophisticated like dignity and status, some are intangible like love and affection. These needs are usually met by the individuals themselves or their family or the society in which they live. But when these needs are unfulfilled they lead to social problems. Some of the social problems present in our society are poverty, inadequate housing, unemployment, loneliness and crime. The whole body of remedial and ameliorative services for the weaker sections of our society are covered by social welfare. These include curative and preventive services. Social welfare contributes to change and adjustment of social institutions to the creation of the required infrastructure of community services and can enable people to accept and provide social change for over all development.

Social welfare is also understood as those formally organized and socially sponsored institutions, agencies and programmes that operate to improve and maintain the economic conditions, health or inter-personal competence of some sections of the population or of all the population. Thus social welfare implies reordering of socio-economic relations in the present society, which is undergoing rapid transformation. Social welfare can be defined as "The organized system of social welfare institutions designed to aid disadvantaged individuals and groups to attain satisfying standards of life and health. It aims at personal and social relationship which permits individuals to develop their full capacities and the promotion of their well-being in harmony with the needs of the community".

**(d) Social welfare agency**

**Ans.** It is an organisation or an institution that provides treatment and preventive services in social welfare. These agencies practice social work, according to the objectives laid down by the agency. Social welfare agencies are of three kinds. First the governmental agencies which function according to the governmental setup, run and controlled by the government and funded by the taxes collected. Second are the voluntary agencies financed by the members of the community with local contributions and donations. Third are the nongovernmental and autonomous agencies promoted and funded by the government. The daily activities of these agencies are performed by voluntary workers and fulltime paid employees.

**Q2. Discuss social administration and social welfare and its related concepts.**

***Or***

**Describe in detail the functions of social welfare administrator in an organisation.**

***Or***

**Write the functions of social welfare administration.**

**Ans.** Social welfare administration is a process through which social policy is transformed into social services. It involves the administration of government and nongovernment agencies. The following definitions will elaborate the meaning of social welfare administration. According to Walter A. Friedlander (1958) "administration of social agencies translates the provisions of social legislation of social agencies and the aims of private philanthropy and religious charities into the dynamics of services and benefits for humanity.

According to Arthur Dunham (1962) administration is the process of supporting or facilitating activities which are necessary and incidental to services by a social agency. Administrative activities range from the determination of function and policies, and executive leadership to routine operations such as keeping records and accounts and carrying on maintenance of services. On the basis of above definitions, we find that social welfare administration is a process that includes definite knowledge, understanding, principles and ways of interaction. Its main focus is on the sustainability and accessibility of social services to the needy. Social work enables the process of administration through guidance, planning, stimulation, organisation, creating structure, coordinating research. To accomplish the well defined objectives of administration, policies are suitably amended; programmes are formulated, and budget, and finance provided, personnel and selection procedures are made available.

Rosemary Sarri (1971) has outlined the activities of social welfare administration as follows:

(1) Translation of social mandates into operational policies and goals to guide organisational behaviour;

(2) Design of organisational structures and processes through which the goals can be achieved;

(3) Securing of resources in the form of materials, staff, clients etc. for goal attainment and organisational survival;

(4) Selection and engineering of necessary technology;

(5) Optimizing organisational behaviour directed towards increased effectiveness and efficiency; and

(6) Evaluation of organisational performance to facilitate systematic and continuous solution to problems.

**Q3. Outline the features of social welfare administration in brief.**

**Ans.** Some distinctive features of social welfare administration are given below:

(1) Social welfare administration deals with social welfare agencies and helps them to achieve their objectives for the target groups for which they are working. It is specifically concerned with identification of social objectives, the formulation and implementation of proposed programmes to achieve the objectives laid down.

(2) From functional point of view, social welfare administration includes three perspectives of social problems: (a) restoration of impaired social functioning; (b) provision of resources, social and individual, for more effective social functioning; (c) prevention of social dysfunction.

(3) Despite variations in size, scope, structure and types of programmes, every agency has a governing board as an apex body for final decision-making. The board is generally represented by the community it intends to serve.

(4) Social welfare administration requires optimum utilization of its available resources together with active community participation, so that the ultimate goal of programmes can be achieved properly.

(5) Social welfare agencies have to allocate certain portion of their resources for survival so that the organisation can continue to exist. But this should not limit their capacity to achieve quantitative and qualitative growth.

(6) Social welfare agencies generally function in a cooperative manner and ensure participation of all the members in administration of their activities.

(7) There is a growing trend in these agencies to recruit professionally qualified manpower. It has helped in introducing professional approach in their functioning.

**Q4. Trace the history of social welfare administration in India.**

**Ans.** After Independence of our country in 1947 the old administrative pattern was more or less continued with necessary changes to suit the social, political and economic set-up that had evolved.

In the field of social welfare, during the First Five Year Plan, Government of India realized that the government alone cannot manage the enormous range of social problems across the length and breadth of our country and sought the help of voluntary organisations to help them in the process, so created a unique administrative machinery consisting of an autonomous board named CSWB (Central Social Welfare Board) in August 1953.

Similarly, social welfare advisory boards were established at state level. The main purpose of the Board (CSWB) has been to provide financial and technical assistance to voluntary organisations working in the field of social welfare. If we look at the history of administrative organisation, we find that before 1964 social welfare programmes were being managed by different ministries such as education, home, industries, health, labor. The Renuka Ray Committee in its report submitted in 1960, recommended the establishment of the Department of Social Security.

Under the Prime Minister ship of Lal Bahadur Shashtri, a social security department was established and located in the ministry of law on 14th June 1964.

Subjects, namely, social security, social welfare, backward classes and khadi and handicrafts were allocated to the Department of Social Security. In 1966, it was renamed as Social Welfare Department. It was located in the Ministry of Education and Social Welfare created in 1971. Its status was raised to a ministry in the year 1979. Its name was further changed to the Ministry of Social and Women Welfare in 1984. With the creation of a separate Department of Women and Child Development in the Ministry of Human Resource Development, it was recognized and its nomenclature was changed to the Ministry of Welfare in 1985 and subsequently it was renamed as the Ministry of Social Justice and Empowerment.

Thus, the central government has set up a full-fledged ministry and organisations subordinate to it, like National Commission for Scheduled Castes/Tribes, Minorities Commission, National Institute of Social Defence, National Institute for the Handicapped, Department of Women and Child Development, Central Social Welfare Board, National Institute of Public Cooperation and Child Development, etc., under its administrative control.

Besides the execution of social welfare projects, schemes, and programmes sponsored and financed wholly or partly by the central government; the state governments and union territory administrations formulate and implement welfare service programmes on their own in their respective jurisdictions. The state government/union territory administrations carry out their welfare obligations and programmes mainly through their Department of Social Welfare and voluntary organisations. In most of the states, either there is full time secretary for social welfare or it is one of the main portfolios of a secretary. Thus, social welfare schemes are still spread over more than one department/ directorate. The pattern of implementation of some of the schemes, like old age pension, widow pension, and supplementary nutrition programmes also vary from state to state. Though most of the states now have district social welfare officers, there is no social welfare functionary at block level.

**Q5. Briefly discuss the nature of social welfare administration.**

**Ans.** Social welfare lends itself to two usages. It stands for the process of administering the social welfare programmes. It is also an area of intellectual inquiry. The first is practice and second is study. As a practice, social welfare administration is decidedly an art.

**Social Welfare Administration as an Art:** Social welfare administration as an art, have been supported by the following arguments:

(1) **Social welfare administration can be acquired:** No doubt art is a natural gift. Music, dance, drama or painting is the examples of this category of art. But natural gifts can find their best expression by proper training, without which even the best artists will die unknown. On the other hand, a painter making a painting and a potter shaping a beautiful piece of pottery are also the examples of art. It is so because they possess the following elements:

(a) Personal skills
(b) Practical know-how
(c) Result orientation
(d) Creativity and
(e) Constant practice aimed at perfection.

Similarly, the art of social welfare administration can be acquired. Talented persons become the best administrators under proper training. Thus so far acquisition is concerned social welfare administration is also like other arts.

(2) **It is subjective in nature:** A chef makes a dish with personal passion for food. A carpenter adds beauty to his creation with his tools. A social welfare administrator with the application of knowledge and skills can make wonders by combining and bringing together available human and material resources to change the very face of the nation. Today success of every welfare programme depends on how a social welfare administrator performs the job.

(3) **Practical application of knowledge:** Art is the practical application of systematic knowledge. It is not merely theory but

putting that into practice. Similarly, social welfare administration is not merely theory but it is application also. And the best knowledge can be gained by practice alone.

Managing human resource needs a lot of skill, experience and balanced personality traits.

**Social Welfare Administration as a Science:** Science is the systematic study of knowledge. Those who believe that social welfare administration is a science point out that there are certain specific and clear principles on which day to day administration of social welfare programmes are being run and managed. They also argue that these principles are based on sound and rational principles, which are also considered universal.

The following arguments have been put forward to justify that social welfare administration is a science:

(1) **Application of scientific methods:** The claim of a discipline to be called a science depends on whether the scientific method of study is applicable to it. Social welfare administration can be called a science, because the scientific method of study equally is applicable to it, as in the case of other social sciences.

(2) **Critical examination:** Critical examination and study of evidence is the prime requisite of any scientific study. This is possible in social welfare administration also.

(3) **Universal guidelines:** universal principles of social welfare administration also provide the coloring of science. Even if we cannot use all the guidelines in a similar manner, these guidelines certainly help the administrator in proper implementation of social welfare programmes.

However, the nature of social welfare administration as a science has been criticized on the basis of experimentation, and objectivity. Thus, it may not be an exact science, but it is a science in its own way. It is also an art, because it is connected not only with formulation of general principles of social welfare programmes but also with actual running of the administration of social welfare programmes.

**Interdisciplinary Nature:** Social welfare administration requires the interdisciplinary knowledge and constant interaction with other social sciences to know the human beings in totality, such as philosophy, psychology, sociology, political science and economics to solve their problems in appropriate manner.

**Administrative Structure:** Social welfare administration is based on the organisational and administrative structure of social welfare programmes at each and every level of implementation stage. Similarly, it is also important to know the role and set up of non-governmental organisations for effectively carrying out their functions.

**Financial Administration:** The scope of social welfare and social security is increasing day by day and more and more people are coming under the coverage of these programmes, and so the need for additional financial support increases. In order to make out proper and effective budgeting of such programme, the knowledge of financial administration is highly essential. Thus it is important that persons must be trained in the techniques and principles of administration.

**Personal Management:** In order to provide effective social welfare services to the needy and suffering, it is essential to have committed, trained and motivated social welfare functionaries at different levels. Thus social welfare administrators need the knowledge of human resource management which includes knowledge from the very beginning, that is recruitment policies, job classification, training and development, staff evaluation, advancement and transfer so that the personnel understand the need and importance of the work they are doing, and they would be effective in implementing the social welfare programmes.

**Public Relations and Participation:** The social welfare administrator needs to be convinced of the importance of public relations with regard to both their own agency and its services, and the community as a whole. The welfare administrators must be comfortable to use mass media, such as TV, radio, newspaper, brochures, books and personal contacts, to interpret their agencies' programmes to the public and reaching community members. It is also required to get associated with the government and non- governmental agencies working in the field, the people or the beneficiaries, whose co-operation and support will add to the effective planning, formulation and implementation of policies and programmes intended for their welfare.

**To Conduct Research and Evaluation Studies:** Research and evaluation studies provide useful information and feedback on impact of on-going projects and about the different dimensions of existing social problems. Research also facilitates effective planning, policy formulation and implementation of programmes.

**Q6. Can social welfare administration be adopted as a profession?**

***Or***

**Explain social welfare administration as a profession.**

**[Dec-2019, Q.No.-4 (e)]**

**Ans.** Profession is an occupation for which specialized knowledge, skills and training are required and the use of these skills is not meant for self-satisfaction but are used for larger interests of the society and the success of these skills is measured not in terms of money alone.

Thus all professions are occupations in the sense that they provide means of livelihood. However, all occupations are not professions because some of them lack certain characteristics of a profession. The various characteristics of a profession can be mentioned as:

(1) Existence of an organized and systematized body of knowledge;
(2) Formal method of acquisition of knowledge;
(3) Existence of an association with professionalisation as its goals;
(4) Formulation of ethical goals; and
(5) Service motto.

**Existence of Knowledge:** Social welfare administration has developed a distinct body of knowledge, in response to the need for managing the complex social problems in a better way. In India, almost all courses of social work offer a course on social welfare administration to the students. Thus, it satisfies the requirement of a profession in the form of existence of knowledge. However, the social welfare administration is still evolving and new guidelines are being developed though this does not affect its status of being a profession.

**Acquisition of Knowledge:** An individual can enter a profession only after acquiring knowledge and required skills through formal training. For example, only formally trained persons can enter the professions of law, engineering or medicine. Thus social welfare administration may be called a profession because schools of social work and schools of public administration provide training in this discipline.

**Professional Association:** An occupation which claims to be a profession should have an association. Such a representative body of professionals regulate and develop the profession's activities. The professional associations may also prescribe the standards for individuals who want to enter the profession. But we are still struggling for an apex body, which would regulate the terms and conditions for Social Welfare Administration like Bar Council of India etc.

**Ethical Code:** Every profession has a code of ethics. Codes provide proper guidance when the situation at hand is choice between a good and a bad decision. Thus code of ethics serves several functions for a profession, including guiding, decision making, assessing competence, regulating behaviour and evaluating the profession. In social welfare administration, the code of ethics provides a guide for professional roles and relationships at various levels of responsibility in relation to clients, colleagues, employers, employing organisations and the society.

Therefore, the social welfare administration is a profession and its code of ethics is based on the fundamental values of the social work profession that includes the worth, dignity and uniqueness of all persons as well as their rights and opportunities.

**Service Motto:** In modern times, all human activities are concerned with money. But in a profession, an effort is made to see that service motto should prevail over monetary considerations. Professionals should keep social interest in their mind while charging fees for their professional services. For example, a doctor helps the patient, even when he charges fee. But he also serves humanity in the process. A lawyer helps the client. Not to charge fee is a help, but to provide justice to the client is most important. Similarly, a social welfare administrator administers the social welfare programmes, not only for money and personal satisfaction, but use his/her knowledge and skills to serve the larger interest of the society.

Thus, on the basis of the above discussion, it can be summarized that social welfare administration is yet to achieve the status of a profession. To become an independent profession, it requires attaining social sanction, professional commitment, governmental approval, a professional association to regulate the profession and involvement of trained personnel in the field of welfare administration, instead of being controlled only by bureaucrats.

**Q7. Discuss the principles of social welfare administration.**

***Or***

**Enlist the principles of social welfare administration.**

**[Dec-2019, Q.No.-3 (d)]**

**Ans.** Principles are guiding assertions or statements that come from experience or research and help us understand the concept. Principles of social welfare administrations are generalizations based on past experiences of different organisations that help in conducting social welfare administration in a particular manner. The principles of social welfare administration are enlisted below.

(1) The social welfare administrator has to run the social welfare agency. So it is necessary that he or she must have a proper understanding of the agency's aims, goals and objectives. They must know the content of the various programmes, and have the technical knowledge and skills required for conducting the programmes of the agency.

(2) The administrator must aim at delegating responsibility among various staff, volunteers and beneficiaries of the agency. The administrator should delegate responsibility in a way he or she is involving and encouraging participation among different segments of population involved with the work.

(3) The administrator must be efficient in formulating proper rules, regulations, practices and procedures for conducting work in the agency. These rules, regulation, practices and procedures must be uniform for all personnel in the agency and at all levels.

(4) The administrator must be extra careful to bring in efficient and dedicated personnel in the agency so that there is congenial environment in the agency. This in turn will help to conduct the programme well and fully accomplishing the targets. Each person associated in the agency must feel the importance of his work and how his work is going to help meet the agency's aims

and goals. In this way the agency persons entrusted with the responsibility will do a better and efficient job.

(5) The administration should organize regular monitoring and evaluation. All the processes, procedures, practices and achievements must be evaluated well so that they are all done in proper way and the targets are fully achieved. India is a welfare state and the government formulates various policies and programmes for the welfare of the weaker sections of the population. The social welfare agencies work at the field level with the general population, as it is difficult for the government to reach out to all in our vast country. The social welfare administrator is actually the person who executes the programmes favouring the common man. If the administrator is efficient, skillful and resourceful, then he will be effective in meeting the goals of the agency and bringing about social change and development.

**Q8. What is the scope of social welfare administration?**

**Ans.** There are broadly two views about the scope of social welfare administration. These are:

The POSDCoRB view this view of social welfare administration takes into account mostly the execution of the government's sponsored programmes. In other words this view corresponds with managerial view. Henri Fayol, L. Urwick, Fercey M. Ovean and Luther Gulick are advocates of this view. According to Henri Fayol the main categories of administration are:

(1) Organisation
(2) Command
(3) Coordination and
(4) Control

P.M. Queen says that the study of administration deals with the three 'm' that is 'men, material and methods'.

L. Gulick has given a magic formula in a word 'POSDCoRB' that is very popular. In POSDCoRB each letter describing one technique. These letters stand for:

**P** Planning
**O** Organising
**S** Staffing
**D** Directing
**Co** Coordinating
**R** Reporting
**B** Budgeting

In the recent years both academics and practitioners in India have added two more meaningful words to complete the techniques namely:

**E** Evaluation
**F** Feedback

Gulick's approach is 'technique-oriented' rather than 'subject-oriented'. Each of these techniques are very important for social welfare administration. The social welfare administrator has to be well equipped with each of these techniques. To be a good administrator it is important to understand these techniques well and to practice them with extreme skill and proficiency.

**Planning:** Planning means working out broad outline of the things that need to be done and the method to be adopted to accomplish the purpose set for the enterprise. Social planning helps us to be efficient, effective and accountable. Planning is important to meet our desired goals. It is important that before any social welfare programme is initiated or any research is started, proper planning with constructive information with knowledgeable professionals is essential. Answers to 'what', 'how' and 'why' must be well contemplated in respect of the schemes and programmes of social welfare.

Even before planning the welfare services the objectives of the service should be considered. So all welfare services are to be planned and organized according to the policy of the agency. The planning procedure is connected to the policy of the agency. A policy is a statement of objectives, purpose, practice of organizing the programmes and the fundamental viewpoint underlying a service. The statement of policy of the organisation must cater to the programmes, methods, principles and the beneficiaries. Policy should be evolved after consideration by all the stakeholders.

Planning for social welfare is strongly based on the nature and extend of social problems existing in the society. The resources of the community are always limited and the number of social problems that need to be tackled are numerous. Thus the social problems need to be prioritized. The social welfare planning needs to choose the best alternative, with maximum benefit at minimum cost. Social planning also needs to look into social development.

The process of planning needs to follow the following steps:

(1) To formulate appropriate objectives,
(2) To identify the problem,
(3) To collect and understand the existing facts,
(4) To analyse the available facts,
(5) To devise a suitable method,
(6) To organizc thc goals and ascertain the priorities,
(7) To locate the resources,
(8) To look for other options,
(9) To predict results of the several options thought of,
(10) To prepare the plan,
(11) To execute the plan,

(12) To evaluate the results and reformulate the methods for increased effectiveness.

**Organisation:** It is the establishment of the formal structure of authority through which the work is sub-divided, arranged, defined and coordinated for the defined objective. Dimock & Dimock (1964) defined: "Organisation is the systematic bringing together of interdependent parts to form a unified whole through which authority, coordination and control may be exercised to achieve a given purpose. Organisation is both structure and human relations."

Organisation can also be compared to the human body. Just like in the human body there are various systems, the respiratory system, the nervous system, the reproductive system all have separate functions and duties, and they work independently, but they are all interdependent too, and they all form a whole and keep the body fit and fine. So also the organisations have separate units and departments which work independently, and interdependently to be more effective in the functioning of the organisation as a whole to meet its various objectives.

Herbert (1960) proposes that organisation affect the persons who work for it in five different ways, these are:

(1) The organisation divides work among the staff. The personnel are delegated specific work in the organisation according to their capacities.

(2) The organisation creates standard practices and elaborate procedures to help the employees to work better.

(3) The organisation follows authority upward, downward and crossways, this helps in smooth flow of decision making.

(4) The organisation follows a system of communication to reach all.

(5) The organisation guides and teaches its members by providing knowledge, skills and loyalties. The training helps the members to work better and take decisions according to the needs of the organisation.

Organisation is therefore not just a structure, it actually accepts a structure for the human beings who directs, organize and who actually do the work in order to achieve the objectives of the agency.

**Staffing:** Staffing is the process of filling all positions in the organisation with adequate and qualified personnel. Thus it means whole personnel, bringing in and training the staff and maintenance of favourable condition of work. Staff planning or man power planning means personnel management in social welfare administration. Staff planning plans for the requirement of the organisation for work and its corresponding need for personnel. This requires specific personnel policy for social welfare. Some of the important components in Staff Planning that needs to be done by social welfare administration are:

(1) Organisational Planning and Development
(2) Career Development
(3) Terms of Employment
(4) Employee Welfare
(5) Personnel Records
(6) Morale and Motivation
(7) Management-Staff Relations
(8) Personnel Research and Review

**Directing:** It is the continuous task of making decisions and embodying them in specific and general orders and instructions and thus guiding the enterprise.

The components of directing are listed below:

(1) Identifying the right person for the right job,
(2) Encouraging the staff to develop interest in his work,
(3) Teach the work to the new staff members,
(4) Evaluate the performance by observing the staff member's understanding,
(5) Administrative changes to observe and put staff to the jobs that they can do best,
(6) Rewarding staff for completing work well with in time and helping others to work better,
(7) Establishing good spirit and teamwork so that staff work skillfully, intelligently, enthusiastically to finish delegated works.

**Coordinating:** It means integration of several parts into an orderly whole to achieve the purpose of the undertaking. In other words, coordinating means the all important duty of inter-relating the work of various divisions, sections and other parts of the undertaking. Co-ordination is most important to ensure the efficient and economical functioning of social welfare agencies. The social welfare agencies in India have shown a tremendous increase in numbers since independence. India is a large country, spread out over a large area, with diverse languages, religion and culture. Thus it has a large variety of problems too and these problems cannot be dealt with by the government alone, because these social problems need personal touch as social problems are complex in nature. It has also been observed that there is unequal distribution of the social welfare agencies. In some areas there are heavy concentration of these agencies, while in the interior parts of the country, in the difficult terrain and regions in the border areas there is paucity of social welfare agencies. Thus in some areas there is overlapping of services and in some areas services are not available. Social welfare agencies are spontaneous and voluntary in nature, and voluntary services are democratic. Any effort to co-ordinate will mean application of external pressure, which will not encourage the voluntary spirit. Co-ordination must be by mutual consent. Co-ordination between agencies and state is easy, but co-ordination among different agencies is very difficult. There has been no effort by the government to co-ordinate all the social welfare agencies.

**Reporting:** It is keeping those people informed to whom the executive is responsible about what is going on. In other words reporting means keeping both the supervisors and subordinates informed of what is going on and arranging for collection of such information through inspection, research and records. The social welfare administration is responsible to maintain all kinds of records. All files are maintained by the administration. Records of all functions, programmes, meetings and the day-to-day functioning are kept by the administration. These records and reports help in evaluation and monitoring the work of the agency. Thus these reports are very important for the agencies that provide the funds to them. Reports are important for the community to understand the objectives and functioning of the agency. Thus it is the responsibility of the administration to carefully maintain all reports and records.

**Budgeting:** It is all that goes with budgeting in the form of fiscal planning, accounting and control. Budgeting involves the financial administration of a social welfare agency. Financial administration is the system that revolves around the finances of the agency. This concerns with the raising, regulation and distribution of the resources for the growth of the agency. The agency collects funds from the community by means of donations, subscription or taxes and these funds are used for the organisational programmes and the running of the agency. A budget is a complete statement prepared showing the various sources of the money raised for a particular period and the activities and programmes conducted with that money. Financial administration is one of the most important responsibilities of the social welfare administration and if this responsibility is not properly taken up, it can have serious consequences on the administration of the agency.

POSDCoRB activities are common to all large scale organisations. They are the common problems of management found in the different agencies, regardless of the peculiar nature of the work they do. Like public administration, social welfare administration is also an instrument with two blades of a scissor. One blade is knowledge of the subject matter and the other is the techniques that are applied. Both blades must be good to make it an effective tool. Thus, the proper scope of social welfare administration should include both the views i.e. POSDCoRB and subject matter.

**Q9. Discuss the types of social welfare organisation.**

**Ans.** Social welfare organisations play a vital role in rendering Social Services in every country, especially in developing and underdeveloped countries. There are various kinds of social welfare organisations that differ in ownership, kind of service providers, source of funding and other characteristic differences. These various types of Social Service Organisation and their working.

**Formal Organisations** refer to a structure of well-defined jobs, each bearing a definite measure of authority, responsibility and accountability. Formal Organisation lays down the pattern of relationship between individuals and the rules and regulations, which guide the behaviour of individuals. Formal organisations follow the functions of POSDCoRBEF in its working.

**Informal Organisation:** Informal Organisation is an outcome of social interaction between individuals in a formal organisation. Whenever people work together, they evolve informal groups bound together by common, social, technological interest. Such groups constitute informal organisation. Informal organisation represents relationships between individuals in the organisation based on interest, personal attitudes, emotions, prejudices, likes, dislikes, physical location and similarity of work. These relations are not developed according to the procedures, rules and regulations laid down in the formal organisational structure.

Informal Organisation comes into existence because of limitations of the Formal Organisation. It represents, "natural grouping of people at work". The birth of small groups in an organisation is a natural phenomenon. These groups may also overlap because an individual may be a member of more than one informal group. In many cases, informal groups come into being to support and supplement the formal organisation. The informal Organisations have the following characteristics:

(1) Customary and not enacted.

(2) No written rules and regulations.

(3) Does not follow an organisational charts in its working.

It must be noted that the informal organisation is based on formal structure and cannot exist without it. The informal organisation allows an organisation a measure of flexibility, which is a functional necessity. However, the greatest weakness of the informal organisation is its instability; its changeability and its unpredictability.

**Structured organisation:** "An organisation is a group of people who are cooperating under the direction of a leader for the accomplishment of a common end". The need for an organisation arises when two or more persons unite together to achieve some common objectives.

Organisation is one of the basic functions of social welfare administration. Its importance lies in the systematically evolved pattern of relationships designed to set in motion the process of managerial functions. Structured organisations are those, which are formed, and functioning with a clear structure or framework of relationship. As structure, organisation is a network of internal authority, responsibility and relationships. It is the framework of relationships of persons, operating at various levels, to accomplish common objectives.

**Unstructured Organisations:** Unstructured organisations do not have a clear structure or framework. Various committees, community organisations, social action groups are some of the examples of unstructured organisations. They may be formed as per the requirement or given purpose, in order to achieve certain limited goals and objectives. Groups of people come together with the similar objective or ideology to accomplish a specific goal. They work in an unstructured manner, as all of them are equal in the role and duties. These organisations are formed for a short duration and they disintegrate when goals are met or cease to exit due to adverse factors.

**Q10. Explain governmental organisations.**

**Ans.** The structure of welfare organisations differs in agencies, which are established under public sector from those, which are in voluntary or private sector. Public or Government agencies are based upon a law, administered within the framework of local, state and central governments and financed by the government. Individuals, or philanthropic, or religious, or humanitarian groups establish private agencies or non-governmental organisations; their management is vested with a board of directors. These organisations are supported mainly by contributions, donations, endowments or trust funds.

Our country has a long tradition of social service. Our sovereign and democratic republic stands committed to ensure social, economic and political justice to the people and usher in a welfare state. After independence, the concept of social justice became part and parcel of our Constitution and is reflected not only in the preamble, but also in the Directive principles of state policy.

At the State level, the state governments and union territory administrations formulate and implement various kinds of welfare services programmes on their own in their respective jurisdiction for the benefit of the socially and economically weaker sections of the society.

The state government or the union territories administrations carry out their welfare commitments and programmes mainly through the departments of social welfare and voluntary organisations. At the state level, the Department of Social Welfare is the responsibility of the welfare minister and the secretary to government is the administrative head of the department. The secretariat helps, guides and advises the Minister in the formulation of policies of the department, in getting the legislation passed by the state legislature, and supervises the execution of the policies, schemes, projects and programmers undertaken by the Directorate. The functions of the State Social Welfare Boards are as follows:

(1) To promote the growth of voluntary social welfare agencies, with special reference to development of welfare services in all areas.

(2) To administer the grant-in-aid programme.
   (a) On behalf of the Central Social Welfare Board for development and capital grants and
   (b) On behalf of the state welfare governments for maintenance grants.

(3) To assist the Central Social Welfare Board in the provision of a field counseling services for aided agencies.

(4) To administer the programmes of rural welfare projects.

(5) To stimulate effective coordination among voluntary welfare agencies at the States and local levels.

(6) To assist the Central Social Welfare Board and State Government in the further development of welfare services.

At the Central level, also called the Union level although the responsibility of formulating overall policy and planning of social welfare programmes rests with the department of social welfare, the initiation and execution of certain welfare services and stimulating the effective coordination among voluntary welfare agencies especially at the national level will rest with the Central Social Welfare Board.

**Central Social Welfare Board (CSWB):** The important landmark in the history of voluntary social welfare was created in 1953, with the provision of ₹4 Crore for the social welfare sector in the First Five Year Plan. The dilemma before the country's planners was whether this amount should be utilized through government machinery or by voluntary agencies, as at that time there was no independent department of social welfare at the center, nor at the state levels. Under the leadership of Pt. Jawahar lal Nehru our then prime minister, it was decided that social welfare needed a special kind of machinery that had components of flexibility, dedication and closeness to the country's people. It was then felt that it should be handled not by the government machinery but by the voluntary workers who had dedicated their service to the needy.

**Q11. Explain non-governmental organisations.**

***Or***

**Discuss the working of government organisation in social welfare at the central level. [Dec-2018, Q.No.-4(f)]**

**Ans.** Non-government organisations are called by different names by way of the inception. Let us discuss some of them:

**Charitable organisations** are those organisations established for helping the poor or needy people. These organisations are mainly formed to serve the needy through a charitable approach. The Missionaries of Charity is one example of such charitable organisations. Most of its workers are fully dedicated to service and they serve without expecting anything back. These institutions provide institutional care to the poor and neglected. They also provide food, clothing and medical treatment for needy people. The charitable organisations are registered under the Charitable Endowment Act–1890. Section 2 of the Charitable Endowment Act defines 'charitable purpose' as including general relief to the poor, education, medical relief and the advancement of any other object of general public utility.

**Societies and Trusts:** The Voluntary Organisation can be registered under the Societies Registration Act – 1860, Indian Trusts Act – 1882 or under Section 25 of the Indian Companies Act – 1956. Most of the non-governmental organisations are registered under Societies Registration Act. 1860. Societies are formed with some deliberate intention following some system in their day-to-day affairs as well as rules for their governing and proceedings. The following activities should be handled properly, since it is vital for better functioning of any organisation.

**Trust:** Welfare programmes are also run by charitable trusts. The Indian Trusts Act –1882 provides room for registering and running Public, Private, Religious and Charitable Trusts. A Trust is an obligation annexed to the ownership of property and arising out of a confidence reposed in and accepted by the trustee(s), for the benefit of another and the owner. The following are the objects of a charitable trust:

- Trusts for the relief of poverty
- Trusts for the advancement of education
- Trust for the advancement of religion and
- Trusts for other purposes beneficial to the community. (Not falling under any other three heads, e.g., renovation of roads, supply of water, repairing of bridges, etc.).

The government of our country has encouraged the emergence of non-government organisations. In the Seventh Five Year Plan the government emphasized the importance of the role of the non-government organisations to take part in the development process of the country. The government wanted the nongovernment organisations to take up an important role in social development, these duties and responsibilities are put down below:

(1) To supplement the efforts of the government to provide choices and alternative to the rural population.

(2) To be the eyes and ears of the village population, so that the laws, legislations, new knowledge and information can be brought to the village people.

(3) The voluntary organisations must take up pilot projects with innovative ideas which if successful can be implemented on larger scale.

(4) To stimulate the delivery systems to provide services to the population at the grassroot levels.

(5) To disseminate information.

(6) To help the communities to become self-reliant and independent.

(7) To initiate manpower resources in communities for community organisation.

(8) To bring in science, technology and innovations to homes in the community. For example teaching the village population of newer and better methods of cultivation.

(9) To train grassroot workers to deal with community problems and to encourage volunteerism.

(10) To mobilize resources of the community.

(11) To encourage community participation, to make the community responsible and accountable of what is happening in the community.

**Q12. Briefly discuss the characteristics and functions of Non-Government Organisation.**

***Or***

**Discuss the characteristics of Non-Government Organisation. [June-2019, Q.No.-4(f)]**

**Ans.** These are the main characteristics of Non-Government Organisation/Voluntary Organisations:

(1) It is registered under the Societies registration Act, 1860, the Indian Trusts Act, 1882, The Cooperative Societies Act 1904 or Sec. 25 of the Companies Act, 1956, depending upon the nature and scope of its activities to give it a legal status.

(2) It has definite aims and objectives and programmes.

(3) It has an administrative structure and duly constituted management and executive committees.

(4) It is an organisation initiated and governed by its own members on democratic principles without any external control.

(5) It raises funds for its activities partly from the exchequer in the form of grants-in-aid and partly in the form of contributions or subscriptions from members of the local community and/or the beneficiaries of the programme.

**Functions of Non-Government Organisation:** The main functions of the non-government organisations are as follows:

**(1)** Human beings by nature are gregarious**:** The urge to act in groups is fundamental to them. People therefore form groups and associations voluntarily for their benefit as also of others with a view to lead a fuller and richer life. This phenomenon is reflected in voluntary associations, which are formed for promotion of recreational and cultural activities, social services and professional interests.

**(2)** A pluralistic society with a democratic system requires a multitude of independent, nongovernment organisations to serve as a buffer between the individual and the state and thus preventing the government from developing monopoly in various fields.

**(3)** Organized voluntary action helps groups and individuals with diverse political and other interests, contributes to strengthening the feeling of national solidarity and promotes participative democracy.

**(4)** The state does not have the requisite financial resources and manpower to meet all the needs of its citizens. The non-government organisations by raising additional resources locally can meet uncovered needs and enrich local life.

**(5)** Community participation can be promoted by nongovernment organisation as they are closer to the people. People respond better to them as compared to government agencies.

**(6)** Creating a sense of responsibility through direct involvement. Non-government agencies due to their personnel touch are in a better position to design and implement programmes in the community.

**(7)** Correcting planner's mistakes. Non-government organisation with people's participation can point out mistakes in planning, policy making, social welfare administration etc.

**(8)** Creating public opinion. The non-government organisation can work for better understanding and positive attitude among the target groups on particular issues. Like organisations working against stigma and discrimination towards HIV/AIDS people.

**(9)** Formulating new policy through public opinion. The non-government organisations can make the policy makers aware of ground realities and the exact need and problems faced by the general public. Nongovernment organisation can also work towards promoting new social legislations for betterment of the society.

**(10)** Flexibility and experimentation. The nongovernment organisation are autonomous and thus have greater freedom to be flexible in their functioning and can experiment new methods and programmes.

**(11)** To compliment and supplement government initiative. India is an enormous country with diverse issues and problems, non-government organisation can help in government programme implementation and in formulating new programmes for the community people.

**Q13. Discuss bilateral and international organisations.**

**Ans.** The word bilateral means, "Agreement made between two countries". In these, two countries make agreement to have duty free entry of donated supplies for relief and rehabilitation of the poor and the needy without discrimination of caste, creed or race. Under these agreements, commodities like food grains, milk power, cheese, processed food stuff, drugs, medicines, multivitamin tablets, hospital equipment and supplies like ambulances, mobile dispensaries, agricultural implements, etc., are received by approved organisations, located in respective countries. Government of India encourages such assistance. The Ministry of social justice and empowerment operates the bilateral agreements on gift deliveries entered into by the Government of India with the Governments of Federal Republic of Germany, Sweden, Switzerland, United Kingdom, and United States of America.

**International organisation:** An international organisation is an organisation with an international membership, scope, or presence. There are two main types:

**International nongovernmental organisations (INGOs):** Non-governmental organisations (NGOs) that operate internationally. These include international non-profit organisations and worldwide companies such as the World Organisation of the Scout Movement, International Committee of the Red Cross and Medecins Sans Frontireres.

**Intergovernmental organisations, also known as international governmental organisations (IGOs):** The type of organisation most closely associated with the term 'international organisation', these are organisations that are made up primarily of sovereign states (referred to as member states). Notable examples include the United Nations (UN), Organisation for Security and Co-operation in Europe (OSCE), Council of Europe (COE), International Organisation (ILO) and International Police Organisation (INTERPOL). The UN has used the term "intergovernmental organisation" instead of "international organisation" for clarity.

The first and oldest intergovernmental organisation is the Central Commission for Navigation on the Rhine, created in 1815 by the Congress of Vienna. The role of international organisations is helping to set the international agenda, mediating political bargaining, providing a place for political initiatives and acting as catalysts for coalition- formation. International organisations also define the salient issues and decide which issues can be grouped together, thus help governmental priority determination or other governmental arrangements. Not all international organisations seek economic, political and social cooperation and integration.

**Q14. What do you mean by donor agencies? List some donor agencies.**

***Or***

**Write a short note on donor agencies.**

**[June-2019, Q.No.-5 (b)]**

**Ans.** Organisation is mobilizing financial support for its activities. A number of national and international organisations are providing funds to the social service organisations. Such agencies are known as donor organisations. They give support to the social service activities on the basis of the project proposals, submitted by the organisation. Generally donor agencies are providing funds and other services to the registered organisations for their various social activities for the needy and marginalized. The amount of their support varies from project to project according to the requirements or the gravity of the problems. The donor agencies mainly raise funds from its citizens and the government. Some of the donor agencies are:

- Global Fund
- Bill Gates Foundation
- William J. Clinton Foundation
- Ford Foundation
- CMMB (Catholic Medical Mission Board)
- USAID (United States Agency for International Development)
- AHF (AIDS Healthcare Foundation)
- Caritas India
- Church Auxiliary for Social Action (CASA)
- Danish International Development Agency (DANIDA)
- Christian Children's Fund
- World Vision
- Co-operative for American Relief Everywhere (CARE)
- Catholic Relief Services (CRS)
- Indo-Global Social Service Society (IGSSS)
- Cordaid, Germany.

**Q15. Briefly list some international agencies in India.**

***Or***

**Enumerate some of the international organisations and the UN bodies working in the fields of social welfare.**

***Or***

**Write the short note on International Organisation.**

**[Dec-2019, Q.No.-5(g)]**

**Ans.** Among the International agencies which first organized their activities in India may be included the Red Cross, the YMCA and the

YWCA. These organisations are now working in India through their national organisations, which are autonomous in all respects. After World War I, the League of Nations initiated certain International organisations, which in due course began to work in India. Among these, the most important was the International labour Organisation. Then, came, after theend of the World War II, the United Nations Economic and Social Council, the UNICEF, the WHO, and the FAO among other agencies, which have recently established their regional offices in India, is the International Union of Child Welfare.

In addition to the agencies mentioned above, the names of some more International Organisations may be added:

- Action for Food Production.
- Cooperative for American Relief Everywhere.
- Catholic Relief Services.
- Indo-German Social Services Society.
- Internation Association of Lion's Club.
- Rotary International.
- Salvation Army.

The United Nations has set up various organisations for groups needing special help. Their contributions to international welfare may be discussed as follows:

**United Nations Children's Emergency Fund (UNICEF):** The United Nations International Children's Emergency Fund (UNICEF) was established by the General Assembly on 11 December 1946. Its purpose is to help developing countries to improve the condition of their children and youth. UNICEF provides assistance in such fields as health, nutrition, social welfare, education and vocational training. It also helps governments to assess the important needs of their children and plan comprehensive programme to meet them. A large part of UNICEF aid is in the form of providing equipment, drugs, well-drilling rigs, school garden supplies, prototype equipment for day care centers and equipment for the production of the textbooks. UNICEF was awarded the Nobel Peace Prize in 1965 and the Indira Peace Prize in 1989.

**United Nations High Commission for Refugees:** The office of the United Nations High Commission for Refugees (UNHCR) was established on 1st January 1951. It provides legal protection, and at the request of a government, material assistance for the refugees.

UNHCR was awarded the Nobel Prize in 1954. There are a number of other U.N. bodies working for the social welfare. Some of these organisations are:

- United Nations Center for Regional Development
- United Nations Development Programme
- United Nations Educational, Scientific and Cultural Organisation
- United Nations Environment Programme

- United Nations Institute for Training and Research
- United Nations Research Institute for Social Development.

**Q16. What are the ingredients of management?**

**Ans.** An organisation is considered to be a web of inter-relationships, which are more often than not, coloured with authority, power and other formal and informal patterns of communication. In common parlance, authority and power are taken as synonymous. In fact, authority is defined as the decision-making right –when a right to take a decision with regard to a particular matter is vested in a particular position, that position is said to possess the said authority. On the other hand, power is one's ability to influence other's behaviour.

Thus, authority is legal or legitimate while power is non-institutional. As each position in the organisational structure is entrusted with a certain responsibility, authority given should be adequate to handle that responsibility. No employee can work effectively if he/she lacks the requisite authority. Authority may be traditional (derived from tradition or norms), charismatic (derived from personal charisma or divine or exceptional powers) and legal authority (derived from principles, rules, regulations laid down by an organisation).

It may be possible that a person with authority may not be having matching personality to command respect and acceptance from his/her subordinates and a person with power may not possess legitimate authority.

Bureaucracy is frequently used and abused word, which in common parlance connotes mindless application of the letters of the rules without any compassion, judgement or empathy. In olden times, organisations were smaller and there was face to face contact with the owner and the workers/employees. With establishment of large sized organisations and employment of huge number of people dispersed over wide geographical locations, bureaucratic administrative framework was considered an ideal type.

A critical look at present day organisations, especially those engaged in social welfare activities, bring out that over-conformity to rules stifles initiative, innovation and flexibility, and leads to delayed decision-making and red-tapism. At times, long hierarchy and cumbersome procedures defeat the very purpose for which the organisation is set up. Specifically, in the case of social welfare administration, these negative outcomes of bureaucracy affect the service delivery system to a great extent.

Motivation is crucial factor to determine the health of the mind of the employees as well as organisational health. It is the process that accounts for an individual's intensity, direction and persistence of efforts towards attaining a goal. Only the ability or dexterity of employee is not sufficient, rather the will to work plays vital role in his/her performance. So, the job of managers or administrators does not end by recruiting suitable professionals for the job at hand, but retaining and maintaining their motivation and morale is also their duty.

Motivation is a highly dynamic and complex variable in organisational behaviour. The advocates of scientific management and classical theories thought that if basic needs of employees (food, shelter, security, etc.) are taken care of and productivity is linked to rewards, their motivation levels remain high. However, contemporary concepts of motivation take into account significance of informal groups, participative leadership, open communication, etc.

Leadership is the ability to influence a group towards the achievement of goals. In the social service sector, it is very crucial. It rests upon leaders and managers to get the organisation realize its objectives. However, the primary task of the leadership also varies according to the stage of the organisational development. It varies from the early leadership which is primarily focussed on demonstrating the usefulness of the new organisation to the donors and the community – to the leadership which is more mature and which mainly involves expanding the scale of operations, mobilization of funds, organisational procedures and networking, etc.

Transactional leaders are those who guide or motivate their followers in the direction of established goals by clarifying role and task requirements. In contrast transformational leaders are those who inspire followers to transcend their own self-interests, and who are capable of having a profound and extraordinary effect on followers. It is maintained that transformational leadership style has an edge over transactional leadership.

**Q17. Describe organisational climate and management process.**

***or***

**List important management practices.**

***or***

**Explain the important factors involved in organisational climate.**

**Ans.** The field of organisational behaviour is concerned with the study of employees' behaviour in an organisation and its effects on the performance of the organisation. Some of the knotty issues you may have to deal with in creating an encouraging work culture.

**High Job Turnover:** Social welfare administration system, in India, is dominated by voluntary sector that is, along with many positive aspects is also characterized by adhocism, regional imbalance, social Darwinism, where programmes are, more or less, fund driven rather need driven. Social work professionals for jobs do not enjoy preference in welfare administration and have to compete with candidates from psychology/sociology and other social science background. There is often job dissatisfaction because of low salaries, insecurity because of ad-hoc/temporary project based jobs and not much independence for implementation of creative and innovative ideas and so on.

**Social Darwinism:** In common parlance, cut throat competition between organisations and also among colleagues is termed as Social Darwinism that leaves lesser scope of team work, coordination and cooperation. The system of funding at the macro level also promotes competition and conflict situations arise in the voluntary sector. Within the organisation, ego-clashes, divergent personality factors, informal group cohesiveness, politics and rumours, different styles of performing tasks all tend to hamper inter-dependence and team work and also service delivery.

**Personal-professional Self:** This issue is quite pertinent to welfare administration and social work professionals.

During formal and informal interactions at workplace, employees tend to develop likes and dislikes regarding their colleagues. Added to this, increasing conflicts, tensions and stressful situations in modern times, in personal life of social workers may hamper their 'professional self' that demand them to be compassionate, empathetic and devoid of their own tensions, pains and frustrations, which is not true at all the times.

**Positive Relationship:** We may infer that creating a positive climate for nurturing positive professional relationship characterized by feeling of mutual respect, trust and interdependence is vital for social welfare administration in order to realize its objectives. It contributes to the success of total enterprise. Persons who are well related to one another seek for even higher standard of performance. Trustworthiness, responsibility, articulating sound philosophy for personal growth, good channels of communication, etc., ensure positive climate. A positive climate is created when agency procedures and policies are clear. Positive climate is also created when sharing of work together happens. Social workers occupying the position of managers/administrators have a role and a responsibility for the creation of such a positive work culture.

**Healing touch:** In the field of welfare administration, employee's behaviour is all the more crucial as, more often than not, it requires 'healing touch' so as to have soothing effects on clients' problems, crises, pains and frustrations. Lack of human touch and compassion on the part of service providers is likely to defeat the very purpose of the programmes and services meant for welfare and well being of the disadvantaged sections of the society. On the other hand, when staff members and volunteers work in harmony there seems to be greater likelihood that the agency would attain its goals and that the clients and care providers would have a good experience together. Working together in harmony, with devotion and conviction would lead to meaningful endeavours.

Bureaucratic characteristics may be necessary for large sized organisations but it is important that inflexibility, too much emphasis on rules and procedures, red tapism, and the like may be avoided so as to maintain human touch and caring attitude in service delivery.

**Q18. What do you mean by communication and social marketing?**

**Ans.** Communication is the act of conveying meanings from one entity or group to another through the use of mutually understood signs and semiotic rules. Nonverbal communication describes the processes of conveying a type of information in the form of non-linguistic representations. Examples of nonverbal communication include haptic communication, chronemic communication, gestures, body language, facial expressions, eye contact, and how one dresses. Nonverbal communication also relates to the intent of a message. Examples of intent are voluntary, intentional movements like shaking a hand or winking, as well as involuntary, such as sweating. Speech also contains nonverbal elements known as paralanguage, e.g. rhythm, intonation, tempo, and stress. It affects communication most at the subconscious level and establishes trust. Likewise, written texts include nonverbal elements such as handwriting style, the spatial arrangement of words and the use of emoticons to convey emotion.

Nonverbal communication demonstrates one of Paul Wazlawick's laws: you cannot not communicate. Once proximity has formed awareness, living creatures begin interpreting any signals received. Some of the functions of nonverbal communication in humans are to complement and illustrate, to reinforce and emphasize, to replace and substitute, to control and regulate, and to contradict the denovative message. Verbal communication is the spoken or written conveyance of a message. Human language can be defined as a system of symbols (sometimes known as lexemes) and the grammars (rules) by which the symbols are manipulated. The word "language" also refers to common properties of languages. Language learning normally occurs most intensively during human childhood. Most of the thousands of human languages use patterns of sound or gesture for symbols which enable communication with others around them. Languages tend to share certain properties, although there are exceptions. There is no defined line between a language and a dialect. Constructed languages such as Esperanto, programming languages, and various mathematical formalism is not necessarily restricted to the properties shared by human languages.

**Social marketing** is the use of marketing theory, skills and practices to achieve social change. It has the primary goal of achieving "social good." Traditional commercial marketing aims are primarily financial, though they can have positive social affects as well. In the context of public health, social marketing would promote general health, raise awareness and induce changes in behaviour. To see social marketing as only the use of standard commercial marketing practices to achieve non-commercial goals is an oversimplified view.

Social marketing seeks to develop and integrate marketing concepts with other approaches to social change. Social marketing aims to influence behaviours that benefit individuals and communities for the greater social good. The goal is to deliver competition-sensitive and segmented social change programs that are effective, efficient, equitable and sustainable.

Increasingly, social marketing is described as having "two parents." The "social parent" uses social science and social policy approaches. The "marketing parent" uses commercial and public sector marketing approaches. Recent years have also witnessed a broader focus. Social marketing now goes beyond influencing individual behaviour. It promotes socio-cultural and structural change relevant to social issues. Consequently, social marketing scholars are beginning to advocate for a broader definition of social marketing: "social marketing is the application of marketing principles to enable individual and collective ideas and actions in the pursuit of effective, efficient, equitable, fair and sustained social transformation". The new emphasis gives equal weight to the effects (efficiency and effectiveness) and the process (equity, fairness and sustainability) of social marketing programs.

The first documented evidence of the deliberate use of marketing to address a social issue comes from a 1963 reproductive health programme led by K.T. Chandy at the Indian Institute of Management in Calcutta, India. Chandy and colleagues proposed, and subsequently implemented, a national family planning programme with high quality, government brand condoms distributed and sold throughout the country at low cost. The programme included an integrated consumer marketing campaign run with active point of sale promotion. Retailers were trained to sell the product aggressively, and a new organisation was created to implement the program. In developing countries, the use of social marketing expanded to HIV prevention, control of childhood diarrhea (through the use of oral re-hydration therapies), malaria control and treatment, point-of-use water treatment, on-site sanitation methods and the provision of basic health services.

**Q19. Enlist the principles involved in social marketing.**

**Ans.** The principles of social marketing can be arranged in five Ps, which are as follows:

**Product** unlike commercial marketing where product is a tangible item, here, in SM, product is the behaviour or idea that the campaign planners would like the targeted individuals/ consumers to adopt.

The product can be an action (e.g., immunizing children) or material item (e.g., condoms).

**Price** includes the costs associated with 'buying' the product, which is sum total of economic cost as well as psychological cost (embarrassment, say, in buying condoms for safe sex) and social cost (e.g., possibility of losing face).

**Place** comprises of the distribution channels used to make the product available to target audiences. When the product is a physical item, it must be easily obtainable by consumers (e.g. condoms available at paan-shops). In the case of product being an idea, say, education of girl child, it must be socially available and supported within the consumers' social sphere.

**Promotion** includes the efforts taken to ensure that the target audience is aware of the campaign. These publicity efforts should be designed to cultivate positive attitudes and intentions regarding the product that pave the way for behaviour change.

**Positioning** means that the product must be positioned in such a way as to maximize benefits and minimize costs. Positioning is a psychological construct that involves the location of the product relative to other products and activities with which it competes. For instance, using condom would bring peace of mind plus freedom from STIs/HIV and pregnancy while not using it would lead to many health consequences with social and psychological underpinnings.

**Q20. What are public relations? Discuss its objectives in social welfare.**

***Or***

**What is the importance of public relations in social welfare?**

***Or***

**Describe the activities that can be taken up under public relation.**

**Ans.** Public Relation (PR) is one of the important functions of social welfare administration which ensures the development of cordial and harmonious relations with the stakeholders. It is the practice of managing flow of information between the organisation and the public.

PR is an essential and integrated component of public policy or service. The public relations activities are meant to ensure the benefits to the citizens, for whom the policies and services are meant for. The Institute of Public Relations, USA, has defined Public Relations as "the deliberate, planned and sustained effort to establish and maintain mutual understanding between an organisation and its publics". Likewise, Edward L. Bernays has given definition of Public Relations as "the Management of Social attempt by information, persuasion and adjustment to engineer public support for an activity, cause, movement or institution". Public relations and publicity are not synonymous but many PR campaigns include provisions for publicity also. Publicity is the spreading of information to gain public awareness for a product, person, service, cause or organisation, and can be seen as a result of effective PR planning.

PR is a planned effort or management function. It is an execution of communication programme for rapport building, creating goodwill, understanding and acceptance as the chief end results sought by public relations activities. It is very important to understand the two components of PR - 'Public' and 'Relations'. It is essential that socio-demographic and cultural characteristics, values, attitudes, perceptions of the 'public' (that includes employees in the organisation as well as the community that the organisation is serving) be studied objectively. 'Relations' means conscious decision of the kind of relation or image the administrators want to create in the eyes of the public the process of public relations.

The process of public relations is categorized into seven phases for better understanding: The first phase includes identifying and listing out the information or message to be disseminated. The second phase of PR process is to ascertain the existing image or awareness level about the issue in the target group or common public. The third phase is developing communication objectives and priorities. The fourth phase of PR deals with developing the message and choosing appropriate media to transmission. The fifth phase of PR is the implementation of 'communication campaign' designed in the fourth phase and coordination or the dissemination of message. In the sixth phase, communication campaign is checked whether message has reached properly and the expected action or behaviour or knowledge on image factors emerged. The seventh phase of PR includes rectification of the communication campaign, in case the message does not reach properly after identification of reasons for the ineffectiveness. It is followed by dissemination of the revised message.

**Q21. Explain the following:**

**(i) Fund raising** **[June-2019, Q.No.-5(g)]**

**Ans.** Fundraising or fund raising (also known as "development") is the process of gathering voluntary contributions of money or other resources, by requesting donations from individuals, businesses, charitable foundations, or governmental agencies (see also crowd funding). Although fundraising typically refers to efforts to gather money for non-profit organisations, it is sometimes used to refer to the identification and solicitation of investors or other sources of capital for for-profit enterprises.

Traditionally, fundraising consisted mostly of asking for donations on the street or at people's doors, and this is experiencing very strong growth in the form of face-to-face fundraising, but new forms of fundraising, such as online fundraising, have emerged in recent years, though these are often based on older methods such as grassroots fundraising. Fundraising is a significant way that non-profit organisations may obtain the money for their operations. These operations can involve a very broad array of concerns such as religious or philanthropic groups such as research organisations, public broadcasters, political campaigns and environmental issues.

Some examples of charitable organisations include student scholarship merit awards for athletic or academic achievement, humanitarian and ecological concerns, disaster relief, human rights, research, and other social issues.

Some of the most substantial fundraising efforts in the United States are conducted by colleges and universities. Commonly the fundraising, or "development"/"advancement," program, makes a distinction between annual fund appeals and major campaigns. Most institutions use professional development officers to conduct superior fundraising appeals for both the entire institution or individual colleges and departments. Examples of this include athletics and libraries.

**(ii) Social auditing [June-2019, Q.No.-5(f)]**

**Ans.** Social audit is a way of measuring, understanding, reporting and ultimately improving an organisation's social and ethical performance. It as a term was used as far back as the 1950s. There has been a flurry of activity and interest in India and neighbouring countries since 1990s. It is based on the principle that democratic governance should be carried out, as far as possible, with the consent and understanding of all concerned. It is thus a process and not an event.

Civil society organisations (CSOs), non-governmental organisations (NGOs), political representatives, civil servants and workers of Dungarpur district of Rajasthan and Anantapur district of Andhra Pradesh collectively organise such social audits to prevent mass corruption under the Mahatma Gandhi National Rural Employment Guarantee Act (MGNREGA). A grass roots organisation of Rajasthan, Mazdoor Kisan Shakti Sangathan (MKSS) is believed to have started the concept of the social audit while fighting corruption in the public works in the early 1990s. As the corruption is attributed to the secrecy in governance, the 'Jansunwai' or public hearing and the right to information (RTI), enacted in 2005, are used to fight this secrecy. Official records obtained using RTI are read out at the public hearing to identify and rectify irregularities. "'This process of reviewing official records and determining whether state reported expenditures reflect the actual monies spent on the ground is referred to as a social audit." Participation of informed citizens promotes collective responsibility and awareness about entitlements.

The findings of the social audit should be shared with all local skate holders. This encourages transparency and accountability. As social workers, we should expand and popularize the concept and process of social audit, which would help in enhancing the objectives of democracy, social justice and empowerment of community people.

**Q22. Discuss the conflict resolution and dealing of social welfare services with burn outs.**

**Ans.** There is need for the social work administrator to understand conflict resolution. There can be numerous situations at workplace leading to arguments and disagreements among colleagues. Some of this conflict is relatively easy to recognize, may not necessarily be easy to resolve. Conflict may manifest itself in a number of ways including angry shouting, in always making contrary points to another person, or even in sullen withdrawal from all interactions. Conflict can also be between departments, agencies, organisations, groups and individuals or vice versa.

Conflict has a positive role too. It makes people better able to cope with further stressful situations and even envisage new breakthroughs and help create a collaborative culture. In fact, managers/administrators need to nurture constructive conflict dedicated to finding new solutions, new services and new understanding of the social situation. Diversity of personalities, perceptions, values, working style and coping patterns cause conflict at workplace.

Conflict resolution denotes final solving of the conflict. There are a number of ways to resolve a problem, argument or difficulty by applying social work methods, techniques and skills. Emphatic, active and attentive listening, on the part of a team-leader/administrator/manager goes a long way in conflict resolution. It is followed by helping the aggrieved party nullify emotions as they can inhibit or distort communication which is critical to resolving dispute.

Burnouts means "become extinguished through a lack of fuel". In our profession there are many situations which put us down and we lose motivation to work. It is necessary to deal with burnouts and some of the suggested ways are as follows:

(1) The social worker/employee should maintain awareness of the changing social climate and a realistic evaluation of its impact on people, including themselves. This would help in widening of the perspective and dealing with burnouts in a better way.

(2) Leaning helps to avoid burnouts. Looking each challenge/work as an opportunity to learn and grow is required.

(3) Working in the field of one's own interest and about which they are motivated to learn more, is the best antidote against burnouts.

(4) Time management and stress management are of vital importance in today's work environment. Learning to manage their individual work loads effectively and responsibly may help

social workers/employees in keeping their motivation and morale high.

(5) It is important to possess and maintain a personal value system consistent with the value system of human service, even if its tenets may run contrary to accepted social values.

(6) For social workers/employees, find a personal life style sufficiently satisfying to enable them to distance themselves from their work is required against burnouts. In other words, keeping professional and personal life separate is needed.

**Q23. Explain social policy.**

**Ans.** Social policy is policy usually within a governmental or political setting, such as the welfare state and study of social services. Social policy consists of guidelines, principles, legislation and activities that affect the living conditions conducive to human welfare, such as a person's quality of life. The Department of Social Policy at the London School of Economics defines social policy as "an interdisciplinary and applied subject concerned with the analysis of societies' responses to social need", which seeks to foster in its students a capacity to understand theory and evidence drawn from a wide range of social science disciplines, including economics, sociology, psychology, geography, history, law, philosophy and political science. The Malcolm Wiener Center for Social Policy at Harvard University describes social policy as "public policy and practice in the areas of healthcare, human services, criminal justice, inequality, education, and labor. Social policy might also be described as actions that affect the well-being of members of a society through shaping the distribution of and access to goods and resources in that society. Social policy often deals with wicked problems.

The discussion of "social policy" in the United States and Canada can also apply to governmental policy on social issues such as tackling racism. In the West, proponents of scientific social planning such as the sociologist Auguste Comte, and social researchers, such as Charles Booth, contributed to the emergence of social policy in the first industrialised countries following the industrial revolution. Surveys of poverty exposing the brutal conditions in the urban slum conurbations of Victorian Britain supplied the pressure leading to changes such as the decline and abolition of the poor law system and Liberal welfare reforms. Other significant examples in the development of social policy are the Bismarckian welfare state in 19th century Germany, social security policies in the United States introduced under the rubric of the New Deal between 1933 and 1935, and the National Health Service Act 1946 in Britain.

Social policy in the 21st century is complex and in each state it is subject to local and national governments, as well as supranational political influence. For example, membership of the European Union is conditional on member states' adherence to the Social Chapter of European Union law and other international laws.

**Q24. Discuss health policy and its programmes.**

***Or***

**Write the short note on Goals of NRHM.**

**[June-2019, Q.No.-5(e)]**

**Ans.** 'Health is wealth' – this old proverb has all the more significance for the government of any nation like India as only healthy citizens can contribute fully for the national growth and development. In this regard, the government has formulated its National Health Policy in the year 1983 that talked about setting up of a well-dispersed network of comprehensive primary healthcare services, with referral system, specialty and super-specialty facilities in a decentralized and integrated manner. The NHP-1983 had envisaged providing 'Health for All by the year 2000 AD', through the universal provision of comprehensive primary healthcare services, which we could not achieve for several reasons. Again, in the year 2002, another National Health Policy was formulated where an attempt has been made to maximize the broad-based availability of health services to the citizenry of the country on the basis of realistic considerations of capacity.

There is dearth of funds for medical facilities, shortage of medical and para-medical personnel, with further disproportionate shortfall in less developed and rural areas, obsolete and unusable equipment in many public hospitals, dilapidated state of the buildings, minimal availability of essential drugs, and the capacity of the facilities is grossly inadequate, which leads to over-crowding, and consequentially to a steep deterioration in the quality of the services. The NHP-2002 addresses all these issues making specific recommendations in these matters.

Mental health disorders are actually much more prevalent than is apparent on the surface. While such disorders do not contribute significantly to mortality, they have a serious bearing on the quality of life of the affected persons and their families. Mental health institutions are woefully deficient in physical infrastructure and trained manpower. NHP-2002 examines these deficiencies in the public health sector and makes suitable suggestions.

IEC initiatives are important for creating awareness about preventive and curative healthcare. It is especially vital for disseminating curative guidelines for the TB, Malaria, Leprosy, Cataract Blindness Programmes, and to prevent HIV/AIDS and other life-style diseases. The Policy, while projecting an IEC strategy, fully addresses the inherent problems like high illiteracy rate in the country.

One of the main components of NHP-2002 is to apply the alternative systems of medicine – Ayurveda, Unani, Siddha and Homoeopathy – in the umbrella of national healthcare framework.

**Administrative Aspects:** After brief discussion on the health policy in India, let us briefly look at the administrative aspects of the health services. The Ministry of Health and Family Welfare is the nodal agency that implements various national health programmes. Healthcare system in India, involves a huge web of primary health centres and sub-centres, community health centres and district hospitals. National Rural Health Mission (2005-12) is one of the very crucial campaigns of the government that seeks to provide effective healthcare to rural population throughout the country with special focus on 18 states having weak public health indicators and/or weak health infrastructure. The Mission is an articulation of the commitment of the Government to undertake corrections of the health system and promote policies that strengthen public health management and service delivery in the country.

***Goals of NRHM are:***

- Reduction in Infant Mortality Rate (IMR) and Maternal Mortality Ratio (MMR).
- Universal access to public health services such as Women's health, child health, water, sanitation and hygiene, immunization, and nutrition.
- Prevention and control of communicable and non-communicable diseases, including locally endemic diseases.
- Access to integrated comprehensive primary healthcare.
- Population stabilization, gender and demographic balance.
- Revitalize local health traditions and mainstream AYUSH.
- Promotion of healthy life styles.

Core Strategies of NRHM are to train and enhance capacity of Panchayati Raj Institutions (PRIs) to own, control and manage public health services; promote access to improved healthcare at household level through the female health activist (ASHA); health plan for each village through Village Health Committee of the Panchayat; strengthening sub-centre through a untied fund to enable local planning and action and more Multi Purpose Workers (MPWs); strengthening existing PHCs and CHCs, and provision of 30-50 bedded CHC per lakh population for improved curative care to a normative standard (Indian Public Health Standards defining personnel, equipment and management standards); preparation and implementation of an inter-sectoral District Health Plan prepared by the District Health Mission, including drinking water, sanitation and hygiene and nutrition; integrating vertical Health and Family Welfare programmes at National, State, Block, and District levels; developing capacities for preventive healthcare at all levels for promoting healthy life styles, reduction in consumption of tobacco and alcohol etc.; and promoting non-profit sector particularly in underserved areas. Supplementary strategies include regulation of Private Sector including the informal rural practitioners to ensure availability of quality service to citizens at reasonable cost; promotion of Public Private Partnerships for achieving public health goals; mainstreaming AYUSH – revitalizing local health traditions and reorienting medical education to support rural health issues including regulation of Medical care and Medical Ethics; and effective and viable risk pooling and social health insurance to provide health security to the poor by ensuring accessible, affordable, accountable and good quality hospital care.

***Major National health programmes are as follows:***

- National Water Borne Disease Control Programme
- National Filarial Control Programme
- National Leprosy Eradication Programme
- Revised National TB Control Programme
- National Programme for Control of Blindness
- National Iodine Deficiency Disorders Control Programme
- National Mental Health Programme
- National Aids Control Programme
- National Cancer Control Programme
- Universal Immunization Programme
- National Programme for Prevention and Control of Deafness
- Pilot Programme on Prevention and Control of Diabetes, CVD and Stroke
- National Tobacco Control Programme

**Q25. Discuss educational policy and its programmes.**

**Ans.** The constitution of India is the ultimate document which guides State policy in all sectors including education. Details of provisions contained in the Constitution having a bearing on education. State governments and local authorities are expected to provide facilities for instruction in the mother tongue at the primary tongue at the primary stage of education.

The National Policy on Education (NPE) is a policy formulated by the Government of India to promote education amongst India's people. The policy covers elementary education to colleges in both rural and urban India. The first NPE was promulgated in 1968 by the government of Prime Minister Indira Gandhi, and the second by Prime Minister Rajiv Gandhi in 1986. The government of India has appointed a new committee under K. Kasturirangan to prepare a Draft for the new National Education Policy in 2017. Since the country independence in 1947, the Indian government sponsored a variety of programmes to address the problems of illiteracy in both rural and urban India. Maulana Abul Kalam Azad, India's first Minister of Education, envisaged strong central government control over education throughout the country, with a uniform educational system. The Union government established the University Education Commission (1948–1949), the Secondary Education Commission (1952–1953), university Grants Commission and the Kothari Commission (1964–66) to develop proposals to modernise India's education system. The Resolution on Scientific Policy was adopted by the government of Jawaharlal Nehru, India's first Prime Minister. The Nehru government sponsored the development of high-quality scientific education institutions such as the Indian Institutes of Technology. In 1961, the Union government formed the National Council of Educational Research and Training (NCERT) as an autonomous organisation that would advise both the Union and state governments on formulating and implementing education policies.

Sarva Shiksha Abhiyan or SSA, is an Indian- Government programme aimed at the universalisation of elementary education "in a time bound manner", as mandated by the 86th Amendment to the Constitution of India making free and compulsory education to children between the ages of 6 to 14 (estimated to be 205 million children in 2001) a fundamental right. The programme was pioneered by former Indian Prime Minister Atal Bihari Vajpayee. As an intervention programme, it started on 2002 and SSA has been operational since 2000-2001. However, its roots go back to 1993-1994, when the District Primary Education Programme (DPEP) was launched, with an aim of achieving the objective of universal primary education. DPEP, over several phases, covered 272 districts in 18 states of the country. The expenditure on the programme was shared by the Central Government (85%) and the State Governments. The Central share was funded by a number of external agencies, including the World Bank, Department for International Development (DFID) and UNICEF. By 2001, more than $1500 million had been committed to the programme, and 50 million children covered in its ambit. In an impact assessment of Phase I of DPEP, the authors concluded that its net impact on minority children was impressive, while there was little evidence of any impact on the enrolment of girls. Nevertheless, they concluded that the investment in DPEP was not a waste, because it introduced a new approach to primary school interventions in India. The Right to Education Act (RTE) came into force on 1 April 2010. Some educationists and policy makers believe that, with the passing of this act, SSA has acquired the necessary legal force for its implementation.

The Kasturba Gandhi Balika Vidyalaya or KGBV is a residential girls' secondary school run by Government of India for the weaker sections in India. It was a scheme was introduced by the Government of India in August 2004, then integrated in the Sarva Shiksha

Abhiyanprogram, to provide educational facilities for girls belonging to Scheduled Castes, Scheduled Tribes, Other Backward Classes, minority communities and families below the poverty line in Educationally Backward Blocks.

Mahila Samakhya Programme is 'Education for Women's Equality' that was launched in 1988-89 and has covered more than 10,000 villages in 10 states. Through women's group, it enables women to use education as a path for their empowerment. District Primary Education Programme is to ensure education of children at district level. It stresses on gender training and has constituted Village Education Committees. Schemes under the development of higher education are with respect to university and higher education and technical education.

**Q26. What are the policies and programmes of social welfare?**

***Or***

**Briefly describe the scope of ministry of social justice and empowerment.**

**Ans.** Ministry of Social Justice and Empowerment as the name suggests is to ensure equitable treatment to such sections of society suffering social inequalities, exploitation, discrimination and injustice. The Ministry is headed by Cabinet Minister and Minister of State.

Next, are the Secretary and then Additional Secretary of the MSJE. The activities of the Ministry are under taken through Bureaus as the Bureau of Scheduled Castes Development, Backward Classes Bureau Coordination, Media, Administration, Disability Bureau, Social Defence Bureau and Project, Research, Evaluation and Monitoring Bureau, each Bureau is headed by Joint Secretary. Let us now examine the salient issues covered by the MSJE:

The basic objective of the policies, programmes, law and institution of the Indian welfare system is to bring the target groups into the main stream of development by making them self-reliant.

**Scheduled Caste Development:** It is responsible for all round development of Scheduled Castes and to bring them in the mainstream of national life and ensure their full participation in socio-economic development of the country. It has initiated a lot of schemes for people belonging to SC community. A few salient ones are – Babu Jagjivan Ram Chhatravas Yojna; Central Sector Scholarship Scheme of Top Class Education for SC students; Self Employment Scheme for Rehabilitation of Manual Scavengers; Central Sector Scheme of 'Rajiv Gandhi National Fellowship' for providing scholarships to SC students to pursue programmes in higher education such as M.Phil and Ph.D.; Post-Matric Scholarship for SC/ST students; Pre-Matric Scholarship for the children of those engaged in unclean occupations; Central Sector Scheme of National Oversees Scholarship for SC candidates; Special Education

Development Programme for SC Girls belonging to Low Literacy Levels; Book Banks for SC/ST students; upgradation of merit of SC Students; Central Sector Scheme of Free Coaching for SC and OBC students; National Scheduled Castes Finance and Development Corporation (NSCFDC); Assistance to Scheduled Castes Development Corporations; Supporting Projects of All India Nature of SCs (under the scheme, financial assistance is provided to reputed research institutions including universities to conduct purposeful studies for the welfare of SC community); and National Commission for Safai Karamcharis.

**Backward Classes Development:** The Backward Classes are those castes/communities that are notified as socially and educationally Backward Classes by the State Governments or those that may be notified as such by the Central Government from time to time. The affairs of Backward Classes were looked after by the Backward Classes Cell (BCC) in the Ministry of Home Affairs and shifted to the then newly created Ministry of Welfare (now called MSJE). The Backward Classes Division in the Ministry looks after the policy, planning and implementation of programmes relating to social and economic empowerment of OBCs. It also looks after matters relating to two institutions set up for the welfare of OBCs: National Backward Classes Finance and Development Corporation (NBCFDC; meant to promote economic and developmental activities for the benefit of Backward Classes and to assist the poorer sections of these classes in skill development and self employment ventures) and the National Commission for Backward Classes (NCBC; The National Commission for Backward Classes Act, 1993 was enacted on the direction of the Supreme Court to set up a permanent body for entertaining, examining and recommending upon requests for inclusion and complaints of over-inclusion and under-inclusion in the central lists of Other Backward Classes (OBCs) of citizens for the purpose of making reservation in civil posts and services under Government of India).

**Salient Programmes for Other Backward Classes** are Pre-matric Scholarship for OBC Students (students from families of below poverty line are given the scholarship and its funding is shared by State and Centre in the ratio of 1:1, while in UTs 100% grant is given by Central Government); Post-matric Scholarship for OBC Students (100% central assistance is provided to State Government/Union Territory Administration for the purpose.); Hostel for OBC Boys and Girls (Out of the hostels set up under this scheme at least one third will be exclusively for girls. 5% of the total seats in these hostels shall be reserved for disabled students); Assistance to Voluntary Organisations for Welfare of OBCs.

NBCFDC has launched Swarnima Scheme to make women of Backward Classes self reliant and Swayam Saksham Scheme for professionally unemployed youth for their self-employment. It has also initiated Education Loan Scheme to provide loans at concessional rate of interest to the student of Backward Classes living below the poverty line for pursuing general/professional/technical courses or training at graduate and higher levels. Under its Margin Money Loan, the loans are given up to 40% of the cost under various sectors viz. Agriculture and Allied, Small Business/ Artisan and Traditional Occupation, Service and Transport. The corporation has initiated certain micro finance schemes like Micro Credit Financing women through accredited NGOs either directly or through self help groups, Mahila Samridhi Yojna to provide micro finance to women entrepreneurs in rural and urban areas and Training Grant Scheme to provide financial assistance to the members of the target groups for up-gradation of their technical skill.

**Persons with Disabilities:** The salient features of the National Policy for Persons with Disabilities. The National Policy recognizes that Persons with Disabilities (PWD) are valuable human resource for the country and seeks to create an environment that provides them equal opportunities, protection of their rights and full participation in society. The policy focuses on prevention of disabilities (awareness and early detection camps) and rehabilitation measures (physical, educational, vocational and economic rehabilitation for a dignified life in society). It talks about awareness, early detection and intervention, counseling and medical rehabilitation, provision of suitable and modern aids and appliances through DDRCs and Accredited Social Health Activist (ASHA) of National Rural Health Mission, National institutes mentioned above and their outreach work. The policy talks about development of Rehabilitation Professionals by giving training to Anganwadi workers, Auxiliary Nurse Midwifes, NGO workers and creating awareness among teachers, panchayat members and community people. Special emphasis is given on education of PWDs in Sarva Shiksha Abhiyan, Integrated Education for Disabled Children (IEDC) scheme. Further, 3% reservation in educational institutions and employment in government institutions and PSUs has been provided. The policy also reinforces the need for barrier free environment in public buildings and transport amenities.

**Social Defence:** The Social Defence Bureau of the Ministry caters to the requirements of neglected and marginalized people, abandoned destitute, neglected and delinquent juveniles who need care and protection for want of support or are in conflict with the society or the law, the drug addicts and offenders, the aged and host of others who need special care, protection and support. For services provided for the care and rehabilitation of juvenile delinquents, Juvenile Justice Act should be read. Likewise, policy on girl child, as well as policies for women empowerment should be read that, among other things, also deal with girls and women in need of care and protection. The programmes and the policies of the Bureau aim at equipping this group to sustain a life of respect and honour and to become useful citizens. In this process, the

Bureau plays the role of a catalyst and has promoted voluntary action. The State Governments, autonomous bodies, NGOs and even the corporate world are involved in formulating and implementing the policies. All the programmes are meant to aid, prevent neglect, abuse and exploitation and provide assistance to those deprived and mainstream them.

**Elderly Care:** In response to increasing vulnerability of elderly, the Ministry of SJE formulated a National Policy on Older Persons (NPOP) in January 1999 to reaffirm its commitment to ensure the well-being of the older persons in a holistic manner. It assures financial security through Old Age Pension Scheme for poor and destitute older persons, better returns on earnings/savings of people in organized sector, skill upgradation, self-employment, continued employment and income generation. The NPOP meeting health needs of elderly through strengthening and reorienting public health system from primary to tertiary levels, as well as implementing health insurance. The policy ensures provision of standard institutional services for the destitute and needy elderly. It further says that the State has to gear up security network to save older persons from criminal offences and police is required to keep friendly vigil. It also maintains strict and effective implementation of social legislations related to elderly. The NPOP further describes the positive roles expected from various stakeholders like Media, community people and mainly the family. It envisages training of human resource in geriatric care.

**Grants in aids:** In keeping with its mandate, the MSJE supports and assists a number of projects in the field of Disabilities, Social Defence, welfare of the Scheduled Castes, Other Backward Classes etc, which are implemented through various Voluntary Organisations.

**Planning, Research, Evaluation and Monitoring (PREM) Division:** The MSJE is implementing a number of schemes for various vulnerable and disadvantaged groups they cater to. Therefore, it is important that the impact of these schemes/programmes should be assessed and evaluated from time to time, so that these can be suitably modified/ revised to make them more effective or phased out if their utility is found to be doubtful. It is also necessary to identify through research, areas where social problems are likely to arise in future so that the Ministry can plan timely interventions. The Ministry, therefore, sponsors research and evaluation studies under PREM division.

***Let us list associated organisations with MSJE:***

- Ali Yavar Jung National Institute for the Hearing Handicapped (AYJNIHH)
- Artificial Limbs Manufacturing Corporation of India (ALIMCO)
- Dr. Ambedkar Foundation
- Institute for the Physically Handicapped (IPH), rechristened as Deen Dayal Upadhyay Institute of Physically Handicapped

- National Commission for Safai Karamcharis
- National Commission for Backward Classes (NCBC)
- National Commission for Scheduled Castes (NCSC)
- National Institute of Mentally Handicapped (NIMH)
- National Institute of Visually Handicapped (NIVH)
- National Institute for Orthopaedically Handicapped, Kolkata
- National Backward Classes Finance and Development Corporation (NBCFDC)
- National Safai Karamcharis Finance and Development Corporation (NSKFDC)
- National Scheduled Castes Finance and Development Corporation
- National Handicapped Finance and Development Corporation (NHFDC)
- National Trust for the Welfare of Persons with Autism, Cerebral Palsy, Mental Retardation and Multiple Disabilities
- National Institute of Social Defence (NISD)
- National Institute for the Orthopaedically Handicapped (NIOH) rechristened as Dr. Shyama Prasad Mukherjee National Institute for Orthopaedically Handicapped
- Officer of the Chief Commissioner for Disabilities
- Rehabilitation Council of India (RCI)
- Swami Vivekanand National Institute of Rehabilitation, Training and Research (SVNIRTAR).

❑❑

# Question Papers

## MSW-009 : COMMUNITY ORGANISATION MANAGEMENT FOR COMMUNITY DEVELOPMENT
## December, 2017

---

***Note:*** *(i) Answer all the* ***five*** *questions.*
*(ii) All questions* ***carry*** *equal marks.*
*(iii) Answer to question no. 1 and 2 should not exceed* ***600*** *words each.*

---

**Q1. Discuss the Sociological understanding of a community. Illustrate with example from your own region.**

**Ans.** Refer to Chapter-1, Q.No.-5

***or***

**Describe the various models of Community organisation.**

**Ans.** Refer to Chapter-2, Q.No.-17

**Q2. Trace the history of Community organisation in India.**

**Ans.** Refer to Chapter-2, Q.No.-9

***or***

**Define social action. Describe in detail the strategies and tactics in social action.**

**Ans.** Refer to Chapter-3, Q.No.-1 and Q.No.-13

**Q3. Answer any two of the following questions in 300 words each:**

**(a) Highlight the various assumptions regarding community organisation as a method of social work practice.**

**Ans.** Refer to Chapter-2, Q.No.-6

**(b) Describe the four basic systems as discussed in the integrated approach to social work.**

**Ans.** Refer to June-2019, Q.No.-3(c)

**(c) Briefly discuss the characteristics of Non-Government Organisation.**

**Ans.** Refer to Chapter-4, Q.No.-12

**(d) Elaborate advocacy as a key strategy of Social Action.**

**Ans.** Refer to Chapter-3, Q.No.-15

**Q4. Answer any four of the following questions in about 150 words each:**

**(a) What are the main characteristics of a community?**

**Ans.** Refer to Chapter-1, Q.No.-6

**(b) Discuss the features of Gandhian model of Social Action.**

**Ans.** Refer to Chapter-3, Q.No.-12

**(c) Enlist the principles involved in social marketing.**

**Ans.** Refer to Chapter-4, Q.No.-19

**(d) List out the skills required for community practice.**

**Ans.** Refer to Chapter-2, Q.No.-27

**(e) Briefly present the main features of tribal communities.**

**Ans.** Refer to Chapter-1, Q.No.-33

**(f) Discuss Britto's popular social action model with examples.**

**Ans.** Refer to Chapter-3, Q.No.-10

**Q5. Write short notes on any five of the following questions in about 100 words each:**

**(a) Nomadic tribes**

**Ans.** Refer to Chapter-1, Q.No.-27

**(b) Collaboration**

**Ans.** Refer to Chapter-3, Q.No.-13

**(c) Social Institution model**

**Ans.** Refer to Chapter-3, Q.No.-11

**(d) Burn out**

**Ans.** Refer to Chapter-4, Q.No.-22

**(e) Jajmani System**

**Ans.** Refer to Chapter-1, Q.No.-19

**(f) Kubumbashree Programme**

**Ans.** Refer to Chapter-1, Q.No.-32

**(g) Budgeting**

**Ans.** Budgeting involves the financial administration of a social welfare agency. Financial administration is the system that revolves around the finances of the agency. This concerns with the raising, regulation and distribution of the resources for the growth of the agency. The agency collects funds from the community by means of donations, subscription or taxes and these funds are used for the organizational programmes and the running of the agency. A budget is a complete statement prepared showing the various sources of the money raised for a particular period and the activities and programmes conducted with that money. Financial administration is one of the most important responsibilities of the social welfare administration and if this responsibility is not properly taken up, it can have serious consequences on the administration of the agency.

**(h) Fund raising**

**Ans.** Refer to Chapter-4, Q.No.-21(i)

□□

## MSW-009 : COMMUNITY ORGANISATION MANAGEMENT FOR COMMUNITY DEVELOPMENT

### June, 2018

***Note:*** *(i) Answer all the **five** questions.*
*(ii) All questions **carry** equal marks.*
*(iii) Answer to questions 1 and 2 should not exceed **600** words each.*

**Q1. Explain the main features of rural social structure in India and discuss the linkages between caste and class in rural society.**

**Ans.** Refer to Chapter-1, Q.No.-19

***or***

**Define community organisation. Discuss briefly the development of community organisation practice in India.**

**Ans.** Refer to Chapter-2, Q.No.-1 and Q.No.-9

**Q2. Describe the steps in the process of community organisation.**

**Ans.** Refer to Chapter-2, Q.No.-16

***or***

**Describe the concept of Social Welfare administration. What are the essential feature of Social Welfare administration?**

**Ans.** Refer to Chapter-4, Q.No.-1 and Q.No.-2

**Q3. Answer any two of the following questions in about 300 words each:**

**(a) Define community. Enlist the characteristics of a community.**

**Ans.** Refer to Chapter-1, Q.No.-1 and Q.N.-6

**(b) What are the major assumptions that influence the method of community organisation?**

**Ans.** Refer to Chapter-2, Q.No.-6

**(c) Enlist the guiding purposes of community organisation.**
**Ans.** Refer to Chapter-2, Q.No.-4

**(d) Briefly enumerate the role of a community organizer.**
**Ans.** Refer to Chapter-2, Q.No.-26

**Q4. Answer any four of the following questions in about 150 words each:**

**(a) What are the basic features of power relations in rural areas?**
**Ans.** Refer to Chapter-1, Q.No.-19

**(b) Discuss briefly the social and economic aspects of urban communities.**
**Ans.** Refer to Chapter-1, Q.No.-14

**(c) Briefly describe the scope of Ministry of social justice and empowerment.**
**Ans.** Refer to Chapter-4, Q.No.-26

**(d) Discuss the models of social action.**
**Ans.** Refer to Chapter-3, Q.No.-10

**(e) Enlist various components of needs assessment.**
**Ans.** Refer to Chapter-2, Q.No.-16

**(f) Explain the relevance of power and leadership in community organisation.**
**Ans.** Refer to Chapter-2, Q.No.-22

**Q5. Write short notes on any five of the following questions in about 100 words each:**

**(a) Social planning**
**Ans.** Refer to Chapter-2, Q.No.-17

**(b) Difference between community development and community work**
**Ans.** Refer to Chapter-1, Q.No.-34

**(c) Stakeholder analysis**
**Ans.** Refer to Chapter-3, Q.No.-14

**(d) Legislative social action**
**Ans.** Refer to Chapter-3, Q.No.-9

**(e) Social auditing**
**Ans.** Refer to Chapter-4, Q.No.-21 (ii)

**(f) Social welfare**
**Ans.** Refer to Chapter-4, Q.No.-1 (c)

**(g) Donor organisation**
**Ans.** Refer to Chapter-4, Q.No.-14

**(h) Goals of National Rural Health Mission (NRHM)**
**Ans.** Refer to Chapter-4, Q.No.-24

Christmas
isn't a
Season
it's a
Feeling

## MSW-009 : COMMUNITY ORGANISATION MANAGEMENT FOR COMMUNITY DEVELOPMENT
## December, 2018

---

***Note:*** *(i) Answer all the* ***five*** *questions.*
*(ii) All questions* ***carry*** *equal marks.*
*(iii) Answer to questions 1 and 2 should not exceed* ***600*** *words each.*

---

**Q1. Define Community Organisation and describe any three models of Community Organisation.**

**Ans.** Refer to Chapter-2, Q.No.-1 and Q.No.-17

***or***

**Discuss the three modes of intervention to Purposive Community Change as developed by Rothman.**

**Ans.** Refer to Chapter-2, Q.No.-17

**Q2. What do you understand by Social Welfare Organisation and discuss in brief its various functions.**

**Ans.** Refer to Chapter-4, Q.No.-2

***or***

**Trace the historical evolution of the concept of a tribe. Highlight the major issues faced by tribal communities.**

**Ans.** Refer to Chapter-1, Q.No.-33 and Q.No.-28

**Q3. Answer any two of the following in about 300 words each:**

**(a) Elaborate on the neighbourhood model as given by Siddiqui.**

**Ans.** Refer to Chapter-2, Q.No.-28

**(b) Explain the assumptions regarding Community Organisation as a method of social practice.**

**Ans.** Refer to Chapter-2, Q.No.-6

**(c) Discuss globalisation and its impact on community practice.**

**Ans.** Refer to Chapter-2, Q.No.-25

**(d) Highlight the salient features of National Health Policy, 2002.**

**Ans.** Refer to Chapter-4, Q.No.-24

**Q4. Answer any four of the following in about 150 words each:**

**(a) What are the objectives of a charitable trust?**

**Ans.** Refer to Chapter-4, Q.No.-11

**(b) Highlight the salient features of tribal community.**

**Ans.** Refer to Chapter-1, Q.No.-33

**(c) Explain Empowerment.**

**Ans.** Empowerment is the degree of autonomy and self-determination in people and in communities. This enables them to represent their interests in a responsible and self-determined way, acting on their own authority. It is the process of becoming stronger and more confident, especially in controlling one's life and claiming one's rights. Empowerment as action refers both to the process of self-empowerment and to professional support of people, which enables them to overcome their sense of powerlessness and lack of influence, and to recognize and use their resources.

In social work, empowerment forms a practical approach of resource-oriented intervention. In the field of citizenship education and democratic education, empowerment is seen [by whom?] as a tool to increase the responsibility of the citizen. Empowerment is a key concept in the discourse on promoting civic engagement. Empowerment as a concept, which is characterised by a move away from a deficit-oriented towards a more strength-oriented perception, can increasingly be found in management concepts, as well as in the areas of continuing education and self-help.

**(d) Discuss Britto's popular social action model with examples.**

**Ans.** Refer to Chapter-3, Q.No.-10

**(e) Mention any two PRA methods.**

**Ans.** Refer to Chapter-4, Q.No.-20 and Q.No.-21

**(f) Discuss the working of government organisation in social welfare at the Central level.**

**Ans.** Refer to Chapter-4, Q.No.-11

**Q5. Write short notes on any five of the following in about 100 words each:**

**(a) Need assessment**

**Ans.** Refer to Chapter-2, Q.No.-16

**(b) Collaboration**

**Ans.** Refer to Chapter-3, Q.No.-13

**(c) Public relations**

**Ans.** Refer to Chapter-4, Q.No.-20

**(d) Burnout**

**Ans.** Refer to Chapter-4, Q.No.-22

**(e) Meaning of rural community**

**Ans.** Refer to Chapter-1, Q.No.-17

**(f) Bilateral organisations**

**Ans.** Refer to Chapter-4, Q.No.-13

**(g) Slums**

**Ans.** Refer to Chapter-1, Q.No.-15

**(h) Kudumbashree Programmes**

**Ans.** Refer to Chapter-1, Q.No.-32

## MSW-009 : COMMUNITY ORGANISATION MANAGEMENT FOR COMMUNITY DEVELOPMENT

**June, 2019**

---

*Note: Answer all the **five** questions. All questions carry **equal** marks. Answer to Question No. 1 and 2 should not exceed **600** words each.*

---

**Q1. Describe some of the community development programmes in rural areas.**

**Ans.** Refer to Chapter-1, Q.No.-32

***or***

**Trace the history of community organisation in India.**

**Ans.** Refer to Chapter-2, Q.No.-9

**Q2. Define social action. Discuss the scope and relevance of social action.**

**Ans.** Refer to Chapter-3, Q.No.-1 and Q.No.-3

***or***

**What do you understand by social policy? Discuss its relation and relevance for social welfare administration.**

**Ans.** Refer to Chapter-4, Q.No.-23

The most common social and political use of the term 'policy' refers to "a course of action or intended course of action, conceived as deliberately adopted, after a review of possible alternatives, and pursued or intended to be pursued". Social Policy is thus, "a statement of the programmes, methods and principles of social agency". The older concept that the policy formulation is the function of politics is hardly tenable today. Earlier it was considered that policy-making is a higher order activity than administration and social planners have recommended that policy-making should be distinctly separated from administration or execution of the policy. Wilson has claimed that administrators were not only subordinate to policy-makers but were presumably value-neutral and efficient. They carried out policy and do not make policy. Regarding execution, bureaucracies are generally the instruments which implement public policy. Bureaucracies are necessary for policies to be carried out with some predictability, equity, and due process. Nonetheless, the negative connotations of bureaucracy (like, red tapism, inflexibility, over-emphasis on rules and regulations, to mention a few) may contribute to withdrawal of public confidence in the efficacy of public policy.

Currently, the essence of administration is policy formulation. The role of administrators is not confined to execution of the policy as they are increasingly taking active part in the formulation of new policies and reviewing and modifying the older ones. Along with this, the administrators are playing crucial role in the execution of the policy. Administrators also participate in another way in the making of policy for the future - they formulate recommendations for legislation and this is a part of the function of policy making. In modern times, the relationship between policy and administration has become so much blurred that it is difficult to say where policy ends and administration begins or vice versa. Therefore, no study of administration could be complete without including the study of policy in it.

Policy gives direction for programme planning and execution at the ground level. Formulation of social policy is, therefore, essential for the successful working of any system of social administration. Unless social administration is assisted by an adequate system of social legislation and sound social policy, it cannot attain its true purpose. Absence of a clear cut social policy often proves to be a major handicap to the development of a sound system of social administration. Hence it would be no exaggeration to say that there can be no successful system of social administration without a social policy.

Next, even a well formulated policy is of no use unless it is implemented effectively. Thus, factors influencing administration (as you have studied in previous units) play crucial role for policy execution. Organisational efficacy has direct and strong bearing on the successful implementation of public policy.

Social policy is vital for social planning. It must be conceptually clear and simple, theorctically sound, and stated in terms of desired changes achieved among target groups. The policy with clear designation of roles and responsibilities of all the stakeholders, clear directives and organizational structures, goes a long way in effectively realizing its set goals. Social policy reflects the government's commitment for the particular cause for which the policy has been formulated. It implies the government's priorities and resource distribution. Hence, technical and budgetary means as well as time frame should be delineated clearly in the policy. However, it may be reminded that policies are merely guidelines and do not enjoy legal sanctity as in the case of social legislations.

Since Independence, the government of India has formulated many policies and reviewed and modified them from time to time. National Health Policy, National Policy on Education, National Policy on Empowerment of Women in India, National Policy for Persons with Disability, National Youth Policy, National Policy on Children and so on and so forth. Many of these policies have been reviewed and revised (say, National Health Policy, National Policy on Education). These policies are comprehensive documents covering the vision and mission of the State, plan of action, targets to be achieved, stakeholders, expected outcome, etc. Though the State cannot be sued if it fails to keep its promises mentioned in the policy, however, in this largest democracy of the world, votes of the common man prove to be a driving force for politicians to try their best in policy execution. Further, in India, social policy plays crucial role in formulation of Five Year plans.

It may be reiterated that without proper execution, social policy, doesn't matter how ambitious and fool proof it is, remains a paper tiger. In administration, committed leadership, inter-ministerial coordination, central-state relationship, political will, representation of various stakeholders including the grassroots people are some of the crucial factors that influence implementation of social policies. In the subsequent sections, you would study about Health policy, education policy and policies in social welfare and associated programmes and schemes administered by the respective Ministries and State machineries.

**Q3. Answer any two of the following questions in about 300 words each:**

**(a) Briefly discuss the elements of community work in India.**

**Ans.** The, essential elements of community work in India are described below:

(1) **Group of people:** Community is a group of human beings. It is not possible to form a community without a group of men and women.

(2) **Definite locality:** A community always occupies a definite geographical area. Locality is the physical basis of community. Without a definite locality, social relations between human beings cannot be established and the 'we' feeling cannot evolve.

(3) **Community Sentiment:** Community sentiment means a feeling of belonging together. It is "we feeling" among the members. The members of a community speak the same language, conform to the same mores, posses the same sentiment, and have the same attitudes.

(4) **Likeness:** The people in a community share a common way of life. Their customs, traditions, mores, language etc. are similar.

(5) **Permanency:** A community is not temporary like a crowd or a mob. It is relatively stable. It includes a permanent life in a definite place.

(6) **Neutrality:** Communities are not deliberately created. They are not made by planned efforts. An individual is born in a community. It has a natural growth of its own.

(7) **A particular Name:** Every community has some particular name. In the words of Lumley, "It points identity, it indicates reality, it points out individuality, it often describes personality and each community is something of a personality ".

(8) **Size:** A community may be big or small. A small community may be included in a wider community. For example, a city and a village may be included in a district. District may enclose small communities-like villages, towns, tribes etc.

(9) **Wider ends:** People in community share several common interests. They associate not for the fulfillment of a particular end. The ends of a community are wider. People work together to fulfill some common interests.

(10) **Regulation of Relations:** Every Community in course of time develops a system of traditions, customs, and morals. Practices, some rules and regulations to regulate the relations of its members. People in a community come together to meet the primary needs through a common set of institutions and organisations.

**(b) Discuss the relationship between community organisation and other primary methods of social work.**

**Ans.** Refer to Chapter-2, Q.No.-12

**(c) Describe integrated approach to social work and social action.**

**Ans.** Social work is an evolving discipline where interventions are geared up towards initiating, exploring, retaining and modifying the ways and means by which persons, individually and/or collectively are helped in resolving disruptions in their social functioning. Like other disciplines touching social life of human beings, social work too needs to design and re-design conceptual frameworks, theories and models related to interventions. As social situations change, the outlook to analyze and measure various social situations should also change. Theories and concepts guiding us through our social interventions also need to be revised, updated, improved and evolved. It is in this context, that Integrated Approach to Social Work was developed that would provide you a comprehensive framework of social intervention based on system's theory, fitting in most of the social situations requiring planned, guided social change.

Pincus and Minahan have given this framework with a view that social work interventions are not unilateral and 'people's participation' is needed in almost all situations. In this approach, social worker enters into a system, thereby consciously altering its previous state and balance as a means of attaining explicit goals. The underlying assumption in developing the unitary method or integrated approach to social work intervention was that regardless of the many forms social work practice can take, there is a common core of concepts, skills, tasks and activities which are essential to the practice of social work and represent a base from which the practitioner can build. The traditional social work theories and methods have been woven around dichotomous terms (person and environment, clinical practice or social action, micro-system and/or macro-system) that, in some way, provided a myopic perspective of viewing social reality. Pincus and Minahan have suggested the following criteria for developing a unitary or integrated model for social work practice:

(1) This unitary model should provide an all-encompassing framework, avoiding conceptualizing social work practice in dichotomous terms like either case work or social action, individualist or collective approach. It is believed that the strength of the profession lies in recognizing and working with the connections between these elements.

(2) The social worker has tasks to develop and maintain relationships with a variety of people in any planned change effort (and not with the clients and his/her family only).

(3) The social worker is required to work with and through many different sizes and types of systems (one to one relationships, families, community groups) in helping a client.

(4) There should be selective and judicious use of theories (ego, learning, communication, etc.) in understanding social situations.

(5) The Model should be applicable in variety of situations and settings.

In the subsequent sections of the unit, you would study at length about this integrated approach based on system's theory, substantiated with enough field examples. You are also advised to make use of this model in your field work practicum.

**(d) Elaborate on the principles of social action.**

**Ans.** Refer to Chapter-3, Q.No.-19

**Q4. Answer any four of the following questions in about 150 words each:**

**(a) What are the main characteristics of a community?**

**Ans.** Refer to Chapter-1, Q.No.-6

**(b) Explain the various models of community organisation.**

**Ans.** Refer to Chapter-2, Q.No.-17

**(c) Mention the role of community organiser.**

**Ans.** Refer to Chapter-2, Q.No.-26

**(d) Discuss Gandhian model of social action.**

**Ans.** Refer to Chapter-3, Q.No.-12

**(e) Enlist skills required by social workers at various stages of social action.**

**Ans.** Refer to Chapter-3, Q.No.-16

**(f) Discuss the characteristics of non-government organisation.**

**Ans.** Refer to Chapter-4, Q.No.-12

**Q5. Write short notes on any five of the following in about 100 words each:**

**(a) Nomadic tribes**

**Ans.** Refer to Chapter-1, Q.No.-27

**(b) Donor agencies**

**Ans.** Refer to Chapter-4, Q.No.-14

**(c) Conscientisation model**
**Ans.** Refer to Chapter-3, Q.No.-10

**(d) SWOC analysis**
**Ans.** Refer to Chapter-3, Q.No.-14

**(e) Goals of NRHM**
**Ans.** Refer to Chapter-4, Q.No.-24

**(f) Social auditing**
**Ans.** Refer to Chapter-4, Q.No.-21(ii)

**(g) Fund raising**
**Ans.** Refer to Chapter-4, Q.No.-21(i)

**(h) Purpose of UNICEF**
**Ans.** Refer to Chapter-4, Q.No.-15

## MSW-009 : COMMUNITY ORGANISATION MANAGEMENT FOR COMMUNITY DEVELOPMENT

**December, 2019**

---

*Note: Answer all the **five** questions. All questions **carry** equal marks. Answer to Question Nos. 1 and 2 should not exceed **600** words each.*

---

**Q1. Define a Tribe. Trace the historical evolution of the concept of a tribe.**

**Ans.** Refer to Chapter-1, Q.No.-22 and Q.No.-33

***or***

**Explain the guiding values and purposes of Community Organisation.**

**Ans.** Refer to Chapter-2, Q.No.-4 and Q.No.-5

**Q2. Discuss the history of social action in India.**

**Ans.** Refer to Chapter-3, Q.No.-2

***or***

**Define Social Welfare Administration. Discuss the nature of Social Welfare Administration.**

**Ans.** Refer to Chapter-4, Q.No.-2 and Q.No.-5

**Q3. Answer any two of the following questions in about 300 words each:**

**(a) What are the major issues faced by tribal communities?**

**Ans.** Refer to Chapter-1, Q.No.-28

**(b) Explain community organisation practice with the marginalised groups.**

**Ans.** Refer to Chapter-2, Q.No.-24

**(c) Explain the strategies and tactics in social action.**

**Ans.** Refer to Chapter-3, Q.No.-13

**(d) Enlist the principles of social welfare administration.**

**Ans.** Refer to Chapter-4, Q.No.-7

**Q4. Answer any four of the following questions in about 150 words each:**

**(a) Discuss, how the issues of tribal communities could be addressed through community development programmes.**

**Ans.** The tribal communities received some help through Special Multipurpose Tribal Development Projects (MTDPs) created towards the end of 1954. These MTDPs could not serve the interests of the tribal people since the number of schemes were numerous. Later the Community Development Blocks where the concentration of tribal population was 66% and above were converted into Tribal Development Blocks (TDBs). Due to failure of this to address tribal communities needs, Tribal Sub-Plan Strategy (TSP) was evolved for rapid socio-economic development of tribal people, and is continuing even now with the following objectives:

(1) Over all socio-economic development of tribals and to raise them above poverty level.

(2) Protection of tribals from various forms of exploitation.

The Scheme/programme and projects under TSP are implemented through Integrated Tribals Development Projects (ITDPs) which were set up in Block(s) or groups of Blocks where ST population is more than 50% of the total population.

The Government of India formed a Ministry of Tribal Affairs in October 1999 to accelerate tribal development. The Ministry of Tribal Affairs came out with a draft National Policy on Tribals in 2004. The draft policy recognizes that a majority of Scheduled Tribes continues to live below the poverty line, have poor literacy rates, suffer from malnutrition and disease and is vulnerable to displacement. It also acknowledges that Scheduled Tribes in general are repositories of indigenous knowledge and wisdom in certain aspects. The National Policy aims at addressing each of these problems in a concrete way.

There are many tribal community development initiatives from the NGO sector that worked closely on the issues of tribal communities, specially their capacity building and sustainable development.

Many of the initiatives concerned with tribal development have adopted participatory approaches made to ensure the successful completion of the project goals. There are many tribal community development initiatives from the NGO sector that worked closely on the issues of tribal communities, specially their capacity building and sustainable development.

During the last 10 to 15 years, with increasing recognition of the importance of people's participation for increasing the effectiveness of development interventions, an extensive array of 'people's' institutions have been created in the villages for the implementation of sectoral programmes. These include joint forest management (JFM) committees being set up by the Forest Department, education committees by the Education Department, watershed associations and committees by the DRDA, water and health committees by the Public Health Department, water users association by the Irrigation Department, and Mahila Mandals (women's associations) by the Women and Child Department.

One of the most successful one is the Andhra Pradesh Tribal Development Project.

The APTDP established a variety of local-level institutions, including SHGs, cluster-level associations of SHGs, user groups/village development committees (such as for education, health, irrigation, soil conservation and grain banks) and a nodal institution in the form of VTDAs. The latter were conceived on the one hand as the forum for the expression of community priorities and concerns and on the other hand as a means of delivering projects and programmes to the communities. The leaders and members of VTDAs were chosen by the communities as their representatives, and generally this selection required the approval of the traditional councils of elders, so that the relationship between the new and the old did exist, albeit on an informal basis.

In addition, one novel concept introduced was the formation of community coordination teams consisting of groups of dedicated young professionals who lived in tribal villages to assist in social mobilisation, awareness building and the identification of needs and priorities around which development interventions could be built.

Overall, the project has created space during implementation for a multi-stakeholder approach with a specific focus on tribal people. The project saw tribal people as partners in the improvement of their own natural resource base and means of livelihood with programme management that is initiated, executed and monitored by the community. The creation of thrift and credit groups has increased their habit of savings. The programmes focused on various aspects like, education, health, income generation activities, agricultural development, self-help groups etc.

**(b) Explain community organisation as a problem solving method.**

**Ans.** Refer to Chapter-2, Q.No.-11

**(c) Explain the elitist social action model.**

**Ans.** Refer to Chapter-3, Q.No.-9

**(d) Briefly describe different types of advocacy.**

**Ans.** Refer to Chapter-3, Q.No.-15

**(e) Explain social welfare administration as a profession.**

**Ans.** Refer to Chapter-4, Q.No.-6

**(f) 'Bureaucracy is a necessary evil.' Discuss.**

**Ans.** Bureaucracy is frequently used and abused word, which in common parlance connotes mindless application of the letters of the rules without any compassion, judgment or empathy. In olden times, organisations were smaller and there was face to face contact with the owner and the workers/employees. With establishment of large sized organisations and employment of huge number of people dispersed over wide geographical locations, bureaucratic administrative framework was considered an ideal type. Certain salient characteristics of bureaucracy are – division of labour (division of work based on specialisation and efficiency), hierarchy of authority (unity of command pattern between scalar and hierarchal pattern of subordinates and superiors), maintenance of formal written documents and extensive filing system, strict abidance of procedures, rules and regulations, expert training (on job orientation and refresher courses for employees), impersonality of interpersonal relations (interpersonal dealings are formal, impersonal and wholly devoid of emotions and sentiments) and rational programme of personnel administration (person's expertise and caliber as criteria for recruitment rather than ascriptive factors and fixed system of salary scale and promotion).

Max Weber, considered as Father of Bureaucracy, and his followers have maintained that these (above mentioned) characteristics of bureaucracy would bring rationality, uniformity, and efficiency in an organisation. In modern times, no organisation is wholly free from bureaucratic characteristics, though the degree may vary depending upon the type, size, structure and purpose of the organisation. A critical look at present day organisations, especially those engaged in social welfare activities, bring out that over-conformity to rules stifles initiative, innovation and flexibility, and leads to delayed decision-making and red-tapism. At times, long hierarchy and cumbersome procedures defeat the very purpose for which the organisation is set up.

Specifically, in the case of social welfare administration, these negative outcomes of bureaucracy affect the service delivery system to a great extent.

**Q5. Write short notes on any five of the following in about 100 words each:**

**(a) Subsistence economy**

**Ans.** A subsistence economy is an economy directed to basic subsistence (the provision of food, clothing, shelter) rather than to the market. Henceforth, "subsistence" is understood as supporting oneself at a minimum level. Often, the subsistence economy is moneyless and relies on natural resources to provide for basic needs through hunting, gathering, and agriculture. In a subsistence economy, economic surplus is minimal and only used to trade for basic goods, and there is no industrialisation. In hunting and gathering societies, resources are often if not typically underused.

In human history, before the first cities, all humans lived in a subsistence economy. As urbanisation, civilisation, and division of labor spread, various societies moved to other economic systems at various times. Some remain relatively unchanged, ranging from uncontested peoples, to marginalised areas of developing countries, to some cultures that choose to retain a traditional economy.

Capital can be generally defined as assets invested with the expectation that their value will increase, usually because there is the expectation of profit, rent, interest, royalties, capital gain or some other kind of return. However, this type of economy cannot usually become wealthy by virtue of the system, and instead requires further investments to stimulate economic growth. In other words, a subsistence economy only possesses enough goods to be used by a particular nation to maintain its existence and provides little to no surplus for other investments.

It is common for a surplus capital to be invested in social capital such as feasting.

**(b) Interdependence of tribal and non-tribal communities**

**Ans.** Refer to Chapter-1, Q.No.-26

**(c) Value orientation in community organisation**

**Ans.** Refer to Chapter-2, Q.No.-5

**(d) Skills in community work**

**Ans.** Refer to Chapter-2, Q.No.-27

**(e) Principle of dramatisation**

**Ans.** Refer to Chapter-3, Q.No.-19

**(f) Social movement**

**Ans.** Refer to Chapter-3, Q.No.-21

**(g) International Organisation**

**Ans.** Refer to Chapter-4, Q.No.-15

**(h) UNICEF**

**Ans.** Refer to Chapter-4, Q.No.-15

□□

**Feedback is the breakfast of Champions.**

Ken Blanchard

You can Help other students.
"Inform any error or mistake in this book."

We and Universe
will reward you for Your Kind act.

Email at : feedback@gullybaba.com
or
WhatsApp on 9350849407

www.ingramcontent.com/pod-product-compliance
Ingram Content Group UK Ltd.
Pitfield, Milton Keynes, MK11 3LW, UK
UKHW021702190726
13853UKWH00001B/401